The
Promontory
People

The Promontory People

AN EARLY HISTORY
OF THE CORNISH

CRAIG WEATHERHILL

Francis
Boutle
Publishers

First published by
Francis Boutle Publishers
272 Alexandra Park Road
London N22 7BG
Tel/Fax: (020) 8889 7744
Email: info@francisboutle.co.uk
www.francisboutle.co.uk

ISBN 978 1 9164906 1 1

Acknowledgements

While not profiting from their direct input, this book would have been impossible to write were it not for the collective endeavours of scores of researchers and writers on early medieval Cornwall. While I may be critical of some of their conclusions in the following pages, I have learnt a great deal from their work. It would be invidious to identify individuals, with one exception. The late Professor Charles Thomas, who did so much to put Cornish archaeology and Cornish Studies on their feet, expressed a keen interest in this project. I dedicate this book to his memory. Finally, I wish to thank Clive Boutle and Alan Kent for their support and help in transforming this book into reality.

Photographs are by permission of J.A. Beare, with the exception of Cornwall Archaeological Unit for the photo on p. 114.

Contents

The author at the Trevethy Quoit portal dolmen, St Cleer

List of maps and illustrations

The Tristan Stone, Fowey: Could this impressive mid 6th century inscribed stone really be closely linked with a world-famous legend? See pages 109-112

Preface

ON the 24th April 2014, people across the UK and further afield were understandably puzzled by newspaper headlines to which they had woken up. These read to the effect that the UK Government had included onto the Council of Europe's Framework Convention for the Protection of National Minorities a small and somewhat obscure people called … the Cornish.

A widespread feeling of bemusement followed, to be compounded by a statement from Stephen Williams, the Communities Minister, who pointed out that: 'The Cornish and Welsh are the oldest peoples on this island'.

Probably for the first time in many cases, people were beginning to ask each other: Who are the Cornish? Aren't they just a variety of English people, down there at the bottom left-hand corner of the island, albeit with curious accents, wonderful choirs, delicious pasties, baffling place-names, obscure saints, Doc Martin, Ross Poldark and beautiful beaches, albeit a place of tragic social deprivation? What is it that makes them so different? It seems strange that, in the modern era, so little is known or realised about one of Britain's constituent peoples. This book attempts to answer these questions.

There is also a deep seated modern presumption that the Duchy of Cornwall and its people are remotely positioned, far from the modern centres of commerce and administration, but, for the bulk of Cornwall's history, the very opposite has been true. Far from being remotely sited, Cornwall actually lies at the very centre of a geographical arc of commerce and innovation that is millennia old, and which has shaped the entire history of the Duchy. This is the Atlantic Arc of western Britain, Europe and Ireland, and southward to Brittany, the shores of the Bay of Biscay and the western coast of Spain and Portugal.

The distinctiveness of the Cornish people has been remarked upon by many people over the years. Polydore Vergil, an Italian writer who became a naturalised Briton, and historian to Henry VIII, wrote *Anglica Historia* around 1535, and had this to say: 'The whole country of Britain … is divided into four parts whereof the one is inhabited by Englishmen, the other of Scots, the third of Welshmen and the fourth of Cornish people, which all differ among themselves, either in tongue, in manners or else in laws and ordinances.'

In fact, a number of foreign visitors to Tudor Britain noticed that Cornwall was commonly regarded as a nation in its own right, with the Cornish being acknowledged as a distinct ethnic group. Lodovico Falier, an Italian diplomat at the court of Henry VIII in 1531, noted that: 'The language of the English, Welsh and Cornish men is so different that they do not understand each other.' A few years later, Gaspard de Coligny Chatillon, French Ambassador to London, commented that the kingdom of England was by no means a united entity, for it also: 'contains Wales and Cornwall, natural enemies of the rest of England and speaking a different language.'

After the death of Elizabeth I in 1603, the Venetian ambassador to London wrote that she had ruled over five different peoples: 'English, Welsh, Cornish, Scottish and Irish.' Arthur Hopton, in 1616, wrote something similar to Polydor Vergil's account: 'England is … divided into three great provinces or countries … every of them speaking a several and different language as English, Welsh and Cornish.'

Comments about the peculiar distinctiveness of the Cornish carried on into modern times. Robert Louis Stevenson, of Treasure Island fame, remarked that: 'Lady Hester Stanhope believed she could make something great of the Cornish; for my part, I can make nothing of them at all. A division of races, older and more original than that of Babel, keeps this close, esoteric family apart from neighbouring Englishmen.'

S.P.B. Mais, in *The Cornish Riviera* (1928) was to write that: 'Brunel's Royal Albert Bridge at Saltash is the means … of transporting travellers from … an English county to a Duchy which is in every respect un-English,' while D.H.Lawrence simply remarked: 'I like Cornwall very much. It is not England.'

Counties of England are not distinctly named in other languages, but Cornwall is different. At least 36 languages, as far flung as Mandarin,

Hindi and Russian, have their own words for Cornwall, a few examples of which are listed here:

Basque	Kornualles
Breton	Kernev-Veur
Cornish	Kernow
Gaelic	A'Chorn
Greek	Kornoualli (transliterated)
Hindi	Kornaval (transliterated)
Icelandic	Kornbretaland
Irish	Corn na Breataine
Italian	Cornovaglia
Latvian	Kornvola
Lithuanian	Kornvalis
Polish	Kornwalia
Portuguese	Cornualha
Spanish	Cornualles
Turkish	Kernevekeli
Upper Sorbian	Korniska
Welsh	Cernyw

In 2013, researcher Kevin Cahill studied what he was to call The Second Domesday, a little known survey carried out in 1873, of every landowner in the United Kingdom and properly entitled: Return of Owners of Land. This confirmed that across most of the UK, the absolute owner of the soil was the Crown, and that all individual freehold owners are, in effect, merely tenants who hold their land in Freehold from the Crown ... but not so in Cornwall.

Cahill explained as follows: 'The Crown is not the only absolute owner of the land in the UK. In 1855, the High Court ruled that: 'the whole territorial interest and dominion of the Crown in and over the entirety of Cornwall is vested in the Duke of Cornwall'. So, Cornwall is a separate kingdom! I know the Cornish have been shouting about this for a long time, but they turn out to be right. The Duchy is contesting its description as a public authority before the High Court now, (2011) over the mussel beds case. The original assertion of the claim to the High Court has surfaced again, and the High Court agreed to it as in 1855. And, yes,

Cornwall IS a separate feudal authority, i.e. kingdom.'

Kevin Cahill had stumbled across a fact that is recognised in law, and that many Cornish people already knew, but of which few others were even aware: a peculiar and unique status that is held by the little land in the far southwest of Britain, and which is clearly based upon something that stretches far back into history.

This book aims to relate the early part of this unique history, from the earliest of times to the period of Norman rule. It attempts to explain the origins, language, and development across the ages, of an ancient and enigmatic people who remain the least understood inhabitants of Britain: the Cornish people …

… the Promontory People.

Craig Weatherhill
Hal an Tegen, Pennsans
Kernow
2018

This book contains the following conventions:
BCE Before Current Era)   1,000 BCE = 1,000 BC
CE (Current Era)   1,000 CE = 1,000 AD

Chapter 1

Laying foundations

In the beginning

FOR millennia, the Cornish people have not only been shaped by the sea that almost surrounds their homeland, but by the very nature of the land they live on. 400 million years ago, the plate of the earth's crust that would contain Cornwall, along with the whole of what would become Europe, Britain and Ireland, lay several thousand miles south of its present position. It had previously been butted up against what would become the North American tectonic plate, but was slowly drifting away.

There were several periods when the plate's surface was both forced above, and depressed below, the surface of a warm tropical sea, where mineral and organic sediments drifted to the ocean floor in layers formed in differing environmental conditions. Over more millions of years, these became compressed and hardened into rock. A volcanically active earth then forced additional igneous materials into the forming matrix and had even done so before, Cornwall's oldest rocks being an igneous mass of varying types forming part of what is now the Lizard peninsula. These appear to be as old as 500 million years.

As the plate moved northward, around 300 million years ago, and as the Atlantic Ocean basin began to open up, it collided with the African plate. The result was a lifting and folding of the earlier rocks into a stupendous mountain range stretching from the Pyrenees, across Brittany, Cornwall and South Wales and across to Ireland. It also nudged the ancient Lizard mass against the rest of what would be Cornwall, the heat produced by this collision further altering a large part of the Lizard geology into the unique serpentine rock for which the area is famed.

These tectonic forces then caused molten magma to well up from beneath to form an undulating and elongated dome known as the Cornubian batholith. This extended from Dartmoor to Scilly and perhaps even further west. Welling up beneath the upfolded earlier rocks at 800 degrees Celsius, this would form the granite spine of Cornwall but during that turbulent period, two kilometres or so beneath the surface, it certainly generated several violent volcanoes.

This event, more than any other, would pave the way to Cornwall's future. The sedimentary shales and slates abutting the granite became altered by the intense heat and hardened them into metamorphic form, such as hornfels and greenstone. The upwelling of the granite, followed by the release of superheated steam under tremendous seismic pressure, forced mineral-laden vapours into cracks and fissures extending out into the metamorphosed rocks. After condensing and cooling, these formed veins of metallic ore that, far into the future, would form the basis of Cornwall's economy for over four millennia. These ores were of tin and copper, arsenic, iron and lead; tungsten, uranium and many more – around 90% of all mineral types lie under Cornwall. Indium, much sought by the i-Tec industry, is a recent discovery in a Cornish mine. In places, the breakdown of feldspars in the granite gave rise to the formation of kaolin, or china-clay, the extraction of which is still a major industry today.

Over further millions of years, the softer rocks of the mountain chain eroded away to leave a landscape that more closely resembled the Cornwall of the future. The roof of the granite spine and its metamorphic borders became exposed above the sedimentary rocks in several places: Dartmoor, Bodmin Moor, the St Austell granite, Carn Brea and the Carnmenellis granite, Tregonning Hill and West Penwith. Further west, the granite exposes again as the Isles of Scilly and perhaps as the undersea ridges of Haig Fras and the Great Sole Bank.

Sea levels continued to fluctuate to extremes, almost submerging Cornwall at one point around 25 million years ago. This receded in stages, creating wave cut platforms still evident today; at about the 300 metre (1,000 ft) contour, the 225m (750 ft) level and, most noticeably in today's landscape, at the 120 metre (430 ft) line. The sands of an ancient beach from the last of those pauses can still be found at the southern foot of St Agnes Beacon, then an island.

It would still be a very long time before humankind, or its predecessors, were to make an appearance in this landscape. Meanwhile, a further momentous event, or series of events, were about to approach from the frozen north.

The island of Britain had long since reached its present position on the surface of the globe when, about 2.6 million years ago, the Ice Age began. At least four major, and several minor, glaciations occurred, with ice-sheets advancing and covering much of Britain as far south as the Severn-Thames line. In places the ice grew to a thickness of 3 kilometres. On each occasion the immense weight pushed the northern part of Britain downward into the earth's crust, the south rising in counterbalance. Sea levels dropped by as much as 120 metres (400 feet) lower than today.

Britain and Ireland did not then exist as anything more than a peninsula of northern Europe. The Channel between Britain and France was dry land; a valley for a massive river containing the waters of the Thames, Rhine and Seine, and many more flowing from southern Britain and northern France. The North Sea was also dry; a huge, low-lying plain with a low range of hills which is now the submerged Dogger Bank. Those parts of Britain that remained clear of the ice were inhospitable, freezing wastes of tundra and permafrost.

Between each southward advance of the ice was a period of interglacial respite, when the glaciers retreated and icecaps melted. The climate warmed and sea levels rose, only to fall again with the next glaciation. There is no sign of human or hominid activity in what would be the British Isles until the last two of these interglacial periods, which began 800,000 years ago. This was an interrupted period called the Palaeolithic, or Old Stone Age.

The oldest known human activity in Britain was on its eastern side, with the ice being far enough north to allow small hunter groups to wander up from northern Europe about 850,000 years ago, most likely on a seasonal basis only and following herds of red deer, small horse, mammoth and rhinoceros across expanses of grassland, with an ever-present danger of sabre-toothed cats and hyenas. These people probably followed the Rhine to its confluence with the Thames, and then along its tributaries.

From this early period, only one indication has yet been found that these earliest hunters and herb gatherers made their way as far west as

Cornwall. This was a single stone axe that was found at Leha, St Buryan, in the 19th century. The people who left it there were not yet *homo sapiens*, but *homo erectus* and *homo heidelbergensis*. *Homo neanderthalis* also made a limited appearance around 230,000 years ago.

Periods of intense cold drove all these people south again onto what we would now call the European continent, and there would have been periods when excessive meltwater flow made access to Britain impossible. It appears that, from 180,000 to 60,000 years ago, there was no human activity at all in the area of Britain.

A warmer spell about 50,000 years ago brought grasslands back to southern Britain and, with it, more human activity. This time, more of them came west, resulting in the finds made at Kent's Cavern, Torquay and other cave sites not far from there, which date from 44,000 years ago. *Homo sapiens* first appeared on British soil some 14,000 years later, one of the most famous remains from this event being the 'Red Lady of Paviland' (actually the skeleton of a young man, whose bones had been daubed with red ochre), found in a cave on the south coast of Wales.

The final advance of the ice sheets and glaciers began around 70,000 years ago, slowly creeping south, and lasted for 60,000 years. Again the ice-sheets themselves did not penetrate south of the Severn-Thames line, but once more reduced the ice-free areas to a hostile environment of tundra and permafrost, driving all human activity back across the land-bridge. Across Europe and western Asia, people were pushed far to the south to take up refuges north and west of the Black Sea, and in Iberia. The tip of southwest Ireland also remained ice-free, but a tongue of ice protruded south from the Irish Sea basin. This may have been visible from the north coast of the Land's End peninsula and seemingly touched the Isles of Scilly, where glacial deposits have been found at the northern tips of Tresco, Bryher and St Martins. These contain flint gouged from the Irish Sea basin by the glacier.

As this last glaciation finally began to melt and retreat, again causing sea levels to rise, icebergs breaking from this retreating glacier may well have dumped more of this Irish Sea flint onto an early shoreline of Mount's Bay. This might explain the common occurrence of flint on Loe Bar, the stone not being found anywhere in Cornwall's own geology. A very late, melting iceberg was undoubtedly responsible for dumping a 50-ton boulder onto the foreshore at Porthleven. Known as the Giant's

Rock, this consists of a gneiss which is not found anywhere in Britain. The final melting of permafrost washed a sludge of soil and frost-shattered rock down into valleys to leave thick deposits of what is locally called *head*.

By 15, 000 BCE, the ice sheets and glaciers had begun to thin and retreat. A gradual warming was beginning to create more temperate conditions and there is evidence from Bodmin Moor that grassland was starting to re-establish itself, but even the southernmost parts of Britain remained empty of human activity.

The first Cornish people

BY 9,600 BCE Britain, still a peninsula of northern Europe despite sea-levels rising once again, was completely ice-free. The landscape had become a mixture of grassland and forest, havens of wild life and ready for human occupation. The southern part of the North Sea was still a dry-land plain, and the Channel also remained dry land, bisected by a wide estuary running westward from a point south of the Isle of Wight. The Hurd Deep, now a linear depression on the sea floor to the north of Alderney, was part of this river's valley.

Human activity was on the move, from the Ice Age refuge areas to the north and west of the Black Sea, and from Iberia, south of the Pyrenees. The first would repopulate northern Europe, and eventually mainland Britain from its eastern side, but part of the Iberian concentration was already looking northward, to move up the coast of Biscay and across the Channel estuary. These, the first of the post-Glacial colonists, were to enter the west side of Britain, spreading and settling further north and into Ireland over the land bridge that still existed between northern Ireland and southern Scotland.

This heralded the beginning of the Mesolithic era, or Middle Stone Age and, unlike those who had visited 30,000 years earlier, most were coming to stay. At this point the history of the Cornish people truly begins, because four out of five Cornish people today (79%) carry the intact genetic code that shows direct descent from arrivals from Atlantic Europe between 11,600 and 6,500 years ago This is determined by a dominant H haplotype in maternal gene lines, which originated from the north Iberian refuge, then spread through Iberia, Gaul, western Britain and into Ireland. The dominant paternal gene line, R1b, is recognised through Y chromosome DNA. Found throughout Britain and Ireland, it is much stronger in the west, becoming less apparent as one travels east, and weakest of all on the North Sea coast. Although more complex, these show a dominant R1b-9 ancestral haplotype which originated from a small area in the Basque regions.

Sub-group R1b-15c is the most applicable to Cornwall. Again originating in the coastal Basque region, northward spread was particularly concentrated into the Cornish peninsula, and is dated to the very earliest post-Glacial colonisation of Britain, 11,600 years ago. The figure of people with similar early Atlantic European descent in Wales from this same period is 81% (88% in Ireland) and therefore Communities Minister Stephen Williams was quite correct to state, in April 2014, that the Cornish and Welsh represent the oldest peoples on this island.

Mr Williams's source had been Oxford University's Peoples of Britain genetic survey, headed by Sir Walter Bodmer, and which stated that 'the people of Wales and Cornwall differ from those of southern and central England,' a genetic distinctiveness that had also been identified by Professor Bryan Sykes in 2006. It added that, while traces of the eastern migrant groups were to be found across the UK, these were fewer in Wales and Cornwall than anywhere else. While the individual genetic constructions of the Cornish and Welsh also differed, the survey had also noted their 'fairly large similarities with the ancestry of Ireland on the one hand, and France on the other, which we think is most likely to be a combination of remnants of very ancient populations who moved across into Britain after the last Ice Age.' The Cornish and the Devonians also formed two distinct genetic groups, with the Tamar-Ottery line being the clear boundary between them. Sir Walter Bodmer also pointed out that the Cornish had a particular variant of the Melanocortin 1 receptor gene also found among the Welsh and other peoples recognised today as Celtic.

Eastern Britain, along with eastern and central Europe, was to be populated by people spreading westward from the glacial refuge areas that had lain to the north of the Black Sea, in the regions now occupied by the Ukraine and the Balkans. These were typified by the I1a and I1c genetic groups, although their numbers appear to have been smaller than the western group. These people could cross the North Sea plain that was still dry land and, due to travelling a much greater distance, with pauses en route, these folk almost certainly arrived later, mostly arriving in what is now East Anglia perhaps between 9,000 and 7,000 years BCE.

The initial groups of hunters, gatherers and fisherfolk were coming to an empty and fruitful land, with a mix of forest and grassland. It was not without its dangers: lions and hyenas were initially on the prowl, but were probably extinct in Britain before 8,000 BCE. Horse, reindeer, bison, red deer and woolly rhinoceros were abundant, as were brown bears, foxes, wolves, lynx, badgers, beavers, wild oxen, wild cats and pigs. It was a hunter's paradise, and as time passed, more people ventured north from Atlantic Europe, and westward from northern and eastern Europe to take advantage of it.

By 8,300 BCE, sea levels had risen far enough to almost detach Britain from the European mainland, probably discouraging migration for all but the most adventurous who might have chanced their luck in fragile boats, or those who could still come, dry-shod, from the east across what remained of the North Sea plain. Sea levels still lay 20 metres lower than at present. Scilly, now a large single island, lay sundered from the mainland of Cornwall, with other islands at locations such as the Seven Stones and Cape Cornwall Bank still above surface.

A major and catastrophic event occurred at around 6,200 BCE. In the North American continent, the retreat and melting of the vast Laurentide Ice Sheet, that had covered a large part of the continent, created an immense lake, known as Lake Agassiz. Roughly the size of the Black Sea, this covered much of what are now the Canadian states of Manitoba and Ontario, and southward into Minnesota and North Dakota. The moraines containing it gave way, allowing this vast quantity of cold water to burst into Hudson Bay, and out along the St Lawrence Seaway into the Atlantic, where it had the devastating effect of disrupting the Gulf Stream that kept Britain in a temperate climate.

Temperatures in Britain dropped by several degrees. Sea levels, already rising, rose up to a further 2.7 metres, triggering a major undersea landslide off the coast of Norway. The result of this was a tsunami that rushed down the eastern side of Britain, and signalled the end of 'Doggerland', the plain that had joined eastern Britain to Europe. The scale of this wave can be detected along a stretch of the eastern British coast nearly 400 miles long, from northeastern Scotland south-wards; evidence of the tsunami still being traceable up to 5 metres above present sea level. The North Sea was born, and Britain at last became an island.

The effect of this cold period on the island's population can only be imagined, but it must have led to a sizeable depopulation as people went south again to find more temperate conditions, leaving only the hardiest of souls to tough it out. It would take 150 years for the Gulf Stream to re-establish and restore the previous climatic conditions.

By 6,000 BCE, the climate had recovered and improved to the point where average summer temperatures were above 16 degrees Celsius. Within another 1,500 years average temperatures would become 2 degrees Celsius higher in winter and 1 degree higher in summer than today, with the wildwood wholly established across the island.

The full extent of Mesolithic activity in Cornwall will never be known as many favoured coastal sites now lie under the sea, but society appears to been somewhat nomadic in nature, with no permanent settlements being built for a long time. The population remained fairly sparse, with groups of maybe a dozen families, each circulating in a territory of several hundred square kilometres. Contact with other groups, where implements and information were exchanged, must have occurred, perhaps initialising trade and certainly bonds between future partners. There were probably nowhere near enough people to create any major social friction, although some squabblings over prime hunting or fishing grounds would have been likely.

Mesolithic life seems to have consisted of winters spent hunting in lowland forests then, in spring, moving to the coast, fishing in the sea and in rivers, hunting seals, catching crab and lobster, and gathering edible sea weeds and shellfish. Summer would see groups of families following herds onto upland grasslands, a hunting season that would last into autumn while provisions were supplemented with nuts, roots, fruits and berries. Camps probably consisted of tents or tepees built of hide stitched together with gut or sinews and fitted onto wooden frames. These could be easily dismantled when the herds moved on, or the fish-run ended, to be carried to the next camp location.

The language they spoke was not Celtic, for that had yet to develop, but a clue to it might lie in their place of origin – the region of the Basques in the shadow of the Western Pyrenees. Basque, or Euskara, is of extraordinary antiquity. It is one of the few remaining pre-Indo-

European languages surviving in Europe and it is tempting to imagine the Mesolithic Cornish speaking an early form of that language.

During springtime, in each group's forays to the coastal regions, limpets seem to have been a prominent feature of their diet; middens filled with limpet shells having been found in several locations around the Cornish coast. A popular location was Trevose Head, but Gwithian-Godrevy, on the eastern side of St Ives Bay, was the most prolific Mesolithic site known in western Cornwall. This centred on an estuarine environment, the Red River then having a much wider and deeper tidal estuary than is apparent today. Finds of burnt flint indicate campfires in several places, while activity centres away from the estuary were grouped around fresh water springs.

Inland, Dozmary Pool was another Mesolithic centre of activity, probably during the summer hunting seasons. Many of the flint implements that have been found there, such as scrapers, indicate that animal hides were being prepared for use in clothing, shelter-building and boat construction.

A major activity during these times was the production of edged tools of flint and chert. Neither material occurs in Cornwall's geology and yet flint and chert pebbles turn up in several coastal locations, particularly Loe Bar.

Likely explanations are that flint and chert were washed into the Channel, when dry land, by glacial run-off and erosion, then carried down the large Channel river, to be deposited in large clusters on its former banks somewhere off the Cornish coast, to be washed in by tides and currents. As mentioned earlier, icebergs containing flint gouged from the Irish Sea basin also dumped their loads off the Cornish coast as they melted. Greensand chert occurs naturally in south Devon. This was also commonly used in Cornwall, so could have been brought in along established overland or sea routes as well as having been washed down by meltwater to a position offshore at an earlier time.

Mesolithic folk made the most of these easily worked materials, with many flint-working sites being found right round the Cornish coast, and at several inland sites as well. The tools fashioned from them range from hand axes, awls, arrowheads, scrapers and drill bits, to microliths, these being very small, delicate and exquisitely fashioned cutting blades.

In the later Mesolithic period, after 6,000 BCE, people were starting to use the natural environment to greater purpose. Areas of woodland were beginning to be cut down and burnt to provide game coverts and settle-ment sites. Domestication of animals had also begun, notably dogs, cattle, pigs and horses. The meat from a single auroch, a huge breed of ox, could provide a meal for 100 people. New plants were encouraged in these managed areas, notably those bearing edible nuts, berries, leaves and roots.

Sea-going vessels also appear to have been developed at this time, audacious ventures far out to sea being indicated by finds of the bones of deep-water fish, especially cod, at several late Mesolithic campsites. The people of this time were perfectly capable of fashioning canoes carved out from massive tree trunks and, for more adventurous sea trips, might also have developed boats made from hide stitched over a timber frame, the fore-runner of the Irish curragh. Such vessels, crewed by incredibly brave mariners, might well have established contact with the Continent.

This contact and the beginnings of trade are indicated by recent finds at a now submerged Late Mesolithic settlement site 11 metres beneath the waters of the Solent. Cereal DNA recovered from the site indicates that wheat products were probably being brought into southern Britain from the continent. The wheat was identified as *einkorn*, a variety of bearded wheat that had first been domesticated in Anatolia, Turkey, around 8,000 BCE. This would not be cultivated in Britain until around 4,000 BCE but, at a point halfway between these dates, British Mesolithic inhabitants, existing on hunting, gathering and fishing, were importing it from European farmers who were growing and trading it, and most likely exporting it by boat. It is not impossible that the beginnings of Atlantic and cross-Channel trade might have been established as early as 6,000 BCE. Finds from this submerged site also show that Mesolithic people were not only capable of felling timber, but splitting it, too.

Cornish Mesolithic society has often been likened to that of Native American tribes, prior to the colonisation of America by Europeans. For the most part this was peaceful, productive and very much community-based. We know nothing of its spiritual beliefs and practices but it is not unreasonable to imagine that these would have been very much based upon nature itself, the people being utterly dependant upon the natural world and its unpredictability, even though they had already begun to learn how to adapt that world to suit their own purpose.

Farmers and megaliths

THE Mesolithic period was seeing momentous changes on the continents of Europe and Asia, which would eventually have equally significant effects on the islands of Britain and Ireland.

Around 9,000 BCE, in what has been termed the 'Fertile Crescent' of Syria, Anatolia and Northern Iraq, the new skill of agriculture was being developed. Initially based on bearded wheats such as emmer, spelt and einkorn, this expanded into animal husbandry and additional crops. It was inevitable that this knowledge would spread and it was to do exactly that, to the east of that initial area, and throughout all of Europe to the west.

At about the same time a linguistic revolution was also taking place: the formation of an Indo-European language, which spread to similar areas, perhaps in association with the spread of agriculture. Indo-European, over centuries and millennia, would be the ancestor of an extensive range of linguistic groups. The area in which this development first took place appears to have been to the east and north east of the Black Sea, and to the north of the Caucasus Mountains. This evolving parent of many languages spread eastward across Persia and into the Indian sub-continent. It also spread northwestward to affect the greater part of the European mainland, and along the northern coast of the Mediterranean to the Atlantic, further diversifying as it progressed into many branches. It was this path that would eventually prove vital to the history of Cornwall, as will be detailed in a later chapter.

The beginning of the Neolithic period, 6,500 years ago, saw kinder conditions in Cornwall than we have today. On average, summer temperatures were 2° Celsius warmer than now, and winter temperatures about a degree milder. Much of Cornwall was forested, but the higher parts of its uplands were probably under heather and grassland, with oak and hazel scrub on the higher exposed slopes, and oak woodland on more sheltered hillsides. Valley wetlands held grass and sedge mire, although alder carr was also becoming established at that time.

Farming reached these islands at the beginning of what is called the Neolithic era, or New Stone Age. For Cornwall, further settlers were sailing north from those same coasts of Biscay as their Mesolithic predecessors, via Brittany, and into Cornwall bringing with them the knowledge and skills of agriculture. They would bring all the seed grain they would require, and probably livestock as well, heavily trussed to ensure that their likely reactions of panic and alarm to sea travel would not capsize or wreck the boat.

Although the Neolithic is often seen as a 'Golden Era' of peaceful development, the reality may well have been rather different. The transition to an agricultural society would have been gradual, and not without friction and even conflict. Mesolithic hunters had already been managing the woodlands to some extent to provide grazing areas where game animals could gather. Whether Neolithic farmers understood this or not, such areas were far easier for them to further clear than untouched forest would be, and it is quite likely that they concentrated on these to found their new farms. It is not hard to imagine how the huntsmen felt about that when reaching a seasonal hunting range they had nurtured for centuries, only to find it taken over by new farmers who had radically altered the landscape by clearing forest and game reserves to make way for their fields.

This likely conflict between the new farmers and the established hunter-gather-fishers would take time to settle. Even then, immigrants with new ideas were unpopular and hard to accept, but the new would eventually come to dominate, and then be the norm, with Mesolithic traditions being gradually absorbed into Neolithic culture. Indications are that it was women from the Mesolithic communities who sought partners among the Neolithic farmers, rather than the other way round.

Perhaps it was because of this early period of conflict that the earliest large structures erected by the farmers were the Tor Enclosures, effectively fortified sites on prominent hills with extensive views. About a dozen of these are known in Cornwall and on Dartmoor, usually on hills with impressive natural tor, or carn, formations. Irregularly shaped enclosures were formed by building walls faced with upright stones, linking to natural outcrops of rock. These often contained levelled platforms on which timber buildings could be erected.

In West Penwith, the Land's End peninsula, these oldest surviving of all Cornwall's built monuments can be found on Carn Kenidjack, Carn Galva and Trencrom Hill. West and Mid-Cornwall have the Carn Brea and Helman Tor sites and, on Bodmin Moor, tor enclosures have been identified on Rough Tor, Tregarrick Tor, De Lank, Notter Tor, Stowe's Pound and perhaps Berry Down, St Neot. They also exist at Dartmoor's

Hound Tor, Whittor and the Dewerstone. The extent of most tor enclo-
sures is in the region of 1 hectare, but a few were a great deal larger.
Rough Tor has up to 4 ranks of walling enclosing 8.5 ha and Helman
Tor's double-walled enclosure is around 3 hectares in extent.

The largest and most heavily studied of these sites is on Carn Brea,
above Camborne and Redruth. The initial tor enclosure was around the
hill's eastern summit, where Carn Brea Castle now stands, and covered
an area of 0.8 hectares. Inside this most of the buildings were situated
but, over time, it was enlarged in a piecemeal fashion until both western
and central summits of the hill had been enclosed by a whole succession
of walls and ramparts to form a complex more than a dozen times larger
than the original construction. It was found to be Britain's oldest known
fortified settlement, yielding a date range of 3,900 BCE to 3,300 BCE.
Whatever else it may have represented, the Carn Brea tor enclosure, on a
226 metre high hilltop that can be seen for miles around, even when
soaring above woodland as it would then have done, made a huge
statement: we now own this land – accept the fact, or else!

This was not something that the longer established population was
going to take lying down. That the settlement enclosure was attacked on
at least one occasion was confirmed by the discovery of over 700 leaf-
shaped flint arrowheads in a small area around the main entrance. There
were also indications that the timber buildings had been burnt to the
ground, indicating that the 150 or so inhabitants had either been
massacred or driven out.

The Neolithic inhabitants of Carn Brea used tools and implements of
stone and flint, from edge-grinding stones to axes. Their pottery was
fashioned from gabbroic clay, the sole source of which lay 20 miles away
on the eastern side of the Lizard peninsula. A great deal of Cornish
Neolithic and later prehistoric pottery is made from this type of clay, and
gabbroic pottery has been found as far away as Dorset and Wiltshire,
indicating that the Lizard site must have been a substantial and long-
lived production centre. Surprisingly, the exact location of this source
has yet to be positively identified.

The march of progress can seldom be halted and, eventually, farming
became the dominant mode of existence. Open moorland at Rough Tor
was being managed by grazing between 3,660 and 3,330 BCE, this being
determined by finds of pollen from Ribwort Plantain and Devil's Bit

Scabious, the growth of which is encouraged by cattle grazing. Cereal crops were certainly being grown in Cornwall before 3,000 BCE, in fields worked by stone-tipped hook ploughs known as ards, and stone-tipped hoes. Livestock included aurochs, massive oxen that could be nearly two metres tall at the shoulder, smaller breeds of cattle, sheep, goats and pigs.

Axe manufacture was also established in Cornwall by 4,000 BCE, with hard metamorphic greenstone being a favoured material. At least ten quarry sites for Neolithic axe manufacture have been identified. Eight of them are in the old Penwith Hundred, in the far west of the Duchy; two of them now submerged by rising sea levels. Futher sites near St Stephen-in-Brannel and at Balstone Down, Callington, are also known. The tools were beautifully made, with some even being given a well-polished finish.

These Cornish greenstone axes also testify to an established system of long distance trading, by land and certainly by sea. Axes quarried and fashioned at sites bordering Mount's Bay have been found as far away as Sussex, Essex and Yorkshire; two of them turned up at the iconic site of Stonehenge.

By the middle of the 4th millennium BCE, a new fashion reached Cornwall from across the sea to the south: megalith building. Coined from two classical Greek words, megalith means 'great stone', and could not be a more appropriate expression for these astonishing achievements of effort and engineering. Megalith building is known along the Mediterranean Sea, and up the Atlantic coasts of Europe, then into western Britain and Ireland; this progression most probably reflecting the actual path and spread of the practice. Architectural design of the great megalithic structures altered on a regional basis as the practice spread west and then northward. In Cornwall, it was to be first repre-sented by the great portal dolmens, also called quoits or cromlechs.

Anyone standing beside the great chamber and 10.9 tonne capstone of Trethevy Quoit, St Cleer, towering more than 4 metres above the ground, cannot fail to be astounded by the sheer magnitude of the task that Neolithic Cornishmen and women took on and achieved 5, 500 years ago. Those people did not have the hydraulic crane that replaced Carwynnen Quoit's similar-sized capstone onto its newly re-erected upright support stones in the wonderful restoration scheme by the Sustainable Trust which was completed in 2014. This work followed two historic collapses of the monument, which now stands proudly again near Troon.

Portal dolmens are common in Wales, Ireland and Brittany as well as Cornwall, which retains a dozen of them. Only three of these, Pawton Quoit near St Breock, Trethevy Quoit and Zennor Quoit are true portal dolmens. Others were apparently simple, closed and slab-sided boxes, the mushroom-like Chûn Quoit, Morvah, being by far the best preserved of them. Some, like Lanyon Quoit, Madron, have been so altered or ruined that their original form cannot now be determined. The portal effect at Zennor and Trethevy is achieved by two side slabs of the chamber projecting forward to be fronted by a pair of transverse slabs that are also set upright, these and a further transverse chamber slab forming a small antechamber (Trethevy has lost one of these stones). Pawton was designed differently, its portal being achieved by a set of slabs forming a wide frontal façade without an antechamber.

All, however, consist of large upright stones forming a closed, or sometimes open-sided, chamber roofed by a single enormous slab. Again, one is drawn to wonder at the sheer amount of labour and determination that went into their construction, especially when a Neolithic lifespan was unlikely to exceed forty years of age. Teenagers and even children are likely to have been part of the workforce that erected these great monuments. The heaviest of all the capstones, at 14.6 tonnes, is that at Pawton Quoit and perhaps it is no accident that this has the shortest uprights of all the Cornish dolmens. Even the small chamber at Chûn has a capstone weighing 8.8 tonnes.

Several of these dolmens have traces of a surrounding cairn of circular or oval shape. These were typically constructed of roughly fist-sized stones retained by an outer edge, or kerb, of stone walling. At Pawton Quoit this survives up to 1.2 metres in places. Chûn Quoit's cairn is one of the most obvious and a pair of stones on its southern side (one fallen, the other still set on its edge), may be remains of walls flanking a forecourt leading into the mound to the front of the chamber. In many cases, it is thought that these cairns were roughly drum-shaped, their retaining walls being about a metre tall, with the top of the cairn sloping gently up to the edge of the capstone, which remained visible and exposed, as was the front side of the chamber facing into the forecourt. Trethevy Quoit, however, is so tall that the arrangement was likely to have been different; the cairn only reaching to part way up the sides of the chamber, which must have protruded well above the cairn. What seems certain is that the capstone and chamber were so architecturally impressive that at least part of them was always intended to be seen.

Carwynnen Quoit seems to have been different again. Excavation in 2013 found no trace of any surrounding cairn, so that its tripod form was completely exposed, much as it appears today, and did not form a closed chamber. Its floor was paved with pebbles and it was approached from the north by a pavement of pebble cobbling curving into the west side of the monument. This has been carefully preserved and reburied, with a new pavement built directly above it. The visiting public is invited to bring and lay a pebble to add to this replica pavement, and be part of its ongoing history.

Only two of the surviving Cornish dolmens have been excavated under modern techniques: Sperris Quoit, a badly ruined site just a few hundred metres north-east of Zennor Quoit in 1954 and Carwynnen in 2013-14. Further, minor, examinations have taken place at Lesquite Quoit, Lanivet, and the Devil's Coyt, St Columb. However, being such grandiose monuments, they tended to attract the clumsy spade of the amateur over the last 250 years – explosives were even used at Zennor Quoit. Cremated bone also found at Zennor gave a date range of 3,342-3,024 BCE; similar remains from Sperris Quoit dated to 3,633-3,373 BCE. Finds from beneath the floor of Carwynnen Quoit seem to indicate that this site was younger: bone fragments that could not conclusively be shown as human were dated to 3,025-2,916 BCE. Although this could not date the quoit itself, deposits of burnt bone, with pottery and flints of similar age, suggest that these had been placed as token offerings. This practice seemed to have carried on for several centuries after the dolmens had been built: a perforated whetstone found in the antechamber of Zennor Quoit, tentatively dated to 1,975-1,835 BCE, shows that these monuments were revered and attended for a long time after they were built. Such later finds also support the argument that the front of each dolmen was always left open to view and approach.

Curiously, for such a statement in the landscape as these huge stone monuments make, none of the dolmens stand on hilltops, but are overlooked by higher ground nearby. Even Mulfra Quoit, Madron, which from a distance appears to be on the summit of the hill, actually stands some way below the true summit. Several of the quoits stand at the highest points of field systems that stretch away downhill. These are unlikely to be as old as the dolmen itself, but established at some point during the time that belief practice at the monument was still current. This relationship of quoit and field patterns can still be seen at Chûn, Mulfra and Zennor in particular and strongly suggests that the quoit was considered to be acting as a sentinel or guardian over the productive land below.

It is likely that the dolmens were never built to be tombs, but held a multiple purpose: a territorial marker designed to echo natural rock formations, and a focus for spiritual activity linked with both agriculture and nature, and in which periodical offerings could be left to appease the guardian spirits – perhaps of ancestors – who were believed to dwell or gather within.

Seemingly unrelated to these are the pseudo-quoits that have been increasingly recognised in recent years. For the most part, these are semi-natural granite formations where slabs have been lifted and propped at one end, forming an aperture framing significant landscape features in the distance.

The piece that follows is a conjectural, but plausible vision of Neolithic Cornish life, with the final touches being given to the building of a portal dolmen in the Land's End peninsula, and has been adapted from a scene in the author's own novel *The Tinners' Way* (Tabb House 2010).

Raising the quoit, Zennor Hill, 3,500 BCE

'BENEATH a warm springtime sun, a gathering of many people had assembled on the hilltop. They were small, delicate people, dark of hair and eye. They wore elaborate clothing fashioned from animal hides and wool. The men were bearded, while the women had waist-length hair. Some wore it loose; others tied it back in long ponytails and plaits. Children were there, too, laughing and playful, some playing tag and running in and out of the adults.

'Not one of them seemed to be older than thirty or so, not even the man with grey flecks in his hair who, from the way the others seemed to show him some deference, was some kind of patriarchal figure. At a word from him, all fell silent, even the children, and all turned to face the incomplete but huge structure close by.

'The people gazed with deep reverence upon a group of large stones that had been set upright to form a rectangular chamber within a great drum-shaped cairn of much smaller stones and boulders, its outside edge defined by a drystone wall that stood about chest high. One section of this circular cairn had not been completed but instead formed a long, gentle ramp, at the top end of which a colossal slab of granite that had already been hauled far enough to cover most of the central chamber lay on several wooden rollers. The great slab was festooned with ropes fashioned from woven strips of leather, the loose ends of which were being gathered up for the final pull. Sets of these ropes were attached to harnesses worn by a pair of muscular rake-horned aurochs, the forebears of all domestic cattle, and whose shoulders stood taller than any of the people surrounding them.

'Everyone present was involved. Men, women and even the children took their places on each rope and, on a single command, all began hauling with every ounce of their strength. The aurochs, reacting to the goad, strained forward while, behind the slab, half a dozen men wielding thick stakes used them as levers to inch the ten-ton stone forward.

'Granite scraped on granite. Amazingly, the entire eighteen-foot slab was moving, inch by inch, while the straining people heaved to rhythmic commands. Then, on a sharp word that cut the air, the ropes were dropped, the aurochs were halted, and the people moved back.

'The capstone seemed to be teetering on the very edge of balance and, quite suddenly, the entire slab tilted forward, its rear end rising a foot in the air while the rest dropped onto the upright stones at the front of the chamber with a hollow thud that shook the ground. The men at its rear moved away to allow the wooden rollers, now free of the weight, to tumble back down the ramp. The people watched, holding their breath, as the elder walked up the ramp, stepped onto the capstone and proceeded to walk slowly from one end of it to the other. It did not move.

'A ragged cheer went up. Some of the people were laughing with the release of their tension and out of sheer relief, while others wept with joy, hugging one another, celebrating the success of their astonishing achievement.

'By two evenings later, the work was complete and the entire monument was in its final form. The ramp had been dismantled and the edging wall completed to define a completely circular cairn, whose gently inclined top surface reached to the edge of the exposed capstone so that there seemed to be no entry into the main chamber beneath. Perhaps it would serve as a haven where the revered spirits of the ancestors would gather to hold a vigil of protection over the farm fields below. A walled forecourt pierced one side of the cairn, facing due east and leading to the narrow entrance to a small, blind antechamber behind two crosswise slabs, the tops of which protruded from the cairn itself.

'It had been a kind spring of early growth. On the hillside to the south, fields of half-grown bearded wheat, still green, waved in a gentle breeze. Small black cattle, and the pair of giant aurochs grazed in pastures and on open areas of moorland. The valley bottom was filled with trees and smoke from cooking fires lazily curled from the thatched roofs of small huts scattered among the fields.

'By twilight, the people were back on the hilltop, silently laying offerings of wheat grain within the antechamber of the great dolmen, and there was the elder leading a black calf into the forecourt before turning to face the east, the people moving back outside the forecourt and turning with him. A curved sliver of light on the skyline grew slowly into a huge round moon, whose cold light shone straight into the forecourt, illuminating the wide front edge of the capstone and the tall stone beneath it at the back of the antechamber. At the moment when the complete lunar sphere appeared to be balanced on the horizon, a polished greenstone knife flashed, a gout of bright blood glistened in the moonlight, and the calf collapsed to its knees and then onto its side, dying and then dead. Only now could the spirits of those long-dead ancestors take up residence in their new shrine to protect the living, their settlements, crops and livestock.'

By 3,000 BCE, Neolithic life had become well established. Farmers, fishermen, manufacturers of stone tools, and potters all flourished. So, too, did traders, including mariners of immense courage who not only plied the coastal waters of Britain, but out into the wild Atlantic to trade with the near Continent and with Ireland. The landscape gradually altered as more and more forest was cleared to make way for farmland. A steady trickle of people was also moving into Cornwall from the coasts of the Bay of Biscay, bringing a new language – Celtic – that would become established all along the Atlantic coasts of Europe and Britain and into

Ireland, too, and in several of those areas, remain in use until the present day, the oldest surviving languages of the British Isles.

Apart from the rectangular timber structures in tor enclosures such as Carn Brea, little is known of Neolithic settlements and how they were constructed. It is assumed that the dwellings of the time were timber-built or, if constructed of stone, that the stone might have been reused for building new structures in later times, leaving little trace.

That communities gathered from time to time is suggested by earthwork structures forming substantial enclosures. In 2009, in advance of a controversial green field development site at Higher Tregurra, Truro, a curving ditch, originally V-shaped and 1.8 metres deep, was uncovered. This suggested a circular enclosure some 70 metres across. A single gap faced south-south-west. Grooved Ware pottery was found, suggesting a date range of 3,800-2,400 BCE. Also discovered on the site was a remark-able slate disc, some 30cm across, with one surface covered in an incised chequerboard pattern, a rare example of Neolithic art.

Archaeologists still argue about what the site actually represented, with one faction suggesting that it was a causewayed enclosure. If this was the case, then it would be the only example of its type in Cornwall. More commonly found in central southern England, the nearest known example is at Hembury, East Devon and not very far from that county's border with Dorset. These enclosures consist of circular banks with external ditches, sometimes several of them set concentrically, but with frequent gaps allowing entry at several points in the circuit. Causewayed enclosures generally date from 4,000 to 3,400 BCE.

The opposing camp suggests that the site was a henge, again a circular enclosure but usually consisting of a bank with an internal ditch. Henges are known in Cornwall; at Castilly, Lanivet (somewhat re-modelled in medieval times for use as a plen-an-gwari, or amphitheatre for the per-formance of miracle plays and sporting events); Castlewich, near Callington, which stands close to a Neolithic greenstone axe quarry at Balstone Down; and the Stripple Stones, on Bodmin Moor near Blisland. The latter contains the remains of an internal stone circle, perhaps added during a later re-use of the site.

As only one entrance gap was found at the Higher Tregurra site, it could be that the site was indeed a henge. All that speaks against that is a hint that its ditch once had an internal bank, rather than the external one that is normally found at such sites. However, it would not been unique. At the most famous henge of them all, Stonehenge, the bank had also been set internally.

Both causewayed enclosures and henges appear to have had similar functions as multi-purpose community focus sites. There, several communities could gather, perhaps at significant times of the year, to strengthen relationships and alliances. There, they could host markets, meetings, and ceremonies, and be places where differences could be settled. As centres for society building, these sites were hugely important to the Neolithic population as it grew and developed.

As sites like these were focal points for the living, there were also focal points for the dead, and in Neolithic southern Britain, the long barrow was perhaps the most striking of these by way of their sheer size. In Cornwall, only about eight have been identified with any degree of certainty, and none of them have undergone excavation. Most are ruinous, with that at Bearah Tor, North Hill, now so degraded as to expose the wreck of an internal stone chamber. The most impressive is the Woolley Barrow, close to the Cornwall-Devon border near Morwenstow. Still 2.5 metres in height, this long grassy mound measures 62 metres in length and 21 metres wide. When built, its two longer sides had been flanked by quarry ditches; one of these, on the north side of the mound, was identified during works to the nearby highway.

Long barrows, which were built between at least 3,600 and 2,400 BCE, could be in use for up to a thousand years, and at some examples there have been indications that corpses were left outside to rot and be picked clean by birds and animals, before the bones were brought into what can be best described as a mortuary chamber within the body of the mound. It was evident that, after death, those parts of the body that quickly degraded were not considered to be as important as the spirit that could not die, or as the bones that would endure and perhaps, in the eyes of Neolithic belief, might even have housed the spirit.

Chapter 2

Towards nationhood

The advent of metal

As well as confirming the Cornish as a distinct genetic group, the Peoples of Britain genetic survey also identified a fascinating sub-group confined to the Land's End peninsula and, from archaeological similarities, probably extended to the Isles of Scilly, although no DNA samples were taken there. No further details have emerged, but it is not unreasonable to suggest that this sub-group may date from an arrival around 2,500 BCE of people who may have come from Galicia, at the northwestern tip of the Iberian peninsula.

Like Cornwall, the geology of Galicia contains tin which is known to have been extensively mined in prehistory and, at the close of the Neolithic period, a group of people from there may have sailed northward to West Cornwall, an even richer source of that metal and others, bringing their knowledge and skills with them to establish Cornwall's world-famous history of metalliferous mining.

They found that, in this new land, copper also occurred in abundance alongside the tin. Edged tools and weapons of copper were rather easier to produce so, to begin with, exploitation of that metal was prioritised and, for the first time in British history, metal implements began to appear. A more resilient metal, though, was in demand and the skills of alloying the copper with tin resulted in the wealth of bronze tools and weapons that typified the next thousand years or more.

The arrival of these people coincided with the northward spread of a pottery style known as the Maritime Bell Beaker which, like the Celtic language now being spoken all along the Atlantic coasts of Britain and Europe, had originated in the Tagus valley of southwest Iberia. Over time, some sections of society began to place these distinctive beakers alongside burials, giving rise to a belief in a distinct 'Beaker folk'. It might be more accurate to interpret Beaker burials as a fashionable practice, perhaps of an elite or other social group, rather than attribute them to a particular people, and it was a fashion that spread throughout southern Britain. It seems that this included making sure that the departed soul had something decent to accompany them on the journey to the other-world. Solidified residue in one beaker was found to have been the remains of a particularly potent barley wine.

Two main styles of clay beaker have been found at Cornish sites. The AOC (All Over Cord), or Bell Beaker was of a type that had originated near the Tagus valley in southwestern Iberia to spread northward with the trading ships and perhaps with a movement of people. It was decorated all over its surface by pressing a two-stranded and twisted cord into the clay. The Long Necked Beaker was generally decorated by means of applying a notched comb to the clay, with geometrical designs being popular.

It was also at this time that new forms of monument began to appear, doubtless inspired by those already established on the Atlantic coasts of Europe. The great portal dolmens were still revered, a thousand years after their initial construction, but they were no longer being built. In the far west of Cornwall, and on the Isles of Scilly, a smaller and very localised version was now being built: the chambered cairn or entrance grave.

In their simplest form, these were circular drum or bun-shaped stone cairns, varying from 5 to 12 metres across and retained by a heavy kerb of granite blocks or walling. Each contains a passage-like chamber of large slabs set on edge, or of stone walling, that opened onto the side of the cairn. Roughly a metre both in height and width, this chamber, usually rectangular in plan (but a few are intriguingly boat-shaped), was roofed by a number of pillow-shaped capstones.

Several show a second phase of construction, sometimes a lower collar surrounding the original cairn to produce the stepped appearance best seen at Bant's Carn, Scilly; or a reshaping of the cairn to ritually block the entrance. This is apparent at Tregiffian, near the Merry Maidens stone circle west of Lamorna Cove, and at Tregeseal near St Just. At Bosiliack, on moorland between Lanyon Quoit and Ding Dong Mine

Bosiliack Barrow, Madron: a so-called "entrance grave" of a type found only in West Penwith and Scilly, these apparent shrines from the Neolithic-Bronze Age transition are often associated with ancient field systems.

in Madron parish, inner and outer slabs were set to block the chamber entrance but low enough to leave a slot between their tops and the underside of the roof so that midwinter sunrise could cast light directly into the chamber itself: a miniaturised Newgrange, the great Irish tomb which duplicates this same annual feat on an awe-inspiring scale.

In one or two cases, much grander forms of multi-phase construction is found, carrying on enlargement and adaptation for up to a further thousand years. At the colossal and totally unique Ballowall Barrow, on the cliff top at Carn Gloose west of St Just, it seems that a conventional entrance grave, some 5 or 6 metres across, was the original form before the construction, phased over several centuries, of the huge and complex structure that it became. Another, apparently conventional, entrance grave on the summit of Chapel Carn Brea, above Land's End Airport, was later covered by a massive cairn with several internal retaining walls and later burial cists, one of which can still be seen. This reached a height of some 4.5 metres and, in the 13th century CE, could support on its top a small hermitage chapel dedicated to St Michael, which carried a beacon light for the guidance of local fishermen and travellers from Scilly.

Where the great portal dolmens made a noticeable statement in the landscape, entrance graves generally did not. On the mainland in West Penwith, these were sited on plains, hillsides and valleysides and, being much lower in height, were much more subtle features. The exception is Chapel Carn Brea, built on the very summit of the hill and rather enhancing the hill's naturally breast-shaped appearance by adding an imitation nipple to it; perhaps from a deliberate intent to humanise the landscape. It may be that the position of the hill inspired its construction, being the very last mainland hill of Britain before the vastness of the ocean that lies before it. By the same token, it would also have been visible from several miles out to sea, and perhaps this was also intended. The same consideration might apply to the entrance graves that occupy the twin hilltops of the island of Samson in the Isles of Scilly, the last hills before the open Atlantic. In general, entrance graves were much more closely related to settlements and field systems, and more easily visited from those settlements; the Bosiliack cairn actually stands on a prehistoric field terrace.

The mainland entrance graves of West Penwith number a score or less, but the Isles of Scilly have four times that number and the design similarity of some island examples even suggest the existence of a specialist architect.

No one is certain whether the mainland entrance grave fashion was spread across to the islands, or vice-versa. However, as the Isles of Scilly show no indication of being permanently occupied prior to 2,300 BCE, the consensus of opinion favours the former. Dateable finds from entrance graves are surprisingly recent, given the Neolithic character of their construction. Cremated bone from Tregiffian gave a date range of 2,000 to 1,800 BCE but, from Bosiliack, only from 1,700-1,500 BCE. Trevisker pottery from around 1,500 BCE has turned up quite regularly in the mainland sites, but is not found in the islands, where highly decorated biconical ceramic vessels have frequently been found. The pottery from the mainland sites is generally undecorated. This and other differences between the mainland and island entrance graves suggest the development of a distinct island culture. These finds do not necessarily date the structure itself, and a date range of 2,500 to 1,700 BCE is considered to be acceptable for their construction, with use continuing for a few centuries after.

The entrance graves are unlike anything that is found elsewhere, with the exception of a small group of rather similar monuments found near Tramore in southeast Ireland, a single site in the Isle of Man, and two groups of comparable structures in Scotland, perhaps indicating direct contact between those areas and the far west of Cornwall.

Were these structures tombs or shrines? Some have provided indications that their chamber floors had been covered with a layer of fertile soil, suggestive of a link between them and agricultural fertility. The cremated deposits of human bones, seldom enough to have been complete cremations, seem not to be burials, but more in the nature of votive offerings. These would imply that the entrance grave was more to be regarded as a shrine than a tomb.

Going in circles

As the population steadily increased, so too did the number and type of monuments that were being built. Among the first of these, from 2,500 BCE onwards, were the most iconic and atmospheric of them all: the stone circles. Cornwall has no less than 27 of these, more than in any other area of comparable extent in Britain. Usually a single circle will be found, but pairs are known at Tregeseal, St Just; the Nine Maidens, Wendron; Leskernick and King Arthur's Downs, both on Bodmin Moor. The Merry Maidens is also the surviving circle of a pair. Most remarkable of all is the north-south row of three closely set circles at The Hurlers (a fourth circle has recently been found there), although it is also possible that there was a third circle at Tregeseal, forming a west-east alignment.

Their sizes also vary. In West Cornwall, stone circle diameters are within the 18 to 25 metre range, with a preference for 19 stones and an assumed entrance gap. Further east, on Bodmin Moor, they tend to become as large as 46 metres across (Fernacre) with eighty or more stones of irregular sizes in the ring (Stannon). Further south on the moor, the group at King Arthur's Downs and Leaze more closely resemble the West Cornish circles.

The choice of a circle, in preference to a square or any other shape, might have been inspired by the shape of earlier monuments in the landscape; the circular kerbs that retained cairns containing the portal dolmens and entrance graves, and the henges. At the henge called the Stripple Stones, near Blisland, a stone circle was added to the interior of the existing monument, just as – on a far grander scale – the same was occurring at Stonehenge and Avebury. In this way, continuity with the Neolithic past was being carried through into the Bronze Age. Even so, the stone circles do vary in shape. Some are true geometrical circles, probably laid out by means of a rope and central peg; but others are ovoid or elliptical and often show that their shapes had been carefully worked out by remarkably advanced geometry, long before Euclid or Pythagoras.

Two stone circles, the Stripple Stones and the wonderfully atmospheric Boscawen-ûn, near St Buryan, were given a large pillar set just to the south or southwest of centre. Boscawen-ûn's central stone has a sharp lean, thought to have been an original intention, and a pair of axe carvings that only become distinctly visible at midsummer sunrise. Central stones visible in the middle ring of The Hurlers and at the Nine Stones, Altarnun, are not believed to be original features.

The true purpose of stone circles has never been ascertained but they strongly suggest a ceremonial function with a distinct astronomical significance defined by carefully planned alignments with outlying monuments or natural features to mark the rise or set of sun, moon, or certain stars on particular dates such as the equinoxes or solstices. In this way, they could act as calendars, with an obvious link to agricultural activities. The Boscawen-ûn circle strongly resembles a large sundial, which may not be entirely accidental. On Bodmin Moor, the circle at Craddock Moor was so precisely positioned that, at the Midsummer solstice, the sun rises over the tor enclosure of Stowe's Hill, and sets over Bronn Weneli ('Brown Willy').

Quartz seems to have been viewed as being of some importance: the little Duloe circle, just 9 metres across, has just eight unusually large stones, all of quartz which does not occur naturally near the site. This meant that a great deal of effort went into bringing these stones to the site. At Boscawen-ûn, the centre stone and eighteen of its geometrically flattened ring are of granite. The nineteenth stone, on its southwestern perimeter, is a block of pure quartz.

Stone circles do have the appearance of frozen dances, which is often reflected in their names. Both the Merry Maidens and Boscawen-ûn

Duloe Stone Circle, Duloe: Unusually small for a Cornish stone circle, but formed by a ring of very large quartz stones.

were known as *Dons Meyn* in Cornish ('dance of stones'); the Tregeseal circle was *Meyn an Dons* ('stones of the dance'); and the Boskednan site, on a ridge near Ding Dong Mine, Madron, was *Meyn yn Dons* ('stones in a dance'). Other site names, such as the frequently found Nine Maidens, or *Naw Whor* ('nine sisters'), the Cornish name for the Wendron Nine Maidens, continue this theme. Tales of men or maidens being turned to stone for dancing, or playing the Cornish sport of hurling, on a Sunday almost certainly date from later Christian times, the ancient stone settings being used to illustrate convenient parables told to ensure good behaviour and religious obedience from parishioners on the Sabbath.

Several circles are located in landscapes dominated by a distinct peak that, in some cases, had been the sites of Neolithic tor enclosures. These had been long out of use but it seems that the circle builders still regarded them with a measure of awe and respect, perhaps as sites that had been special to ancestral generations. Processional routes, marked by contemporary monuments, led from the circle to the tor enclosure in several cases. These are best seen at Tregeseal (Carn Kenidjack tor enclosure); the Boskednan Nine Maidens (Carn Galva) and the Hurlers (Stowe's Pound). Rough Tor, with its own large Neolithic enclosure, became the focus for at least three stone circles, perhaps more.

Something of how these peaks must have been regarded is apparent to this day. For example, from the Tregeseal stone circle, the weird form of Carn Kenidjack dominates the whole landscape. From time to time, the cloud base lowers to render the Carn itself invisible while the slopes below it remain in clear view. Were times like these seen as moments when the ancestral spirits, acting as guardians of the agricultural landscape downslope, gathered in the old enclosure, secure within the mists from the prying eyes of the living?

Something of this must have remained in folk memory for millennia for, when Methodism took hold in Cornwall, belief in the benign spirits of the distant past became legends of malignant devils and demons engaging in strange sports or rituals on Carn Kenidjack which, from a place to be regarded with reverence, became a place to be feared and to risk damnation if approached after sunset.

Where stone circles often have landscape features as their focus, so they became a focus in themselves. Most are in the close company of contemporary and related monuments of various kinds: menhirs ('standing stones'), holed stones, barrows, chambered cairns and hilltop enclosures, many of which are again related to alignment with topography and astronomical events. The close relationship between people, the structures they built, the nature of landscape, sky and season, and with agriculture, can be plainly discerned.

The stone circles are frequently surrounded by outlying monuments of the same era. Associated with the Merry Maidens, by way of example, are six menhirs (standing stones), including two pairs, a number of barrows, three holed stones and a chambered cairn or entrance grave, all in its immediate vicinity. A number of medieval stone crosses nearby might represent an attempt to Christianise the pagan nature of the locality.

Menhirs are intriguing, often impressive, and were plainly erected for more than a single reason. In the Merry Maidens complex of monuments, six of them clearly act as sightlines to or from the circle. Isolated menhirs, such as Trye, Madron or Tresvennack, Paul, sometimes marked burials. Mên Vagar, or The Longstone, which sadly had to be relocated to Roche to make way for china-clay expansion, was the last of a succession of monuments on the original site: firstly a timber pillar, then a stone one, and finally the existing stone, a pointed slab some 3.2 metres tall. Some were barely the height of an average man while others were colossal. Mên Pearn, Constantine, stood 7 metres tall before being destroyed and split into gateposts in the 19th century. The tallest in Cornwall today, at 4.6 metres, is the northeast Piper, near the Merry Maidens, while Mên Gurta on St Breock Downs is the heaviest of all Cornwall's prehistoric erected stones at 17 tonnes. That alone illustrates the huge effort that went into erecting them which, in turn, emphasises the importance that was placed on them. A further example of this is the Dry Tree menhir in the centre of Goonhilly Downs. 3.2 metres tall, but with a total length of 4.5 metres, this was transported at least two miles to where it was erected, as it consists of gabbro from Crouza Downs, much nearer to St Keverne.

Stone alignments or rows are common on Dartmoor but, for many years, it was thought that Cornwall only had one; the Nine Maidens row between St Columb Major and Wadebridge. In recent decades, several more have been found, notably on Bodmin Moor. At least one occurs in West Penwith and another on the Isles of Scilly. One stone row near Lezant was no sooner discovered than it was destroyed, a sad reflection upon some modern attitudes.

The Dartmoor examples are often seen to lead to, or be aligned with, an outlying feature such as a barrow or menhir. The Nine Maidens once aligned with a menhir on higher ground some 500 metres to the northeast. Variously called the Old Man, the Fiddler or the Magi Stone, its shattered remains can still be seen. It is a feature of several stone rows that, as one travels along it to one end or the other, a hitherto invisible vista opens up, revealing a distant feature such as a hill or headland that is precisely on the same line as the stone row itself. Most of the Bodmin Moor and Dartmoor examples consist of fairly small, low stones but, in contrast, the Nine Maidens row has much taller stones that are within the range of human height. How the stone rows were used, and what part they played in local society, remains a mystery.

Further enigmas of the period occur in the shape of holed stones, many of which are directly associated with stone circles. The famous

*Dry Tree Menhir, Goonhilly Downs: An impressive 3.5 metre tall standing
stone comprised of stone that only occurs some two miles from its site.*

Mên-an-Tol (*men an toll*: 'stone of the hole') was actually an integral
component of a stone circle some 17 metres across, part of which can still
be seen. In most cases, the artificial hole, usually countersunk on one
side or both, is scarcely large enough to admit a human hand, but the
Mên-an-Tol and the Tolvan, near Gweek, have holes that are large
enough to allow an adult to pass through, leading to beliefs of supernatural healing qualities. On the slope to the south of Carn Kenidjack, near St
Just, is a curious alignment of four holed stones, with two more forming
outliers to the west and northeast. These seem to be part of a proces-

The Tolvan, Gweek: In spite of legends that claim powers of healing for these enigmatic holed stones, their true purpose remains a mystery.

sional way from the Tregeseal stone circle, past a pair of chambered cairns and the holed stones, then passing up the hill to the strangely shaped natural tor (locally 'carn') on the hilltop, with the remains of its Neolithic tor enclosure. It may be that the local population followed this route at set times of the year to pay homage or tribute to the ancestral spirits who dwelt on the Carn, the most dominant feature of the local landscape, and who kept the agricultural landscape below under their protective gaze. We can only speculate about this, but it does seem to be a likely scenario.

The most common of all Bronze Age monuments in the landscape of Britain are the barrows, and Cornwall is no exception to the rule. Often marked on the map as 'Tumulus' or 'Tumuli', they are everywhere: on hill and ridge tops, and on lowland or coastal sites. Some stand alone; others form groups or 'cemeteries', either concentrated groups known as nucleated cemeteries (such a group at Pelynt, in which ten survive, is a particularly fine example) or laid out in a line like the eight that are strung out in a line along a ridge crest at West Taphouse. Barrows are mounds of earth, or stone-built cairns, and a range of architectural styles are apparent.

Their tradition began around 2,500 BCE, with the small mounds erected over Beaker burials. After this, they expanded into the range of styles we see in the landscape today. Bowl barrows are the shape of an upturned bowl; bell barrows of similar profile, but with a splay at their foot that separates them from the encircling quarry ditch that most earth barrows had. The most remarkable of these is the triple bell barrow near Advent. Here, a closely set line of three barrows is encircled by a single quarry ditch, and this is one of only three triple bell barrows that are known in the whole of Britain. Disc barrows are rare in Cornwall, as are the platform barrows, which have short, steep sides and a wide flat top. An unusual exception is a line of four platform barrows set in a north-south line on the flat top of Botrea Hill, near St Just in the far west of Cornwall.

Ring cairns consist of a ring-shaped bank of small stones surrounding a central area that may be featureless, or it may enclose a natural feature, usually a prominent rock. The most spectacular example is at Showery Tor, the northern shoulder of Rough Tor on Bodmin Moor. Here, a substantial circular bank of stones had been built around a remarkable tor formation that is not unlike the famous Cheesewring on Stowe's Hill and may have been seen as spiritually significant.

Many of the stone-built cairns were retained by substantial kerbs of large stone set upright or laid as walling, much like those of the earlier chambered cairns or entrance graves. Up to three courses of walling survive in the kerb of an impressive cairn capping a shoulder of Watch Croft, West Penwith's highest point, while another stone cairn, with an attendant menhir, is set on the hill's very summit.

Barrows have been assumed to be burial sites, but this was not always the case. Some seem to have been used only for ritual purposes while many of the hilltop cairns suggest that their building were attempts to contribute to the landscape by providing a summit with an artificial tor

or carn, and possibly providing the population with additional astronomical sightlines from monuments lower down to assist them with a
more accurate assessment of the yearly calendar.

The size of Bronze Age barrows varied wildly, from mere pimples in
the landscape to colossal undertakings like Carne Beacon, Veryan. 33
metres across and 6.5 metres high, this is one of the largest bowl barrows
in Britain and, in view of its position, the sheer scale of this monument
may have been intended for a purpose. It stands high above Gerrans Bay
and can be seen for miles out to sea. That it was primarily built to act as a
landmark for mariners is an inescapable conclusion, and is even hinted
at in a legend that claims it to be the burial site of a Cornish king, apparently Gerent I, whose body was laid out in a golden ship with silver oars
which had borne his body across the bay. Immediately below the barrow
is a safe landing beach, and a valley that allows easy access inland. That
this was one of many landing places for trading ships is an idea
supported by the later building of a remarkable Iron Age fort on the
valley-side below the barrow that seems to have provided protection for
the landing beach, and where the actual process of trading might well
have been carried out.

Carne Beacon was excavated in the 19th century. Sadly, there was no
king in his golden ship, but it had been a burial site, most probably of a
person of high status. The cremated remains lay in a large stone box
known as a cist, and with secondary cremations laid close by. Consisting
of four upright slabs topped by a capstone, cists resemble miniature
dolmens, and have been found in many barrows. The word cist (properly
kist, and pronounced with a hard C) is one of the few words from the
Cornish language to enter common use in English. It translates as 'box,
chest', and is the likely origin of the Cornish surname Keast.

Burial practice varied according to fashion. Cremations were the
norm during the Neolithic period, while both cremation and inhumation were practised in the early centuries of the Bronze Age. After that,
cremation again became the usual practice. With those barrows that
were intended for burials, the remains were either placed in a shallow pit
or inside a cist. This was often then surrounded by one or more rings of
posts, or by a ring cairn, before being covered by the final mound, either
of earth or stone. Recent study of barrows in the area north of St Austell
suggests that, for a period, a barrow could be covered with a layer of

bright yellow clay that would have made them prominently visible in the landscape. Secondary burials requiring a reopening of the mound were common, while people occasionally reused the ancient portal dolmens and chambered cairns right up until about 1,500 BCE. Sometimes they would place a cremation, and at other times they would leave an offering such as the perforated whetstone found in Zennor Quoit's antechamber. Perhaps the idea was driven by caution; to appease whatever spirits might still dwell within those ancient structures, just to make certain that none be offended.

In some cases, cremations may have been carried out on the spot. One of the pair of large bowl barrows on the clifftop north of Trevelgue Head, Newquay, had been built over the site of a huge funeral pyre that must have brought a great many people to the event.

Many Cornish barrows have yielded grave goods that had been laid with the human remains, hinting at a strong belief in an afterlife. One of the most remarkable finds, in 1818, was the renowned Rillaton gold cup, which accompanied an inhumation burial. The body had been laid full-length, rather than the more common foetal position, within an unusually large cist. Beside it lay a grooved bronze dagger with an ogival shape, and the famous cup. This was basically a version of a beaker, but made of corrugated sheet gold, with a handle.

After discovery, the Rillaton Cup went missing, but it turned up years later in King George V's dressing room, where he had been using it to keep his collar studs in. It is now in the British Museum, but an exact replica is on show at the Royal Cornwall Museum in Truro. Precise dating of the cup has not been possible, but the large Rillaton barrow in which it was found occupies a ridge-top site to the NNE of, and prominently visible from, the trio of stone circles called the Hurlers, which roughly align towards it. It is therefore likely to have been contemporaneous with the circles themselves.

Other grave goods from Cornish barrows include the beautiful gold lunulae, crescent-shaped neck ornaments, found at Harlyn Bay and now on display in Truro, as is the equally impressive bronze dagger or short sword from one of the barrows in the Pelynt group. Axeheads of bronze and barbed, tanged arrowheads have also turned up in a number of barrows along with the large bi-conical and ribbon-handled urns known as Cornish or Trevisker ware.

The acid soils of Cornwall preserve little organic matter from this time, giving us little idea of how people of the Cornish Bronze Age would have looked. Parallels could, however, be drawn from other areas in northern Europe. These show a pattern of sophisticated clothing made from animal hide and from woven wool, fastened with buttons made from bone or copper. Men wore long skirt-like garments that reached from the shoulders and tied at the waist, often with an outer cape that was not unlike a poncho. Close-fitting woollen caps were also in vogue. Women of the period wore long dresses with half-length sleeves during wintertime while, in summer, thin, square-necked jumpers were fashionable. Also popular were corded skirts worn with a belt that often had a plate metal fastener. They often held their hair in place with pins made of jet, bone or copper, and sometimes wore a cap or net on their heads.

Jewellery and other body ornamentation was popular, gold or bronze ear rings often being found with Bronze Age female burials, while male burials could include copper knives, arrowheads and bronze battleaxes, frequently pristine and unused as though they were only for ceremonial use, or merely intended to accompany the dead on the journey beyond. Many of these axeheads were made to be fitted onto a wooden shaft.

There has also been evidence for Bronze Age surgical practices. Skulls have been found with clear evidence of a technique known as trepanning, where a section of the skull was removed and replaced. Presumably, this was carried out in attempts to relieve or cure complaints such as epilepsy, migraines or forms of mental illness. Amazingly, healing of trepanned areas of skull show that some patients even survived this drastic form of surgery.

From an early point in the Bronze Age, perhaps as early as 2,500 to 2,000 BCE, Cornish copper was being exported to the Continent, with tin being added to the export trade by around 1,500 BCE, along with cereal produce. This may have had an effect upon society in general, with a class system becoming established that is generally looked upon as an embryo aristocracy gained from land ownership, a warrior class and a poorer working class. This social trend was to continue well into the succeeding Iron Age. It is from burials belonging to the upper two classes that the bulk of grave goods are found: the daggers, swords, faience beads and amber jewellery. The trend towards this society structure might even have started with the class who had shown a preference for beaker burial.

Bronze – an alloy of native tin and copper and lead – may not have been produced in Cornwall until about 1,500 BCE. More resilient than copper, it was quickly adopted for edged tools and weapons, which were very often of sophisticated design and manufacture.

It is from about 1,500 BCE that an ordering of the farming landscape can be discerned in a form that has lasted to the present day. Stone-built round houses, which would have been fitted with conical roofs of turf or thatch stand amongst systems of stone-walled arable and pasture fields, usually with access lanes through them and on towards areas of upland used for summer pasture. It was a pattern of mixed farming that farmers of only a century ago would have recognised in their own practice. From the beginning of the Bronze Age, a pastoral life was prevalent, with people tending sheep and cattle, and growing bearded wheats and barley in a dryish climate with long, warm summers. This happy state of affairs was soon about to change.

The earliest field patterns had been noticeably curvilinear in shape, and could be developed with more fields being added to their outer perimeter as and when required. Within a short time, the practice shifted to a different co-axial form. These field patterns consisted of long, parallel boundaries with internal sub-division, and terminating at boundaries at right angles on the edges of higher open ground. These could spread over substantial areas, and are best seen on more expansive landscapes such as Bodmin and Dartmoor, where the famous reeve systems are a particular feature of the prehistoric environment. These systems lasted for up to 500 years until about 1,000 BCE.

The co-axial systems then altered to a more intensive practice, with denser patterns of small rectangular fields. On hillslopes, many of these developed terraces or lynchets at their lower edge, due to the downhill movement of soil, especially when aided by regular ploughing. These were to last well into the succeeding Iron Age and Roman periods.

However, it is only from about 1,500 BCE that we begin to see the permanent settlements of round houses that have survived for us to view today. Indications are that, previously in the Bronze Age, transhumance was the main practice. This involved bi-annual movement on a fixed stretch of land from a winter farm to one that oversaw summer grazing, and back again. This may have been the birth of the summer grazing settlements, or shielings, known in Cornwall as the *havos*, literally 'summer dwelling', and found in place-names in forms such as *hewas*. These reflected common farming practice right through to the Iron Age and on into the early medieval period.

Evidence from elsewhere in Britain and in Ireland suggests that the *havos* was tended by the womenfolk, particularly teenage girls and young unmarried women. Driving the livestock to the expanses of rough grazing around the beginning of May (*Beltaine* in Ireland and *Cala' Me* in Cornwall), the community would repair winter damage to the *havos* and leave the young women there to tend to the livestock, and to make butter, cheese and salted buttered curds. The rest of the community would return to the home farm, or *hendre*, to deal with sowing, maintaining and reaping the arable crops. *Hendre*, in the form *hendra*, is the most common place-name in Cornwall, occurring in nearly fifty places. Hallowe'en (*Samhain* in Ireland and *Cala' Gwav* in Cornwall) was the time for the young women and livestock to return to the *hendre*. That the times of departure and return coincided with the two major festivals of the ancient year, marking the beginning of summer and winter, was almost certainly no accident.

Pottery types of the period, excepting the earlier beakers, included Food Vessels, wide bowl-shaped and often heavily decorated ware; and Collared Urns. These were tall vessels with a decorated collar around a wide neck. All of these were manufactured to a high standard and, if ever there was such a thing as a 'golden age' of prehistory, then the Early Bronze Age, from 2,500 to 1,500 BCE, would have been it. Sadly, it was not to last.

There's gold in them thar hills!
IN 1999, near the town of Nebra in the Saxony-Anhalt region of Germany, a hoard of Bronze Age objects were found. Outstanding among these was the Nebra Sky Disc, dated to c.1600 BCE and judged to be the oldest known depiction of the heavens.

The sky disc is 32cm (12.6 inches) in diameter and made of bronze, with gold insets depicting a crescent moon, the sun and stars, including a group of seven stars representing the Pleiades. The bronze had been smeared with rotten eggs, causing a chemical reaction that tinted the bronze to a deep violet colour to emulate the night sky. Two opposing arcs of its circumference had gold borders, the upper and lower limits of each being thought to mark the angles of sunrise and sunset at the winter and summer solstices, and another golden arc at the lower part of the disc might represent a solar barge. In ancient times, people did not know how the morning sun appeared in the eastern sector of the sky when it had set in the west, so they imagined that it was transported there overnight in a celestial barge.

However, even in the Middle Bronze Age, people did know that, every so often, they had to add a lunar month to the usual twelve in order to keep their feasts and festivals at the correct time of year and synchronous with the seasons (a lunar year is 354 days, rather than the solar year of 365 days) and the disc is believed to have provided a method of calculating when this should take place.

The tin content in the Nebra sky disc is of Cornish provenance, but the gold was originally thought to have been brought from the Carpathian Mountains; that is, until it was subjected to detailed analysis. This not only showed that the gold was Cornish, but also narrowed its point of origin right down to the Carnon River, between Falmouth and Truro.

This find shows that, by 1600 BCE – or even earlier as the sky-disc is likely to have been in use for several generations – exports of Cornish metals were not only being transported along the Atlantic Arc seaways, but also eastwards to continental North Sea ports.

That gold had been found in, and extracted from Cornish locations, has been known for a long time, but the amount was always thought to have been small. It has always been assumed that the gold used to make the beautiful lunulae found at Harlyn Bay, and other places; the Rillaton Gold Cup and other gold objects of the Bronze Age found in Cornwall had originated in Ireland. Findings from Southampton and Bristol Universities in 2015 have changed all that. Far from being a minimal and limited resource, Cornish gold had been a major produce.

Even though Ireland, in the Bronze Age, was a copious producer of gold, it was also a principal customer for Cornish gold, from 2,500 BCE to 1,600 BCE. The gold in more than fifty objects of the period currently stored at the National Museum of Ireland was examined and found to have been sourced in Cornwall.

Dr Chris Standish, lead author of the resulting report, suggested that, although gold was known and extracted in Ireland, a foreign, 'exotic,' source might have been seen as adding extra symbolic status to the various gold objects and to their owners. He added that, at that time, and compared with Ireland, much less gold was circulating in Cornwall and southern Britain, implying that gold was being exported because the Bronze Age Cornish felt it to be of greater advantage to trade their gold for other desirable goods than it was to keep hold of it, and use it for themselves.

Co-author of the report, Dr Alistair Pike of Bristol University, considered that this showed that, in the early Bronze Age, gold was not so much linked with wealth, as with belief and symbolism. In several societies, gold was considered to contain supernatural power, and it might well have been the same for the Bronze Age Irish. Dr Pike said that the first gold coins did not appear until 2,000 years later; prehistoric societies were clearly driven by factors more complex than the trade of commodities, with belief systems playing a major role.

As much as 200 kilos of gold – about £5 million worth of it in modern terms – came out of Cornwall, to be transported not only to Ireland, but to North Wales and Anglesey, where the magnificent Mold gold cape may well have been made from Cornish gold. Likewise, the priesthood and chieftains of the area around Stonehenge may also have obtained their gold from Cornwall. Were the various items also made in Cornwall, or was just the raw material transported to its various destinations where it would be fashioned to local design specifications? The probability is that both took place. Items such as bracelets or the beautiful lunulae, broad, crescent-shaped necklets, might been exported as finished items, but a production such as the Mold cape is so unique that it was probably made in north Wales, the gold being exported from Cornish shores as raw material.

Gold was most likely a by-product from the extraction of tin and copper, which, at the time, was largely obtained in Cornwall and Western Devon from the sands and gravels of streams leading off the high granite moorland areas. One method of extraction would have been to lay woolly fleeces in the streams to catch the minute grains of both tin and gold, as still practised to obtain gold in the foothills of the Caucasus Mountains in Georgia, the ancient Colchis, home of the Golden Fleece sought by Jason and the crew of the Argo.

Geologist Simon Camm believes that the headwaters of many Cornish and West Devonian rivers would have been much richer in gold deposits in the Early Bronze Age than today, and that it might well have attracted a prehistoric Klondyke-style rush, with prospectors gaining at least 150 grams of gold per year, and up to twice that amount if luck was on their side. North coast havens such as the Camel estuary and the Hayle estuary were the likeliest export points for the Irish and Welsh markets.

From better to worse

AT some point in the Middle Bronze Age, between 1,600 BCE and 1,000 BCE, farms on the higher uplands of Dartmoor and Bodmin Moor started to be abandoned due to a marked deterioration in climate to a cooler, wetter regime that also led to the formation of peat layers. The cause of this is not fully understood. Some suspect the stupendous eruption of the Santorini volcano in the Aegean Sea as a possible cause. This cataclysm, the tsunamis from which devastated the Minoan culture on Crete, is adjudged to have been several times larger than the famous eruption of Krakatau in 1883, and to have pumped huge quantities of ash into the upper atmosphere to create a prolonged 'nuclear winter' effect.

Whatever the cause, upland farmers in southwestern Britain were forced to move to lower ground, and this could only create a great deal of social friction and open conflict. With increasing populations, much of that land was already taken. It may have been because of this that fortifiable hilltop enclosures, to become the hill forts of the succeeding Iron Age, began to be built.

It was during this period, with its cooler, wetter conditions, and the deterioration of soil quality on the uplands, that the pattern of farming became one of summer grazing on clifftops, uplands and towans (expanses of sand-dunes), while farmland grew fodder and crops in summertime; a pattern that was to last for more than 2,000 years, and to form the basis of the Cornish farming we see today. During the 1st millennium BCE, neglected uplands quickly became open areas of grassland interspersed with scrub, heath and a limited amount of woodland. At the higher edges of farmland, oak and hazel woodland became cleared to establish pasture that was rich in herbs.

The climate deterioration had other effects. Use of stone circles and other social and ritual sites were abandoned as though it had been felt that the old gods had deserted the people, although barrow burial continued for a while before being replaced by the flat cemeteries that were favoured during the Iron Age. Perhaps it was during this period that belief systems moved on to create the pantheon of gods and goddesses that became prevalent in the Iron Age and later.

A social decline echoed the climatic one. Standards of craftsmanship noticeably deteriorated and there is even some evidence that some migration to the Continent might have taken place. Pottery of the Middle and Late Bronze Age illustrates this decline rather well. The Deveral-Rimbury ware and the typically Cornish Trevisker pottery of the period were of inferior standard to the previous ware, and made with coarser material than the sophisticated pottery of the Early Bronze Age. It was as though the whole of society had taken a backward step. The pottery of this later period, mostly from domestic sites rather than burial locations, came in barrel, bucket and globular shapes decorated only with the fingertips, or with bands of clay, and with nothing as fine as the intricately incised work of before.

This seemed the likeliest time for the most senior members of society to become an elite, and it was perhaps in the Late Bronze Age that the kingdoms of, first, Dumnonia and, much later, Cornwall, began to take shape and endure for 2,000 years.

Coinciding with the building of the first hill forts at around 1,000 BCE came a surge in the manufacture of weapons and, in particular, more advanced types of spearhead. Clearly, the move to lower ground had increased the likelihood of inter-community conflict. Soon, weapons would be made from an even more durable material than bronze. Society was pretty much on the decline, but the wheel of fortune always turns and better times lay ahead.

The spoken word

WE will never know what language our Palaeolithic and inter-glacial visitors spoke, nor are we likely to know for certain the language that the first post-Glacial Mesolithic settlers of Cornwall spoke. However, of the latter, there is one very intriguing suggestion.

Geneticist Stephen Oppenheimer, author of *The Origin of the British* (2006), put forward a suggestion which is now generally supported by archaeologists, and by further genetic research, that these settlers had come from the Iberian peninsula, and an initial glacial refuge area in the lee of the Western Pyrenees where, to this day, a curious language survives.

This language is Euskara, or Basque, which not only appears to be unrelated to the family of Indo-European languages, but to pre-date it. Might an early form of this have been the language spoken by Britain's first colonists? It is, of course, impossible to know, let alone prove, but Oppenheimer's suggestion that it may have been is perfectly feasible.

Just as there is a distinct and ancient genetic divide between the people of western Britain and Ireland, and those of the eastern side of Britain, so there was almost certainly an early linguistic one. It is an interesting aside to question which language had been spoken by those other early colonists on the eastern side of the island. They had entered Britain across the plain that is now the North Sea, from other Ice Age refuge areas north and west of the Black Sea, and because of the longer distance they had to journey, probably came into Britain some time later than the western colonists. They must also have spoken a pre-Indo-European language, but can it be identified?

Three language families of this antiquity not only survive in the hinterland of the Black Sea, but also flourish. These are Kartvelian, with 4 million speakers – its best-known language being Georgian; Northwest Caucasian, with 2.5 million speakers; and Northeast Caucasian, with 3.8 million speakers, including the 1.5 million speakers of Chechen. Did the first Mesolithic colonists of eastern Britain speak a precursor of one of these languages? The nature of such a suggestion is highly speculative but, like Oppenheimer's idea for the language first spoken in western Britain and Ireland, perfectly feasible.

However, the language of those first western colonists was not yet Celtic, which is a branch of the Indo-European family. How, where and when Celtic evolved from Indo-European has been hotly disputed for many years and centuries but, at last, we have a much clearer picture. This, however, requires a brief look at Indo-European, the basis of most modern European languages.

The favoured hypothesis is that the Indo-European language family first developed c.9000 BCE in the region of the Black Sea, probably to its north-east, and to the north of the Caucasus mountains. From there it spread, alongside the spread of agriculture, evolving and adapting as it went, northward, eastward and westward. The eastern movement took it into Persia and across the Indian sub-continent, but it is the opposite branch that concerns us the most.

The western spread seems to have followed the European shores of the Mediterranean, firstly to Greece by about 6,000 BCE, where it was to form into Classical and, eventually, Modern Greek. It would travel further, through Italy, southern France and southern Iberia, to form the Celto-Italic group. The further west that it spread, the more it would change. In Italy and southern France it began to form what would eventually become the Romance languages, but it was in south-western Iberia that a significant evolution was to take place, the likeliest place for this event being in the hinterlands of the Tagus estuary, a major centre of prehistoric innovation. Here, Celto-Italic formed into proto-Celtic, most probably around 4,000 BCE.

The route that Celtic then followed was the Atlantic seaway route northward, eventually to be adopted as a *lingua franca* of the sea-trading nations along the route's entire length. It became spoken throughout western Iberia, replacing most of the earlier languages (although Euskara survived in the Basque region), and along the coasts of Biscay into Armorica, and deeper into Gaul along the river valleys. From the Armorican peninsula, it went north into Ireland and western Britain as far north as Orkney, becoming established in those regions by 3,000 BCE. This approximate date is close to that of the northward spread and extent of megalith building, and it is very possible that the two events coincided.

A second spread of early Celtic from Iberia also followed overland trade routes, mostly along major rivers and eastward into Europe across the whole of Gaul and the Low Countries, and into the Alpine areas. This eventually entered Britain from a southeasterly direction, covering that part of Britain that was not already Celtic speaking by 2,000 BCE, and, in time, it also entirely replaced the earlier pre-Indo-European language.

It is possible that this secondary spread evolved a separate dialect over time and distance, becoming P-Celtic, and that the older one had been Q-Celtic, the basis of the modern Irish, Manx and Gaelic languages. Certainly Gaulish was to be a P-Celtic language and, after spreading into eastern Britain, this dialect began to push westwards until eventually, perhaps in the Bronze Age, it had pushed Q-Celtic out of Britain and confined it to Ireland. If this hypothesis is correct, then the Neolithic and

Early Bronze Age Cornish would have spoken Q-Celtic, not becoming P-Celtic speakers until somewhere between 1500 and 1,000 BCE.

From then until the post-Roman centuries, P-Celtic, or British, as it would become known, differed little from northern Scotland to the tip of Land's End, except for regional accents. Certainly the language as written down in southern Scotland during the pre-Norman centuries was so indistinguishable from Old Welsh that it is quite reasonable to describe the British, or Brythonic, of that time as Old Welsh, as Cornish had yet to develop from it into a distinct language.

From Cornwall, a few names have trickled down to us from Iron Age sources, particularly from Pytheas of Massalia (Marseilles), then a Greek colony. This Greek geographer and explorer visited West Cornwall in the late 4th century BCE, the first known person from the Mediterranean ever to do so. *Belerion*, a name he recorded for the Land's End peninsula, is not Greek, but stems from a Celtic root with the meaning of 'shining', perhaps connected with navigational beacons on its high cliffs. The tidal island port he also described, Iktis, might be from British *ek-tiro-s*, 'off-land' (this was surely St Michael's Mount, now archaeologically confirmed as a prehistoric and Roman period trading port).

Later, in the 2nd century CE, the Greco-Egyptian geographer Claudius Ptolemaeus (Ptolemy) gave several names in Cornwall that may have been sourced from Pytheas. Like most Mediterranean scholars of the classical period, Ptolemy himself never visited Britain but had full access to the Alexandria Library containing Pytheas's work. His *Belerium Promontorium* confirms Pytheas's *Belerion* as Land's End. *Cenion* and *Voliba* remain unlocated, but are recognisably Celtic words. *Tamari Fluvii*, 'river Tamar' has scarcely altered in the last 2,000 years.

There is one curious entry in Ptolemy's list: *Ocrinum Promontorium*, which he gave to Lizard Point. *Ocrinum* does not appear to be Celtic, but from a Greek root, *okris*, 'rugged point'. The origin of this is obscure, but perhaps this came from a lost passage by Pytheas, in which the explorer saw the Lizard while in Mount's Bay, with the bristling rocks lying off its furthest point, but did not hear its native name. A description of the Lizard as a 'rugged headland' in his own native Greek would have been expected, and might provide the explanation for the name given by Ptolemy.

The Celtic name for the Lizard may have been *Pretannikon*, 'British (headland)', as its long low shape would have been a distinctive landmark for mariners approaching from the ocean. Still preserved as a place-name on the western side of the Lizard peninsula as Predannack, this retains the original P initial of the island's name, *Pretannike*, which was altered by later classical Greek and Roman writers to the more familiar *Britannia*, although modern Welsh still writes *Prydein* for the island's name.

The *Ravenna Cosmography* contains further place-names in Cornwall. Compiled c.700CE from sources some 300 years older, this is a list of routes all over Europe and Britain. One such route travels from Exeter (*Isca Dumnoniorum*) westward to the Camel estuary and three of its listed names refer to Cornish locations. Once the heavily corrupted entries are deciphered, it is clear that *Tamaris* is the same as Ptolemy's *Tamari fluvii*. Here, though, it may refer to a specific crossing of the river Tamar, perhaps at (North) Tamerton. Two more names to the west of that location are also given: *Durocornovio* and *Portus Alaunus*. Both are identifiably British Celtic in Latinised form, but still not distinctly Cornish.

British, or Old Welsh, would further evolve. In the north, it became Pictish and Cumbrian. In the west, it would become the basis of modern Welsh while in Britain's south-western peninsula, the Kingdom of Dumnonia, it began to change into early Cornish, this process being hastened by a restriction in landward contact due to the westward advance of the West Saxons and their victory at the Battle of Dyrham near Bath in 577 CE, the second time that the Germanic speaking Saxons had attempted to break through to the western coast of Britain, after the Battle of Badon c.500.

It is difficult to determine when Dumnonian British became distinctly Cornish. Prior to the 9th century CE, no written records of it survive, except for Celtic names on inscribed memorial stones dating from the 5th century, and the Roman records given above. Even on these inscriptions, the names are rendered in a rough Latin form, but the occasional hint of an early local linguistic distinctiveness can be found. For example, the RIALOBRAN of the Mên Scryfa near Madron would, in British, have been *Rigalobran(os)* In the Cornish of today, the name would be written as *Rielvran*.

Fragments of script from the 10th century CE show that Cornish had by then become distinct from Welsh, although still close enough to cause some initial confusion. The discovery in the Cottonian Library of what is termed the Old Cornish Vocabulary (*Vocabularum Cornicum*), dated to the 12th century CE, was at first glance thought to be written in a dialect of Welsh called Gwenhwyseg before it was realised by Edward Lhuyd, shortly after 1700, that it was, in fact, Cornish, and Cornish in a state of further transition.

This was a process called assibilation, which was a softening of certain hard vowels and a process that failed to occur in the closely related languages of Welsh and Breton. To give a few examples, Welsh and Old Cornish *nant*, 'river valley' would become *nans*. *Bod*, 'dwelling' softened to *bos*, and *gwint*, 'wind' to *gwyns*. Even Celtic personal names underwent the same process, so that *Cadoc* would become *Casek* in Cornish, the process being evident in the changing orthographies of place-names containing such personal names. In the *Old Cornish Vocabulary*, a list of 961 words with their Latin glosses, some entries are assibilated, while others are not.

Anglo-Saxon, already becoming Middle English, had made certain inroads into parts of eastern Cornwall during the 10th century, with place-names in that language almost completely replacing Celtic ones in the area to the north of the River Ottery, a second area bordering the Tamar to the south of Launceston, and a third in the Rame peninsula at the Tamar's mouth. Elsewhere it made very little impact and Norman administration after 1066 had only a minimal effect. Only the merest scattering of Norman-French names appeared in the Cornish landscape; Catchfrench, the various Barrippers and Bereppas, Reawla and Grampound being examples.

The new Norman overlords appear to have acted wisely in their administration of Celtic-speaking Cornwall, by appointing Breton speakers to an equivalent of viceroy representing the King, and with several Celtic speakers in their own retinues. This was a unique arrangement, as the Norman king himself held direct sway elsewhere. At this time, Breton and Cornish were virtually indistinguishable.

Breton had descended from the British language by way of a migration and colonisation from southwestern Britain, the former kingdom of Dumnonia, in the mid 5th century. The infusion of south western, or Dumnonian, British (later to become Cornish) into Brittany became dominant in that peninsula and, to this day, Breton and Cornish remain the two most closely related of the surviving British languages. The third, of course, is Welsh.

An increasing amount of settlement from England from medieval times, and an equally increasing dependency on links with the east, placed a great deal of pressure on the Celtic language of Cornwall which, at no one given moment from the Norman period onward, was spoken by more than 40,000 people. A golden age of literature in Cornish in the 14th century was short-lived and became increasingly sporadic. More attritional pressure in the 16th century and a refusal to allow a Prayer Book or Bible in Cornish, placed even greater pressure on the language which was steadily forced westward. Not until 2011 was a complete Bible in Cornish produced. From the 16th century, the language suffered a stigmatisation, largely driven by Cornwall's own gentrified classes, of having become a tongue used only by the poorest members of society: in effect, reduced to the status of a peasant language.

By 1700, community use of Cornish was confined to the Land's End and Lizard peninsulas and, 100 years later, was just about hanging on in remote parishes of Penwith. In the mid-19th century, local scholars realised that a vital part of their heritage, and one that defined their identity more than any other, was on the verge of being lost forever. The last known monoglot speaker of Cornish, Chesten (Christine) Marchant of Gwithian, had died at the end of the 17th century and, from then on, all speakers of the language were bilingual in both Cornish and English.

It was a close run thing for Cornish. When those 19th century enthusiasts began to pull together all that was known of the language, record it in a scholarly fashion, and initiate a revival, just a few families still retained traditional knowledge of the ancient tongue. One of those last traditional Cornish speakers, Richard Mann of St Just, but formerly of Zennor, was still alive at the age of 80 in 1914, by which time the language's revival was well under way. From a mere handful of speakers then, to an estimated 5,000 users of Cornish now (with 1,200 more learning the language in 2015) is a remarkable comeback. Interestingly, this figure represents about 12% of the maximum number of Cornish speakers that would have existed at any given moment since the Norman period. Listed by UNESCO as a Seriously Endangered Language, Cornish is now protected under the European Charter for Regional and

Minority Languages. As any modern visitor to Cornwall will affirm, bilingual signage is, with official aid, springing up everywhere and it is to be hoped that the Cornish language can enjoy a rosy future.

The promontory people

ONE can easily imagine a Celtic trading ship calling into a southern British port sometime around 800 BCE, or soon after, with a Continental merchant eagerly exhibiting, for the very first time, types of edged weapons or tools made from an exciting and hard wearing new material: iron. One can just as easily imagine what excitement that would generate among the local populace who would have crowded and jostled around, eager to look at and handle this new metal, and to see demonstrations of its effectiveness.

The merchant might well have brought experts along to show how easy this metal was to work up from ore to finished article, and word would have spread through the island like wildfire. No one knows where the knowledge of iron first entered Britain, but the people of the far southwest would have heard about it in short order.

The next stage would be local searches, all over the island, for sources of the ore itself and, for the people of Dumnonia, within in their own mineral-rich region? Elsewhere in Britain, iron was plentiful in areas such as County Durham, the Forest of Dean, Water Newton and the Sussex Weald. In Devon, high-grade ore could be found near Brixham, North Molton and Ilsington on the eastern side of Dartmoor and, in Cornwall, in a broad band from Perranporth to St Austell. Evidence for prehistoric mines for the material have not been found, probably because they were completely obliterated by later and more intensive mining.

The people were never to look back. Most importantly for them, farming and other crafts such as carpentry would be that much easier, with tools that would last far longer, and be more effective than copper or bronze.

The social decline in the later Bronze Age, coupled with an ever-increasing population, had already given rise to the building of some hilltop forts. In the new Iron Age, this trend was really to take off, but not necessarily as a reaction to greater violence. In fact, little evidence has ever emerged from them of actual conflict. In a few cases, existing and, even then, very ancient hilltop enclosures were brought back into use

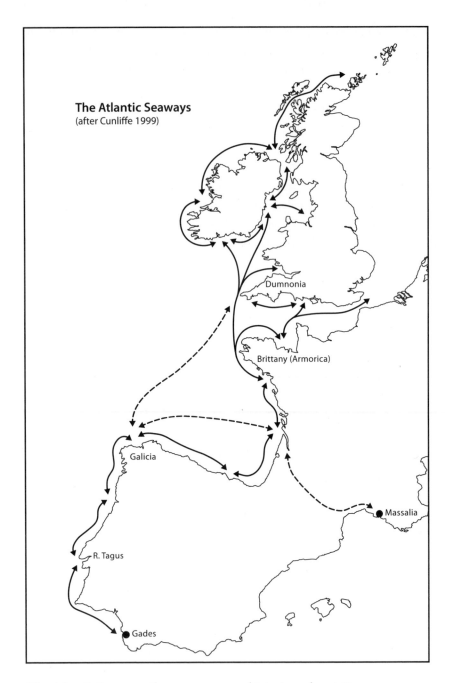

The Atlantic Seaways: the prosperous prehistoric and post-Roman maritime trading network that linked the entire Atlantic seaboard from Orkney to the Mediterranean.

and adapted to suit. The great Neolithic tor enclosure on Carn Brea became a hill fort and the several round house foundations that can be seen inside its giant system of ramparts date from the new re-use of the site. Similarly, the tor enclosure on Trencrom Hill was brought back into active use.

Castle-an-Dinas (Penwith) and Caer Brân in the same peninsula utilised existing Bronze Age ring cairn enclosures, adding concentric outer defences to the older site, which in each case survived because the hill forts themselves were never completed.

The siting and distribution of the hill forts suggest that they were statements that declared the identity and territory of local communities. A more peaceful use appears to have been indicated, especially in the Land's End peninsula where there are signs that they may have been built for a mutually cooperative purpose. From each of the peninsula's several hill forts, a number of others are clearly visible. Chûn Castle was also built on a site with a much earlier hilltop enclosure but, unlike the other two forts, it overlapped the older site, which can only now be seen as a faint arc of bank and outer ditch outside its southwestern perimeter. Had it been built concentrically around the older enclosure, the Caer Brân fort would not have been visible in a shallow saddle of hills to the south but, in its chosen site, this very limited intervisibility was achieved. This can only have been a deliberately precise siting. Might the intention have been to secure a system of alarm signals, from one fort to the next, should any external threat to the peninsula and its valuable mineral resources have materialised from the sea?

Chûn Castle had also been built astride an ancient ridgeway track that linked the rich tin-producing areas around St Just to ports at both St Ives Bay and Mount's Bay. One of the few hill forts that had been completely constructed of extremely strong stone walling forming two concentric rings, Chûn's connection to the tin trade was confirmed by the finding of a tin ingot and an elaborate smelting furnace inside the fort itself.

The building of cliff castles, also known as promontory forts, may have given rise to the first naming of the Cornish (*Cornovii*: 'promontory people') as a sub-group of the Dumnonii, the Celtic tribe occupying the southwest peninsula of Britain from the Somerset Levels westward. No less than 33 of these sites are known in Cornwall and the Isles of Scilly. Some are known of in Devon, but with nowhere near the number of

Castle-an-Dinas, St Columb Major. The huge ramparts and ditches of one of Cornwall's finest Iron Age hill forts dominate the landscape for miles around its 214-metre high hilltop.

these structures that are found further west. They also occur in Brittany and one school of thought suggests a movement of people from there into Cornwall that might have initiated their building.

Firstly, a suitable headland would be chosen, then defended from the landward approach by earth ramparts, or stone walls, with external ditches running right across the width of the headland from one cliff to the other. Some have just a single line of these; others have several, right up to the series of seven defensive lines at Trevelgue Head, Newquay. The remainder of the headland had the natural defences provided by its own cliffs.

The oldest of these appears to the 4th century BCE Maen Castle, between Sennen Cove and Land's End. Overlooked by an extensive system of earlier fields, this headland, defended by a single massive stone wall and deep external ditch with a substantial counterscarp bank along its outer edge, contained no proven habitations. Conversely, The Rumps, near Polzeath, had a thriving community of round house dwellings within its triple lines of defence which gave evidence of trading links as far afield as the Mediterranean.

Clearly, different cliff castles had different functions. Some, like The Rumps, or Pentire Fort as it was named in the 16th century, were defended settlements, perhaps only used on a seasonal basis. Those lying close to safe landing beaches would provide a secure location for maritime trading. Some may have been built to provide refuge and protection should the local community ever come under threat, just retaining lookouts for the most part, while others seem to have had more of a spiritual significance.

An outstanding example of the latter is the great fort at Treryn Dinas, near Porthcurno, whose four principal lines of defence may have been built at different times. The tip of this spectacular headland is a castle built by nature itself of cubiform piles of granite that, in turn, include two naturally poised rocking stones. One, the Lady Logan (a dialect word that should properly be spelt and pronounced 'loggan', and meaning 'swaying'), guards the landward entrance to this amazing natural stronghold. Within, and perched on top of a vertically-sided crag, is the great Logan Stone itself, a massive elongated cube of poised granite estimated to weigh 70 tonnes.

Prior to an act of 19th century vandalism carried out by the crew of a Royal Navy cutter, this great boulder was so sensitively balanced that a strong breeze could set it rocking. One can easily imagine the awe and reverence it would have been held in by the local Iron Age population as they witnessed this colossal rock ponderously swaying all on its own in a way that must have seemed supernatural. (It should be mentioned that both logan stones on this headland can still be rocked but, since the larger one was required to be replaced after being forced from its perch, it does take some effort to initiate its movement).

Until the development of courtyard houses in West Penwith during the Roman period, the usual dwelling type continued to be the round house, in the same tradition as those built during the preceding Bronze Age. In the rockier areas, these were built with thick, circular stone-built walls standing to about chest-height, and roofed with a conical construction of timber and thatch. Excellent modern reconstructions exist at Bodrifty, near Newmill in West Penwith, and at Trewortha on Bodmin Moor. In other areas, the house wall was constructed of wattle and daub

Maen Castle, Sennen: The oldest and most westerly of Cornwall's many Iron Age cliff castles, or fortified headlands.

and, again, reconstructed houses of this type can be seen at Saveock Water, to the west of Truro. Some stand in isolation, or dotted throughout a contemporary field system; others are grouped together in small hamlets.

A new development began to become prevalent in Cornwall from around the 4th century BCE: the rounds. These were settlements of round houses enclosed within an earth and stone bank, usually with an external ditch. This enclosure was probably not intended as a defence against human hostility but to keep four-legged predators at bay: wolves and bears still flourished. It has been suggested that the enclosure bank of a round may have been planted out with blackthorn: as impervious a barrier that could be devised.

The rounds remained popular until at least the 4th century CE, and at least 3,500 of them are known in Cornwall, with more being discovered every year. In West Penwith, at least two examples had courtyard houses added to them, at Goldherring, Sancreed and Porthmeor, Zennor. These were the beginnings of the land-holdings or farming estates (*trevs* in Cornish) that would last almost to the present day. They were to form the basis for the *villae* mentioned in pre-Conquest charters, the *maneria* of the Domesday survey, and the landholdings of the Tithe Apportionment of the 1840s.

In the northern part of the Land's End peninsula, a remarkable series of ribbon-like holdings were laid out and, for the most part, still survive. These run from rough clifftop grazing areas, across the more fertile field patterns on the 120 metre coastal bench, then up to the watershed of the moorland hills that provided summer grazing areas. There they terminate at the ancient ridgeway track, the 'Old St Ives Road', or 'Tinners' Way', that can still be followed today, and may date from as early as the Neolithic period. In several places, the land boundary between holdings is marked by a shared droveway leading from the crop and pasture fields uphill to the summer grazings on the moor. In most of these holdings, the remains of the prehistoric farms can still be found, usually upslope from the current farmhouses that, in most cases, may stand on the site of their medieval predecessors.

From these ancient landholdings come the oldest settlement names that survive in the Cornish language. Names in *Tre-*, or *Trev-* before a vowel, denoted the holding itself. Although now translated as 'farm' or 'settlement', its original meaning would have been 'farm estate'. Names with *Ker-*, *Car-*, 'fort, enclosure' were also applied to complete landholdings, but those which had been centred upon one of the many rounds. The third ancient place-name generic is *Bos-*, 'dwelling,' (older *Bod-*). These seem to have been given to small new and secondary farms formed by splitting off a portion of the original holding to accommodate a new generation of the landowning family.

The sheer number of rounds and open settlements that date from the Cornish Iron Age suggest that the population of Cornwall at around the 1st century BCE was in excess of 100,000 people; about a fifth of its population recorded in 2011 and a remarkably high number.

Those people would often have been a colourful sight to behold. Men generally wore their hair long, and were either bearded, or shaved to leave a heavy drooping moustache. They wore sleeved shirts and trousers that could be belted, or fitted with waistband drawstrings. Full-length cloaks, fastened at the left shoulder with a penannular brooch, were commonly worn when the weather required it. Women wore long skirts and preferred to plait their hair; the plaits either being worn loose, or coiled around the head to be held in place with a bronze pin.

Clothing was woven on elaborate looms and in brightly coloured patterns that included checks, the origin of tartan plaids. Shoes were usually of leather and not dissimilar to the moccasin. The higher classes of both men and women were fond of jewellery. Beautifully crafted armlets, bracelets, torcs worn around the neck, and brooches of copper, gold and bronze, often decorated by enamel inlays, have been found in many places. Appearances were important and, occasionally, beautiful bronze mirrors turn up, notably those from Trelan, St Keverne and from Scilly. The items of jewellery and the backs of the mirrors also feature the influence of the lovely, complex curvilinear designs and art styles that had originated from the la Tène culture of transalpine Europe, imported into Britain and Ireland and copied from around 200 BCE. The adoption of this continental art-form has led to it being somewhat misnamed as 'Celtic Art.'

Weapons included swords, spears and daggers. Shields were normally circular and on the small size, although deeper, sub-rectangular shields are known from this period. Craftsmanship in the Iron Age had progressed significantly: the sheer beauty and quality of the metalwork and jewellery speak for themselves, whilst woodworking was also of a very high standard. Iron Age Britons had developed an entire carpenter's kit, and perfected the spoked wheel, even to the fitting of iron tyres.

Horsemanship, developed in Britain from at least the Middle Bronze Age, was masterful, while their bits, bridles and horseshoes scarcely differed from those we use today. Maritime skills had also become a fine art, which is only to be expected from a maritime people. While river and coastal fishermen used small boats of hide stitched over wooden frames, such as the coracle and curragh, longer and more arduous voyages were undertaken by the massive, plank-built ships described elsewhere in these pages.

On land, the people of the Iron Age made frequent use of the network of trackway routes that had existed since the Neolithic and been expanded upon ever since. Elsewhere in Britain, it was a selection of these that would be further adapted and used by the Romans, rather than creating their own as commonly believed.

Cornish pottery of the Iron Age was also of a very high standard. From about 400 BCE to the 1st century BCE, the commonest was a type known as South West Decorated Ware. Made from the very same gabbroic clay sourced from the St Keverne area of the Lizard peninsula that had been used since the Neolithic period, these wares were thin, regular and very highly crafted, with incised designs. Later, distinctive cordoned vessels began to appear, apparently influenced by similar ware that was being produced across the water in Brittany. These were jars that were often quite tall, with cordons on the shoulders. Some were even big enough to be used as storage jars. Bowls with an S-shaped profile were also in local production, and the standard of all these types of ware was of the very highest order.

From about the 4th century BCE, a peculiar type of structure began to appear in West Cornwall: the mysterious fogous. Their name deriving from *fogow*, a Cornish word for 'cave', these are clustered in West Penwith, with one just east of the Hayle-Marazion isthmus, and a further group of three clustered on either side of the Helford River.

To this day, no one knows the true purpose of these enigmatic, impressive and highly atmospheric structures. In general terms, a fogou consists of a stone-lined and roofed passage, often with subsidiary passages and chambers, but only about a dozen are known. They bear a certain resemblance to the souterrains of Brittany, except that those are almost exclusively tunnels dug through earth and clay with little stone structure to be seen; and to similar souterrains in Ireland and Scotland. However, those date from a rather later period than the Cornish fogous.

Often described as underground structures, only some are truly underground. Four are semi-underground and the remainder were built above ground. Theories of them having been concealed refuges have been virtually discounted, and a suggestion of them having been nothing more than storage chambers is thinly argued and with obvious weaknesses. The majority opinion is that they held some sort of spiritual significance, and this is supported by a carving on an entrance stone of the fogou at Boleigh (Rosemerrin), near Lamorna Cove, of the upper part of a human figure with upraised arms: one holding a staff or spear, the other a diamond-shaped object, with something twined around the wrist. Some have interpreted this as a serpent, which has long been regarded as a symbol of healing.

Ian McNeill Cooke's painstaking study over many years of individual fogous finds that the orientation of fogou long passages often coincides with sunrise/set or moonrise/set on significant dates of the year, and that they also coincide with the direction of local mineral lodes, without the structure itself having any mining function. With a single exception, fogou walls were built in a corbelled fashion, narrowing towards the top and the better to hold the heavy roofing slabs, and their long passage often reveals a gently curving plan.

The magnificent fogou at Carn Euny, Sancreed remains the most intensively excavated and studied, and it still stubbornly refused to give up its secrets. It had been built in three phases: the first, from the 4th century BCE, consisted of its remarkable round chamber and a low entrance passage from the southeast. The second phase came a couple of centuries later, with the long passage cutting across and truncating that entrance passage. Both ends of this seem to have been closed, leaving the sole entry to the entire structure to a tiny 'creep'passage angling to the surface from the lower end of the long passage.

The final phase came when the courtyard houses were built on the site, and the northeast end of the long passage being opened to connect with one of the new houses. Strangely, the design of the first phase structure of the Carn Euny fogou is echoed almost to the inch by an above ground structure at Bosporthennis, Zennor, several miles away and known as the 'Beehive Hut'.

In general, Iron Age life in Cornwall seems to have been a time of relative peace, despite the formidable hill forts in which little that indicates actual warfare has ever been found. Small-scale and inter-community squabbles almost certainly occurred over land disputes and the cattle-rustling raids that seem to have been a feature of Celtic life but, for the most part, people got on with life, in farming, mining, trading, and in honing their considerable wealth of skills and crafts. This is very much the picture of the 'civilised' and 'hospitable' way of Cornish Iron Age life that was remarkably recorded by an unexpected but welcome visitor from the Mediterranean, as a following chapter will detail.

Whereas the spiritual beliefs of the Mesolithic, Neolithic and Bronze Age Cornish can only be gleaned from the monuments they built, and the objects placed within them, it is known that Iron Age culture, in Britain, Ireland and in Gaul, had developed a Celtic pantheon of gods and goddesses. Among these were Dis Pater, the Great Father, and sometimes known as the Dagda; Taranis the thunder god; antlered Cernunnos, lord of nature and the original of Herne the Hunter; Coventina of the sacred springs; Belenos the sun god; Govannon the smith; Sucellos, the god of agriculture and always depicted with a long-handled hammer; Manannan MacLir, god of the sea; Epona, the horse goddess, who was readily adopted by Roman cavalrymen; Teutates, protector of the people, and many more. Few are alluded to in Cornish culture, but the cult of Brigantia, a goddess whose name means 'the high one', was powerful enough for her to be adopted into Christianity as St Brigid.

The goddess Sulis, 'the watcher' (pronounced 'SILL-iss'), gave her name to the Isles of Scilly and her cult was particularly strong at Bath, where the Roman name *Aquae Sulis*, 'waters of Sulis' were applied to the famous hot springs. The Romans themselves adopted her, and equated her with a parallel deity of their own, thus naming her Sulis Minerva.

The god Lugh Làmhfhada, 'bright one of the long hand', famed in Ireland, known in Gaul as Lugus, and in Wales as Lleu Llaw Gyffes 'Lleu of the strong hand', seems to have been known in Cornwall. Here, the fascinating legend of the Giants of Towednack seems to preserve elements drawn from genuine mythology. Its multi-skilled character Jack the Tinkeard, or Jack of the Hammer, parallels the equally adept Irish character in many ways, not least in his associations with the summer festival of Lughnasa.

Figures of Cornish legend are almost certainly folk memories of prehistoric peoples. Mighty structures such as the Neolithic dolmens are ascribed to the giants because, to medieval folk, only they could possibly have moved such enormous stones. Nonetheless, almost every story of the Cornish giants associates them with ancient fortifications. Perhaps the high social standing of the community leaders who did build them became translated into physical height, while the stupidity commonly ascribed to the giants embodies the time-honoured fashion of lampooning authority figures.

The elusive Small People, too, are fascinating and might recall the reclusive and disparate life-styles of late Mesolithic hunter-gatherer-fishers at the time of the first Neolithic farmers. Detail in one story of the Small People being star-worshippers who had no place in their society for the institution of long-term marriage may be telling us something about the life-style of prehistoric people from that era, or even later.

The oak-seers

THAT Celtic peoples included a priesthood – the Druidic Order – is well known, although a great deal of nonsense has been written about them, including claims to know their rituals in detail. The truth is that we do not, because the Druids themselves wrote nothing down. All that we do know is mainly from highly slanted accounts by Roman writers who tended to emphasise, and maybe exaggerate, their bad side over their good one. The Irish cycle of myth does give some insight into Druidic practice but, for the most part, the Druids remain enigmatic.

Druidry was common throughout Iron Age Gaul, Britain and Ireland but the Roman writers claimed that its centre, and perhaps its origin, lay in Britain. Druidic instruction took up to twenty years, with everything being committed to memory. There were three Orders, the lowest being the Bards. These were the archivists who created songs and poems about the history of each tribe and kingdom, and knew by heart the genealogies of the kings and chieftains. On suitable occasions, they would relate these, often accompanying the sung or spoken word with music from a stringed instrument such as the harp.

The Ovates were the next highest Order, these being the healers and seers. Above them all were the Druids themselves, the priests, philosophers, lawmakers, judges and teachers who had the power to place any member of society – even a king – under *geis*; a prohibition from performing some specific action. The penalty for breaking *geasa* was dishonour and sometimes death.

There was an overall prohibition in Celtic society against harming anyone from the Druidic Orders. This taboo continued long after the departure of the Romans and into early British Christianity when priests could travel widely and without fear of harm, be they Celtic or Saxon, and even when journeying into each other's territory. This long-lasting convention, which had begun with the Druids, would permit the Celtic King Gerent II of Dumnonia to befriend a Saxon bishop, Aldhelm, c. 700 CE and, a century and a half later, the Saxon King Alfred could accept a Celtic bishop, the Welshman Asser, as long-term friend, confidante and biographer.

Roman writers placed an emphasis on Druidic sacrifices, both animal and human, but it is likely that these – largely of the animal kind – were restricted to significant festivals such as solstices and equinoxes, or at the four great fire festivals of the year. In Ireland, these fire festivals were known as: *Samhain* (Nov.1st), *Oimelg* or *Imbolc* (Feb. 1st); *Beltaine* (May 1st), and *Lughnasa* (Aug. 1st). The Cornish equivalents of these names are, respectively: *Cala' Gwav, Cala' Whevrel, Cala' Me* and *Calan Est*.

Human sacrifice may have been restricted to appeasing the gods after disastrous events. The body found in a peat-bog at Lindow Moss, outside Manchester, in 1984 was investigated by Dr Anne Ross and Dr Don Robins in their 1989 book *The Life and Death of a Druid Prince*. In this remarkable piece of archaeological deductive work, they suggest that the body was that of a druid or member of the nobility (his manicured fingernails and uncalloused hands were not those of a working man or warrior) in his mid-twenties, who had offered himself for sacrifice following the twin disasters of the Roman massacre of the Druids and destruction of the sacred groves on Ynys Mon (Anglesey), and the defeat of Boudica's revolt against Roman rule, both of which took place in either 60 or 61 CE. Such disasters could only require a human sacrifice to bring the gods back onto the side of the people. He had undergone the threefold death of having his throat cut, then garrotted and finally drowned, three being a magical number in Celtic lore. However, a skull injury suggests that he had firstly and mercifully been rendered unconscious. A fox-fur armlet on the otherwise naked body may, according to Ross and Robins, have been a totem indicating his name, which they suggest was *Louernios*, 'fox' (Cornish: *lowern*).

The Druidic Orders possessed a deep knowledge of geography, astronomy and nature, and were not solely confined to the male gender. Female druids were also recorded in the classical accounts, and were at the forefront of the opposition to Suetonius Paulinus's vicious invasion of Ynys Mon. One of the significant beliefs held by the druids was of rebirth in another body after death, after a period of time, and the lasting nature of this belief would certainly have aided integration with early Celtic Christianity which may also have adopted some other aspects of Druidic practice.

18th century antiquarians, including Cornwall's own Dr William Borlase, developed such a fascination with Druidry that they began to ascribe all manner of things to the druids, even natural formations such as the rock basins found on several granite outcrops, or the stone circles of an earlier era. The latter is not beyond possibility as we simply do not know when Druidry first became established.

That Druidry was present in Cornwall and Dumnonia is beyond dispute. It is known that the druids favoured woodland glades for their ceremonies, particularly where oak was present. The cutting of mistletoe from oaks with golden sickles was an established practice of Druidry and, indeed, their very name is believed to mean 'oak-seer'. In early Celtic, these sacred glades were termed: *nemet-on*. *Nemetostatio* was a location recorded in the *Ravenna Cosmography* listing Roman routes, and probably to be identified with Bury Barton, to the west of Crediton in Devon.

In Cornish, the root of this word, *nemet-*, became *neved*, then *neves*, and this element can be identified in four widely distributed place-names: Lanivet (near Bodmin); Carnevas (St Merryn), Trenovissick (St Blazey) and Trewarnevas (St Anthony-in-Meneage). The first of these is of particular interest, as it marries a word for a pagan sacred site to another, *lann*, which is applied only to early Celtic Christian enclosures. The inference is that, in less Romanised areas of Britain such as Cornwall, Druidry survived its supposed eradication and was still being practised in remote places when Christianity arrived here. The fourth name is also of interest as *neves* is qualified by the prefix *gor-*, 'over, very' signifying importance and suggesting a major druidic centre in forested land on the southern side of the Helford River.

An unexpected visitor

IT was geographical position, rather than accident, that gave Cornwall – and specifically the far west of Cornwall – the distinction of being the first place in the whole of Britain to be written about, and described in any sort of detail. The writer, a Greek explorer, geographer and scholar named Pytheas, was also our first known visitor from the inland sea of the Mediterranean in the late 4th century BCE. The best estimate for the date of his voyage is c.325 BCE.

Pytheas was a citizen of Massalia, now the French city and port of Marseille, but then a Greek trading colony. He had doubtless heard from Gaulish traders about the sea and lands to the north of Gaul, and knew that the source of tin that passed through his home port came from one of those lands, called *nesos Pretannike* (island of Britain), inhabited by a people called the *Albiones*.

Pytheas of Massalia may not have been the first Mediterranean person to venture as far north as the British Isles. Himilco, a Carthaginian mariner and explorer, is said to have done so a century previously, but all that remains of this claim was summarized in a poem called *Ora Maritima*, ('Sea Coasts') penned by Rufus Festus Avienus in the 4th century CE. The wording of this suggests that, after sailing up the Atlantic coasts of Iberia and Gaul, Himilco made landfall in Ireland. The poem states that it is two days sail from 'the gulf Oestrymnian' (Bay of Douarnenez, Brittany): 'Out to the "Holy Isle" (so named of yore), wide on the water spreads out its glebe where folk Hiernan dwell on it afar: There too, nearby, spreads out the Albiones' isle.'

This is all the record that remains of the alleged visit of Himilco. The *Hiernan* are the people of Ireland, but the existence of the island of the Britons (*Albiones*) is merely noted, as though no actual visit to its shores was made. On this thin and somewhat unsafe evidence, it would seem that Pytheas's claim to have been the first Mediterranean visitor to British shores remains secure.

Pytheas seems not to have been a man of particular wealth or standing in the community of Massalia, but he does stand out as being a man of some academic brilliance. Not only did he wish to explore these unknown regions, but to plot their position by fixing the latitudes of places he would encounter. He was quick to note that Atlantic tides were far greater than the minimal ones he was used to in the Mediterranean, and even correctly thought that the moon played a part in creating them.

Whether he travelled alone, or took along a retinue of Gauls local to Massalia, and bilingual in Greek and Celtic, is not known. It is possible that he himself was bilingual in these languages, as both were commonly spoken around his home town. Did he commission a single ship to take him all the way, or did he hop from ship to ship along the trading routes? The latter seems likely, as their captains would have been familiar with the waters they were heading for, and experienced in navigating them. Pytheas also knew that the overland route from Massalia to the shores of Biscay was much quicker and easier than sailing right around the Iberian peninsula. Bearing in mind that the Carthaginians were controlling and blockading the Strait of Gibraltar at that time, it is quite likely that he travelled along that overland route, and took ship from the Garonne.

Pytheas was to circumnavigate Britain, from Cornwall and up the Irish Sea. He sailed far enough north, perhaps to Iceland, or up the Norwegian coast, to encounter sea ice, and maybe even into the Baltic to seek out the source of amber. He likened Britain's shape to that of a triangle, naming the three points as *Belerion* (Land's End); *Orkas* (Orkney), and *Kantion* (Kent). He even estimated the lengths of the three sides, coming up with figures that were impressively accurate.

The demise of his written account of his voyages, probably when the great Library of Alexandria was criminally destroyed, is one of history's great losses. It was all contained in one work, entitled *Peritou Okeanou* (On the Ocean) but parts were quoted by as many as 19 classical writers, few of whom ever themselves ventured beyond their Mediterranean homelands. Some, like Strabo, writing in the first quarter of the 1st century CE, were to view his account with incredulity and Strabo even referred to him as a liar, especially when it came to Pytheas's description of ice on the surface of the open sea at the northernmost point of his voyage (which, of course, no other Mediterranean person had ever seen, let alone envisaged). For the likes of Strabo, such an outrageously fanciful observation could only have been drawn from the realms of fantasy and an overactive imagination! From Cornwall's viewpoint, a vital survival was an extensive quotation written down by Diodorus of Sicily between 60 and 30 BCE, and which can only have been sourced from Pytheas's *Peritou Okeanou*.

This originally eye-witness account gives a tantalising glimpse of West Cornwall in the Iron Age, and confirms that an important part of its local economy was the production and trade of tin.

> 'The natives of Pretannike who live on the promontory called Belerion are especially hospitable to strangers and have adopted a civilised way of life due to their contact with external traders.'

The Celtic name of Britain, with its original P initial (as preserved in Welsh Prydain, and the Cornish place-name Predannack) is here confirmed as being of great antiquity and in use at least as early as the Iron Age. Belerion, the Land's End peninsula, is also a Celtic name, not Greek or Roman; its root being *bel-*, 'bright, shining', and found in the name of the Celtic sun-god, Belenos. The place-name, sadly abandoned long ago, may have meant 'shining one', perhaps alluding to clifftop beacons that were lit to aid shipping. It is evident from these few words that Pytheas received a warm welcome and felt very comfortable with these remote islanders, whose language would have differed little from that of the Gauls he encountered on a daily basis.

> 'It is they who work the tin, treating the layer which contains it in an ingenious way. This layer, being like rock, contains earthy veins and, in them, the workers quarry the ore, which they then melt down to purify it. Then, they work the tin into ingots shaped like knuckle-bones, and convey it to an island called Iktis, which lies off Pretannike; for at the ebb-tide, the land between this island and the mainland dries out, and they can take the tin over to the island in their wagons, and in large quantity'.

From this it is evident that the people of West Cornwall were not secretive, but were quite happy to convey Pytheas inland to see for himself where tin came from, how they extracted it, and how they purified and smelted the metal. He may have been taken along trackways that, to a large extent, still survive to this day. His use of the word '*ingenious*' shows that this civilised Greek visitor was highly impressed with a people who were far less primitive than he might have expected. They used wheeled wagons to transport their produce, although he did not mention if they were drawn by oxen or by ponies.

The method of mining described in this account is of interest, too, as it seems to identify lodeback excavation. This digs down into lodes of tin that outcrop to the surface, so the mines would have resembled deep trenches of a type which can still be found on West Penwith's moors and cliffs. Deep shaft mining was still a great many centuries away. Doubtless, alluvial and eluvial streaming was also commonly practised in prehistory, but these methods are not what Pytheas seems to have been shown. Sadly, the surviving account makes no mention of the farming settlements and hill forts he would have encountered on his guided trip inland, but Pytheas's original work might well have done so.

The island trading port he described in some detail can only be St Michael's Mount which, by his time, was very much the tidal island it is today, and within easy reach of the sources of tin in the Land's End peninsula and around Tregonning Hill. Archaeological work on the

St Michael's Mount: the iconic site of an Iron Age cliff castle and trading port whose use lasted well into the Roman period.

Mount in the 1990s discovered faint remains of two defensive ramparts on the slope facing the mainland and, near the present harbour, sherds of Mediterranean ware which testify to the use of the island as a trading port in the Iron Age, Roman and post-Roman periods. The name he gives for it, again in native Celtic, is Iktis, which could well be a slight misrecording of British *ek-tiro-s*, 'off-land'. This remarkable, rugged 70 metre (230-foot) cone of rock rising from the waters and sands of a wide bay would have been as much a centre of attraction then as it is now. In Pytheas's day, that attraction centred upon trade with the Continent and, although he mentioned no such thing, it is not difficult to imagine a great beacon on the bare summit of the island to guide those trading vessels to their destination.

> '(And a peculiar thing happens in the case of the neighbouring islands lying between Europe and Pretannike for, at flood-tide, the passage between them runs full and they have the appearance of islands but, at ebb-tide, the sea recedes to leave dry a large space and, at that time, they look like peninsulas).'

This can only be one location, and it appears that, before making landfall in Mount's Bay, Pytheas had visited the Isles of Scilly, well into the process of being shattered into an archipelago by a combination of gradually rising sea levels and land still settling back from the uplift of southern Britain in the glacial period. It is a pity that he did not name them, or describe them further, being too fascinated by the range and effect of oceanic tides to do so.

> 'On the island of Iktis, the merchants purchase the tin from the natives and carry it from there across the Straits of Galatia (that is, the Channel), and finally, making their way on foot through Gaul for some thirty days, they bring the goods on horseback to the mouth of the Rhône.'

The destination of the tin produce was, of course, well known to Pytheas, for he lived there. He would have known the Gaulish overland route, probably the very same one that he might have travelled between Massalia and the Garonne to begin his own journey. He is quite likely to have harboured ambitions to trace this route back to the source of the tin for some years before he actually did so.

Here we see at least part of the prehistoric Atlantic seaway trading in operation. The use of coinage was not known in southwestern Britain at this time, or for some time to come, so the method of purchase would have been bartering. The ingots of Cornish tin would have had a long established exchange rate in wine, oils, metalwork and other continental and Mediterranean produce, some of which has turned up on excavated prehistoric sites in Cornwall.

It is fascinating to conjecture what the ships in which Pytheas sailed were like if one can assume that they were Celtic. Boat and ship design in prehistory tended to be slow to change, so some basic designs could easily have endured for several centuries. In 56 BCE, Julius Caesar described the Celtic trading fleet of the Veneti, a southern Armorican people based around the Gulf of Morbihan, as massive carvel-built planked vessels built of oak, with what looked to him like tough rawhide sails. Their cross-timbers were a foot square in section, and the iron nails used in construction were as thick as a man's thumb.

These, Caesar wrote with a certain amount of grudging admiration, could risk crossing shoal water with ease (his own galleys running the risk of being smashed to matchwood if they attempted to follow). Their sides also rose too high from the water to be boarded with ease. They were not oar-powered, but relied on sail. Steering was effected by either one or a pair of steering oars near the stern, the midships rudder having yet to be invented. The fluked anchors of these ships were of iron, scarcely different from those of a century or two ago, and were attached to lengths of heavy chain. In 1889, one such anchor, 1.5 metres (5ft) long, with about 6m (20ft) of its massive chain, was discovered in the Iron Age hill fort of Bulbury, just north of Poole harbour, itself a smaller version of the Gulf of Morbihan, and Caesar had given a hint that the south-western Britons had similar ships to those of the Veneti, by stating that the Veneti and, presumably, their fleet, had been reinforced from 'Britain which faces that part of Gaul'.

Just such a ship was discovered in St Peter Port harbour in the Channel Islands in 1982, with conservation work still ongoing (2018). This ship dated from about 250 CE, but scarcely differed from those that Caesar had described three centuries earlier. Confirmed as being Celtic-built, the Asterix, as she has been dubbed after the Gaulish cartoon character, had burnt to the waterline from an unfortunate on-board fire, but she was also oak-built with massive structural members fixed with thick nails. She was 26 metres (85ft.) in length; 6 metres (20ft.) in the beam and with an estimated freeboard of 3 metres (10 feet). A single mast was stepped at about one-third of the ship's length back from the bow. Her hull section was gently curved, with a flat central section on the bottom about 2.1 metres (7 feet) wide, and a horizontal keel that would have aided beach landings.

An astonishing discovery was that this ship had been equipped with a bilge pump, with bronze fittings. Pottery found aboard her came from as far afield as Spain and Algeria, and it is clear that she was quite capable of sailing considerable distances. Whether she had been built in Britain or in Gaul is still not known. Earlier versions of such a ship could have facil-itated the voyage undertaken by Pytheas with ease.

Having taken ship from Cornwall to continue northwards across the Celtic Sea and up the Irish Sea, Pytheas of Massalia was to achieve great things and safely complete a momentous voyage of discovery. For Cornwall itself, his lasting legacy was this unique first-hand glimpse of life and people at the furthest end of this long peninsula; a Celtic-speaking people whose lives had already been shaped and honed by both the land and the sea, and whose descendants are, for the most part, still here. A deep debt of gratitude is due to the man who was, in essence, Cornwall's first known foreign tourist.

A word needs to be added regarding the enduring myth of Phoenician traders regularly visiting Cornish shores. There is simply no evidence that this ever took place, and no demonstrably Phoenician material has ever been found in Cornwall or Britain. All that we do have is the afore-mentioned vague poetic reference by Avienus to an alleged voyage of a Phoenician (Carthaginian) mariner named Himilco, perhaps a century prior to Pytheas's visit to West Cornwall.

In fact, it was during the Elizabethan era, an age of historical romanti-cism, that the story was dreamt up by a schoolmaster named John Twynne. It was an attractive notion, based upon no facts at all, but which soon caught the imaginations of an unwitting public. It proved so popular that it has somehow endured to the present day and is still occa-sionally mooted in publications as 'fact'.

The Phoenicians were a Semitic people, descendants of the Canaanites, and who populated the coasts of present-day Syria, Lebanon and Israel. From there they became master mariners, developing a major mercantile fleet that plied the Mediterranean Sea from around 1,500 BCE to 332 BCE. By 550 BCE, they had established colonies in the western Mediterranean, along Africa's north coast from Libya to Morocco, and on the south coast of Spain. Not until then would they have had either opportunity or reason to venture out into the Atlantic.

The most notable centre they then had was Carthage in Tunisia and, to all intents and purposes, their regional identity became more Carthaginian than Phoenician. This western sphere of influence extended to just outside the Straits of Gibraltar, so that their most westerly port, for a while, was Cadiz, the former *Gades*. Here they undoubtedly linked with the long established, and Celtic speaking, Atlantic trading merchants from whom they could purchase any goods they might require that had originated in Britain. There is no doubt, however, that they jealously guarded and controlled the Straits of Gibraltar during that period.

The major part of their western Mediterranean influence was lost during the Second Punic War of 218-201 BCE ('Punic' derived from 'Phoenicia'). Carthage itself fell to the Roman general Scipio Aemilianus in 146 BC, and Phoenicia itself lost its identity when absorbed into the Roman province of Syria in 64 BCE.

So, from where might John Twynne have wrongly assumed a direct Phoenician involvement in the Cornish tin trade? He may have read Diodorus Siculus and his quotes from Pytheas about that trade, and then read Julius Caesar's account of the Veneti, the Celtic people of southern Brittany who were heavily involved in the trade during the late Iron Age. The words Veneti and Phoenician are not phonetically dissimilar, and a mere confusion of the two may well be the simplest solution.

The Romans are coming!

WE can be certain that, by the mid 1st century BCE, the people of Cornwall and southern Britain were detecting alarm signals from across the narrow sea. All along the south coast, through their frequent contact with Celtic-speaking Gaul, they were becoming increasingly aware of the expanding might of the Roman Empire. Cornwall had particular reason to fear the future, after the violent ending of Celtic control over the sea-trading routes by Gaius Julius Caesar in 56 BCE.

By that time, principal management of those routes had lain in the hands of the Veneti, a Celtic tribe of southern Armorica (modern Brittany) who inhabited the region surrounding the Gulf of Morbihan and modern-day Vannes. The Veneti operated the sizeable fleet of massive oak-built, and sail-powered, merchant ships already described, that could easily deal with oceanic conditions and were also proving difficult for the Roman legions to subdue.

Caesar, in *De Bello Gallico* ('Of the Gallic Wars'), wrote of the Veneti coastal forts on headlands and islands, much like Cornwall's cliff castles, into which the natives would shelter against the onslaught of Rome. Caesar's forces were compelled to undertake huge engineering operations to tackle the defences of each fort only to find that, when on the verge of a Roman breakthrough, the defenders would signal their ships to come and evacuate them, then transport them on to the next fort, where the Romans had it all to do again. Caesar soon learned that the key to breaking the Veneti was to break their fleet.

Under his instruction, a young naval commander named Decimus Brutus oversaw the building of a war fleet of small but fast *actuariae* in the estuary of the Loire river which, when complete, set out to take on the great lumbering merchantmen of the Veneti in the Bay of Quiberon, outside the mouth of the Gulf of Morbihan. The Celtic fleet numbered some 220 ships and Caesar's journal states that the Veneti: 'secured the alliance of various tribes in the neighbourhood … and summoned reinforcements from Britain which faces that part of Gaul', implying that both men and ships from southwestern Britain were also involved. One wonders whether Caesar felt any sense of foreboding as, twelve years later, this same young naval commander was to take part in his assassination alongside his relative Marcus Brutus.

The sea-battle, watched from the mainland by the Roman army, with Caesar himself at a vantage point atop the colossal Bronze Age barrow known as the Mound of Tumiac, lasted from 10 o'clock in the morning until sunset. At first, the heavy Celtic ships used the wind with great skill, and adopted tactics such as leading the fast, but rather fragile, *actuariae* into shoal waters that they themselves were sturdy enough to withstand. Their gunwales stood so high above water that boarding from the low Roman vessels was well-nigh impossible, even when they tried erecting turrets on their own craft to aid that intention. Spears had to be thrown in a high arc to clear the lofty sides of the Celtic ships, so lacking any real force, whereas the Celtic Veneti could hurl theirs downward with devastating effect.

In the end, it was nature that defeated the Celtic fleet, when the wind suddenly dropped. Powered only by sail, and not by oar as were the sleek *actuariae*, they lay becalmed and helpless. The Romans moved in to throw grappling hooks into their rigging and tear down their sails. It was all over, and only a very few of the Celtic ships survived being put to the torch. Celtic control of the Atlantic seaways, after a good many centuries, was over.

The involvement of British reinforcements only served to harden Caesar's resolve to move in on Britain itself, and now that the Empire had firm control over all maritime trade and contact, the Britons would have no choice but to come to terms with him.

The Britons of the far southwest almost certainly came to know of Caesar's two abortive attempts at conquest in the southeast of the island in 55 and 54 BCE. They already knew of the might and discipline of the Roman army, and had most likely heard of the huge, nightmarish monster that the Roman general brought with him on his second attempt

– a war elephant that the Britons had never seen before, and which must have utterly terrified them.

They might not have heard of the later attempt to conquer Britain led by the deranged emperor Gaius Germanicus, nicknamed Caligula, 'little boots', in 40 CE, which ended on a beach in northern Gaul and went no further. The story is told that Caligula ordered his troops to gather seashells but the truth may be that he merely told them to pack up the engineers' tents for the return journey (the Latin word *musculi* was applied to both shells and engineers' tents).

The true conquest of Britain, or at least as far north as the Clyde-Forth line, did not commence until 43 CE, at the order of Emperor Claudius and led by Aulus Plautius. Claudius, the reluctant emperor, was far from being the stuttering, bumbling fool often portrayed, although he does appear to have had symptoms of what might have been cerebral palsy. He was an intelligent and intensely studious man who had learned well from Julius Caesar's recorded mistakes and, while Emperor, oversaw many outstanding feats of engineering. His tenure gave Rome a brief period of sanity between the madnesses of his predecessors Tiberius and Caligula and that of his successor Nero. Under Claudius, the plan to take Britain was carefully laid and, from the moment his forces landed at Reculver in Kent, the Roman invasion of Britain happened at lightning speed and with devastating effect.

The Roman Empire had complete control of Britain south of the Humber-Severn line within 4 years, and appointed to lead the force to conquer the south west peninsula was the legate Vespasian, a man destined to become Emperor of Rome from 69 to 79 CE. He had gained command of *Legio II Augusta* two years earlier when it had been stationed in Germania. Now the *II Augusta* was in Britain and, after contributing to Roman victories on the Medway and Thames rivers, was heading west from *Noviomagus Reginorum* (Chichester).

Vespasian concentrated his attack on the great hill forts of the Hampshire and Wiltshire region before taking Maiden Castle, Hod Hill and several other forts in Dorset, making much use of devastating weapons such as the *ballista*. This was basically a huge catapult that hurled massive spears with stunning force, and certainly something that the native Celtic inhabitants had never before encountered. On the way, the *II Augusta*, under Vespasian's command, also invaded and gained control over *Vectis*, the Isle of Wight. He then advanced to the great native fort of South Cadbury Castle, close to the border of the most southwesterly British kingdom, Dumnonia, taking that and establishing a Roman station inside. In several of these captured forts, he ordered the building of military stations, fully recognising the strategic value of these hilltop sites.

He finally reached the Exe and there set up the fortress and legionary headquarters of *Isca Dumnoniorum* (Exeter), subsequently to become the administrative centre of what is now Cornwall and Devon. Roman knowledge of Britain had improved dramatically since Julius Caesar's failed attempts at conquest. All that lay west of Isca was a long, sea-girt and tapering peninsula that lay isolated and helpless. Vespasian was sure that no further heavy-handed military advance was required. With Rome in charge of the whole of southern Britain and the waters of the Channel and Biscay, the land west of *Isca Dumnoniorum* would either have to cooperate with the Empire, or starve.

Roman intelligence also knew what resources lay there. Julius Caesar knew that Britain had tin but did not know where, thinking it to come from the mid-part of the island. He had tried to force the Veneti to tell him, but they had bravely refused. Vespasian and his contemporaries now knew very well where it came from, and that the remaining land to the west also held other mineral resources of significant use to the Empire. These would now come under Roman control, leaving the extraction and processing to the natives who best knew those arts, but taking charge of export and revenue. Tin was an important commodity to a Roman society that heavily favoured wares made of pewter, of which tin is a constituent.

To that end, and over the next two decades, Roman forces established three forts in Cornwall: one large one at Calstock, and two small ones at Restormel (just SW of the famous Norman shell-keep) and Nanstallon. Each lay on the western side of then navigable parts of the Tamar, Fowey and Camel rivers respectively. The first two would deal with movement along and across the British Sea (as they named the Channel); the third to deal with export to Wales. The Welsh market may have become too minor to be profitable: the small Nanstallon fort only appears to have occupied and used between 65 and 75 CE, and then abandoned. The Restormel and Calstock forts seem to have had a much longer life, from the mid 1st century to the early 4th century CE.

On this pattern, it would be reasonable to expect another fort somewhere on the western side of the fourth major river, the Fal. Here, though, Roman administrators might well have settled on using an established native fort, the sub-rectangular site at Carvossa, between Probus and Grampound. This is just the length of a short, ancient trackway (which still exists) away from a part of the Fal that was almost certainly navigable at that time, but which is so no longer due to heavy silting from much later mining and china-clay operations further inland. Just a mile or so downstream, near Golden Mill and another large Iron Age fort that might be an alternative to Carvossa, was 'Haul-boat Rock', where sizeable boats were moored as late as the 16th century. Now, at this point, the river is just a few metres wide, in the middle of a broad and level flood plain at the foot of the valley and which indicates its former width.

Built in the pre-Roman Iron Age, Carvossa's most active period of use was between the years 60 and 130 CE. Excavation between 1968-70 revealed a great deal of imported pottery that included amphorae – large jars that contained wine or olive oil – from the Mediterranean, glass, and native ware made by the Celtic Durotriges, 'fort-dwellers', tribe in what is now Dorset. There was also evidence of iron smelting on the site. Carvossa and the three Roman-built forts all lay close to mineral-rich areas, a fact that may be very significant.

From the 2nd century CE, the fashion of stone-built villas as centres of agricultural estates began to spread out from the most Romanised south-eastern area of Britain. The number of known villas, however, decreases as one moves westward. From 37 in Hampshire and 36 in Somerset, only 19 have been found in Dorset, and just three in Devon. Cornwall has just the single example at Magor Farm near Illogan. Nothing of it is visible today, but excavations in 1931 and 1932 found that it had three phases of occupation. It was built in the second half of the 2nd century. Then, around 230 CE, it was enlarged before being abandoned within a few years. A hoard of Roman denarii dated this phase. In the late 3rd century, squatters associated with tin mining moved in for a decade or so. The Magor villa was peculiarly substandard in comparison with other villa sites. It had none of the facilities that are often found in villas, such as an underfloor heating system or hypocaust. Nor was its plan precise, with hardly a true right angle to be found. Because of this, it is generally thought that the villa had been built by a Cornish native who had been in service to the Empire, then retired back to his homeland with the idea of building a home similar to those he had seen elsewhere.

It is often said that the Roman occupation of Britain gave us the art of road building but, for the most part, parts of long-established native trackways were merely upgraded, with some having stone surfacing added to them. In Britain's southwest peninsula, those that were adopted for regular use were few and far between. Main routes from the east to *Isca Dumnoniorum* were restricted to just two. The first was the Fosse Way, which stretched from *Lindum* (Lincoln), via *Ratae* (Leicester), *Corinium* (Cirencester) and *Lindinis* (Ilchester). The second was the Portway from *Londinium* (London) to *Durnovaria* (Dorchester) via *Calleva* (Silchester) and *Sorviodunum* (Old Sarum, Salisbury). From *Durnovaria*, an unnamed route ran westward, close to the south coast, to *Isca*.

Maps generally show no Roman route west of *Isca Dumnoniorum* but, in fact, there were at least two. Neither were paved in the Roman fashion, so would have been native tracks of considerable antiquity. The most significant of the two is listed in a work known as the *Ravenna Cosmography*, a detailed itinerary of the Roman Empire originally compiled c.400 CE, although the surviving copy was made 300 years later.

The names in this copy are grotesquely corrupt but, for the route that ran west from Exeter, these have been carefully deciphered by Professor Charles Thomas. The route is given thus: *Scadu namorum* (*Isca Dumnoniorum*: Exeter); *Giano* (Glano: unlocated); *Eltabo* (*Fl(umen) Tavo*: River Taw); *Elconis* (*Fl. Cenio*: unlocated, but Ptolemy had earlier named a *Cenionis Fluvii*, also unlocated, in Dumnonia); *Nemetotacio* (*Nemetostatio*: North Tawton or Bury Barton); *Tamaris* (*Tamara*: a crossing on the River Tamar, perhaps North Tamerton); *Purocoronavis* (*Durocornovio*, probably Tintagel); *Pilais* (*P(ortus) Alaunus*: a location on the Camel estuary near Polzeath. The lower reaches of the River Camel were formerly known as the *Allen* (*Alan* 1200), a name that the Ordnance Survey has wrongly transposed to the River Layne.

The name *Durocornovio* or, as V in Latin represented U or W, *Durocornouio(n)* is of particular interest as, for the first time in written record, it gives us the native name of Cornwall (*Cornou*; modern *Kernow*), and its people (*Cornouion*; modern *Kernowyon*) as a sub-division and sub-tribe of Dumnonia and the Dumnonii.

That this route was indeed factual is confirmed by two Roman mile-stones found close to Tintagel. These are actually misnamed, as they give no distances but were merely waymarks inscribed in honour of the current emperor of Rome. One of these is dedicated to Gallus and Volusianus, dating it to their joint reign in 251-3 CE. The other is to Licinius, 308-24 CE, which tells us that the Romans made use of an established track linking a port on the Camel estuary with Exeter in the 3rd and 4th centuries CE.

The second routeway is something of a mystery, for it is mentioned in no record; nor does it link with any known Roman fort or settlement. Instead, three surviving 'milestones' confirm a route from the tin-rich area of Gwennap to Mount's Bay and the known exporting centre at St Michael's Mount. Found at Busveal near Gwennap Pit, Breage and St Hilary, these stones are respectively dedicated to the emperors Gordianus, Postumus and Constantine the Great, giving a date range from 238 CE to 308 CE for the use of this probably ancient route under Roman administration.

Living under the Eagle

THERE is little indication that, during the occupation, life for the general population of Cornwall altered very greatly from that which they had enjoyed before the Roman legions ever came. Most native people probably never encountered a legionary, except around the immediate areas of the three known Roman forts. Traders were a different matter, arriving by sea or travelling in along overland routes. Many of these were likely to have been Britons from the most Romanised areas of the island, or similarly Romanised Gauls from across the sea to the south, and bilingual in Latin and Celtic.

It is also worth noting that very few of the Roman military personnel in Britain throughout the 400-year occupation were, in fact, Roman or even Italian. Most had been recruited into the army from other parts of the Roman Empire, from Sarmatia to Iberia, although the bulk of the army and administrators sent into Britain were most likely Gaulish and, therefore, Celtic-speaking.

It is during the Roman occupation that records first appear of people called the Dumnonii occupying the southwest peninsula of Britain, and of their far western sub-tribe, the Cornovii, names which are likely to have been far older, for, like many of the tribal and place-names recorded from this period, they are latinised, but already established, Celtic names. Dumnonia covered the whole of Cornwall and Devon, and as far east as the Somerset Levels. The meaning of Dumnonii, and the kingdom of Dumnonia, is unclear. Its root is British *dubno-*, *dumno-*, which can mean 'deep, dark, mysterious' or even, as a noun, 'world'. A parallel can be drawn to the Fir Domnann of Ireland, a people who were of British stock, according to Irish sources. These were worshippers of an ancestral god or goddess named Domnu, or in British Dumnonos, perhaps 'the deep, or mysterious, one'. Dumnonii might then translate as: 'worshippers of the god Domnonos'. In Welsh, the name of Dumnonia became Dyfnaint, which the later West Saxons adapted to their own tongue as Defna. This, in turn, led to the modern name of Devon.

Professor Charles Thomas has argued that the Cornovii, 'people of the horns or promontories' might have been so named by the Dumnonii because of the many cliff-castles that had been built in the Iron Age around the coast of its western half. This is a perfectly feasible explanation of the name which survives today as Cornwall's native name, Kernow. A tribe of the same name existed in what is now the approximate area of Shropshire and Cheshire. Unlikely to have been directly related to their southwestern namesakes, their own 'horn' or 'promontory' might have been the prominent hill called The Wrekin or perhaps the Wirral Peninsula.

The Dumnonii never produced their own coinage. The British Celtic tribes who did so were in the southeastern and most Romanised portion of the island; those closest to cross-Channel trade across the Straits of Dover and easier contact with the wider Roman Empire, and their immediate inland neighbours. This is not to say that the Dumnonii had no use for coins, for many have been the finds of Roman coins as far west as the Land's End peninsula and the Isles of Scilly. With these, they could trade quite happily with other Roman-controlled areas and evidently did so, bringing in goods of Roman make such as the Samian ware pottery that has been found on many native sites of the period.

During this period the enclosed farmsteads known as rounds, which had first started to appear around 500 BCE, remained popular. At the latest count, 3,500 of these existed in Cornwall alone and, from that figure, it is estimated that the population of Cornwall in the late Iron Age-Roman period may have been in excess of 100,000, or roughly a fifth of its population in 2011. These and the unenclosed farmsteads of the time were to become the farming estates of the present. Across most of Cornwall, the rounds, which were themselves usually under 1 hectare in extent but were the centres of individual holdings, occurred once every 3 square kilometres. In West Cornwall, the incidence was higher, with 80% being within 1.5km of their neighbours. Evidence of metalworking has been found in several of the excavated examples. Rounds remained used until around 600 CE, when replaced by new farm settlements (or *trevs*) established nearby and within the same land holding.

A further native development of the Roman period sprang up in the Land's End peninsula but, strangely, did not spread elsewhere except for a single late example in the Isles of Scilly. This was the courtyard house, a massive oval structure whose entrance, paved with granite flags, led into a central open courtyard onto which opened a variety of rooms. Stone-lined and capped drains brought fresh rainwater in, and to take foul water out. These impressive structures could be anywhere from 15 to 30 metres in length and up to 20 metres wide, and were so solidly built that a good many survive to this day. Chysauster is the best-known example, with as many as a dozen houses, nine of them in a carefully planned group and including the remains of a fogou.

These courtyard house villages have been likened to a kibbutz, or commune, where several families co-farmed on a subsistence basis, with some sidelining in tinstreaming. The field system around Chysauster is impressively large. Partially fossilised by current field boundaries, but elsewhere surviving in their original form as small rectangular enclosures, these fields, at least 2,000 years old and almost certainly older still, cover a good mile length of the southwest facing hillside and abut similar systems to the northwest, which are associated with further courtyard house settlements at Carnequidden and Trye.

Roman merchant ships called into Cornish ports on a fairly regular basis; certainly into the Tamar, Fowey, Fal and Camel, and also into Mount's Bay, perhaps en route to the Isles of Scilly, known to them as *Sylina Insula*. This use of the singular supports the fact that the main

Roman Altar, Tresco, Isles of Scilly: A rare type of monument and the only one of its kind ever found west of the River Tamar.

islands of today (except St Agnes and The Gugh) still formed part of a single large landmass, with smaller ones to the southwest. Its main harbour was then an inlet between present day St Martin's and Nornour, the northernmost of the Eastern Isles, and the site of a remarkable discovery in the 1960s.

On the southern side of this tiny island, overlooking what would then have been an expanse of farmland, is a closely set collection of eleven circular stone huts. These had been founded at around 1,500 BCE, and then continually added to and extended right up to 400 CE. Two conjoined huts, sharing a single external entrance, were found to have served as a mariners' shrine and a depository for votive offerings; presumably in thanks for a safe crossing from the mainland. Placed inside were no less than 280 brooches, 84 Roman coins, 35 bronze rings, 24 glass beads, 11 bronze bracelets/bangles and two bronze spoons. In addition, fragments of many glass vessels were found, some miniature pots and clay figurines that had originated in Gaul. One of these was of a nursing mother; the other was a goddess figure. Very possibly, this represented the Celtic goddess after whom the islands were named: Sulis (with the U pronounced more like the I of 'pin'), who is detailed on an earlier page.

Also found on Scilly was a rare Roman altar stone, its four sides decorated with panels, in two of which are relief carvings of a cleaver and an axe. Any inscription this altar might have had can no longer be traced. Found on St Mary's, it is now displayed in Tresco Abbey gardens, but it remains the only Roman altar to have been found anywhere west of the Tamar. The axe and cleaver suggest that it may have been dedicated to the soldiers' god, Mithras.

That Dumnonia's tin-trade had now fallen under Roman control seems to be confirmed by the finding of an ingot bearing an official Roman stamp at Carnanton, St Mawgan-in-Pydar, and 42 ingots were found on the site of a Roman shipwreck in Bigbury Bay. Presumably, this ship had come to grief after setting out from Plymouth Sound bearing tin from SE Cornwall and Dartmoor. Not far from Carnanton, at Caerloggas, many luxury Roman items came to light: imported amphorae that may have contained fine wines or oils, flagons and high quality pottery wares. It is tempting to see the owner of Caerloggas, a typical native 'round', as a native mine owner, finding a great deal of success in his dealings with Roman merchants.

In this era of early written record, it is a little sad that the names of only two Dumnonian citizens of the Roman period have survived, and only then on an inscription in Cologne to a man serving as a sailor in the Roman fleet on the Rhine, and also naming his father: Aemilius, son of Saenis, civis Dumnonius ('citizens of Dumnonia').

The legions depart

BY the mid 4th century, 300 years of Roman administration had created a Britain in a state of civilised security. Already an embryonic Christian society, it was relatively peaceful. It was well defended and avaricious eyes abroad knew it, as they were already beginning to eye up this fertile and highly desirable island.

During the final decades of the Roman occupation, an already scant Roman presence in Cornwall, and even Dumnonia as a whole, probably became virtually non-existent. The Empire had already split into two parts; one ruled from Rome, the other from Constantinople – formerly Byzantium (modern Istanbul). It was in a state of flux, and falling apart. Under attack from all sides, dissention over its leadership was growing and especially in Britain, which was now being seriously neglected.

To the fore rose one Magnus Clemens Maximus, of Iberian stock, and a proven commander who had successfully put down serious attacks from the Picts and the Irish Scotti in the north of Britain, and expanded on a scheme begun by his predecessor, the *comes* ('count') Theodosius, of handing defence responsibilities onto regional Celtic leaders.

It was clear to Maximus and the Roman army in Britain that their colleagues on the Continent were not faring as well as themselves. They were only too aware that, if Gaul were to collapse under the pressure being ruthlessly applied by Germanic tribes in particular, then it would be only a matter of time before an isolated and vulnerable Britain would follow it down into the darkness. They laid the blame firmly at the door of the joint Western Emperors Gratian and Valentinian II. Disillusioned by their ineffectual leadership, the army in Britain proclaimed Maximus as Emperor. Judging that Britain was secure, at least for the moment, Maximus crossed the Channel into Europe, taking the bulk of the Imperial forces with him.

In less than five years, Maximus swept all before him, subduing Gaul, Spain and North Africa, and killing the Emperor Gratian in the process. His final thrust for Rome, however, proved a step too far. He was captured and executed in the Imperial city by Valentinian in July 388.

The army of Maximus never returned to British shores, but he had forged immortality for himself in the memories of the Britons. Welsh mythology hails him as Macsen Wledig (W. *gwledig*, 'lord, prince, ruler'), and he appears in a late medieval Cornish miracle play as Prince Massen.

It is certain that his achievements in both Britain and Europe, along with those of a British king 90 years later, became absorbed into the future legend of King Arthur.

Roman military presence in Britain was now desperately weakened. In 395, Niall 'of the Nine Hostages', High King of Ireland, took full advantage and led an invasion force that burned *Deva* (Chester) and *Venta Siluram* (Caerleon-upon-Usk) to the ground. British pleas for aid succeeded at bringing in the Imperial general Stilicho in the following year. A Germanic Vandal in origin, this man succeeded in ridding Britain of Irish, Pictish and Saxon raiders, although sporadic raids remained a problem. Once again, the defence of Britain was handed back to its regional Celtic leaders when Stilicho withdrew his own troops to go to the aid to Italy.

The defence of the island was now largely dependent upon a mobile cavalry and infantry force of about 6,000 men, led by a *Comes Britanniorum* ('Count of Britain') appointed by the regional kings, and which had some limited success. In 405, these won a decisive sea battle against the Irish, killing King Niall and reducing the threat from that quarter. However, matters on the Continent were again alarming the Britons. In December 406, Germanic forces of Vandals, Alans and Suevi crossed the Rhine and moved into northern Gaul and headed towards its Channel ports: a direct threat to Britain itself.

Once again, the army reacted to what it saw as another let-down by their Imperial masters and, as they had done with Maximus, proclaimed an alternative Emperor, Marcus. He failed to find support, so was replaced by a civilian administrator, Gratian, who fared no better. Finally a soldier named Constantine was chosen. Believed to have been a native Briton, he was proclaimed Constantine III and, again like Maximus, crossed the Channel with his son Constans, and what remained of the army in Britain, in a bid to to put matters right.

Constantine began well, defeating the Germanic invaders, but Rome viewed him as a similar threat to that which had been posed by Maximus. Firstly the latest of the Western Emperors in Rome, Honorius, enticed him with a vow to recognise him as Emperor if he would help in defeating the Goths led by Alaric, but treachery was planned. No sooner had Constantine set off to cross the Alps, than Honorius had his Master of Horse arrested and charged with conspiring with Constantine to usurp the Imperial throne. Constantine headed back the moment that word reached him, only to find that Gerontius, a man he had appointed as lieutenant to his son Constans, had mutinied in the lands that Constans had under control in the Pyrenees. Constantine immediately relieved Gerontius of command; Gerontius reacted by setting up an Emperor of his own, another man called Maximus, who may have been his own son.

The situation had now become farcical, for no less than six actual or would-be Emperors were vying for power over the rapidly disintegrating Roman Empire: Theodosius in Constantinople; Honorius in his provincial seat at Ravenna; Attalus in Rome, put in place by Alaric of the Goths; Maximus at Tarragona; Constantine and Constans at Arles.

Gerontius now took the foolhardy risk of gaining an alliance with the same Vandals, Alans and Suevi who had been ravaging northern Gaul. This massive force forced Constans to retreat before killing him at Vienne, and this very same disastrous alliance later resulted in North Africa and Spain being lost from the Empire.

Honorius saw Gerontius as by far the greater threat, launching a surprise attack against him and forcing him back into Spain, where his Germanic allies turned on him, setting the house in which he sheltered ablaze. With his wife Nunechia and his squire begging him to kill them rather than let them perish in flames, Gerontius stabbed them both to death, before driving the knife into his own heart.

Honorius now turned his troops against Constantine and his second son Julian, besieging them in Arles for three months. Constantine's only hope of relief, the Frankish general Edobich, was defeated, and Constantine was left with no alternative than to throw himself on the mercy of Honorius. Given a promise of safe conduct, Constantine and Julian allowed themselves to be sent to Honorius who, treacherous as ever, executed them both in September 411.

The defence of Britain was now desperately weakened and raids from across the North Sea were on the increase. The British Councils, considering their island to have been abandoned by Rome, declared themselves independent of Roman rule. They dispatched a letter to Honorius to say that, while they no longer regarded themselves to be subject to his rule, they remained part of the Empire and, as such, were entitled to an adequate defence.

Honorius was unimpressed. Stung by Constantine's unsuccessful coup, and realising that the Empire's own situation was too fragile to risk depleting his own protection by sending more troops to Britain, his reply was both terse and final: 'Look to your own defence.'

The British Councils then expelled all the Roman administrators who still remained, armed themselves, and cleared their cities of barbarians from abroad; actions later emulated in Armorica (Brittany) and the provinces of Gaul.

There is a shadowy record of a Roman force returning briefly to Britain in 418, apparently to conceal or recover certain treasures, but the Roman rule of Britain was over, and the flood gates had begun to open.

Chapter 3

Dumnonia and Cornubia

Saints and seaways

THE collapse of the Roman Empire in western Europe meant that Dumnonia had the chance to regain self-rule and rebuild its own prosperity. No longer was trade, especially overseas trade, to be owned and controlled by Rome. No longer would the sale of native produce be subject to crippling Imperial taxes. No longer would the Empire claim the lion's share of the profits. After a 400 year hiatus, the Atlantic seaways of old could be put back in place, and under Celtic control once more. It would seem that Dumnonian entrepreneurs were quick to ensure that they would be the ones to control those seaways.

Nothing else can effectively explain the early to mid 5th century colonisation of Armorica and Galicia by Dumnonians, for there were no internal pressures in western Britain to force such a move abroad. Some have argued that the migration was caused by Anglo-Saxon incursions into eastern Britain, but these would have no effect on Dumnonia for several centuries to come. Others have identified Irish movements into the area as the cause, but these were far too minimal to have caused any such effect and, apart from the later Tristan and Isolde legend claiming Irish demands for Cornish tribute, relations with the Emerald Isle appear to have been cordial.

Much has been said elsewhere about Irish invasions, migrations or raids on Cornwall from the mid 5th century but, in truth, evidence for this is noticeably lacking, apart from a few Irish names on inscribed stones of the period, and the arrival of several Irish priests. The Sanas Cormaic, written about 900 AD, mentions a *Dún maic Liatháin*, a fort held c.450 AD by the *Uí Laitháin* clan from an area near Cork, and who had migrated to South Wales, that was: *i tírib Bretan Cornn,* 'in the lands of the Cornish Britons'. Charles Thomas considered this might have been the hill fort on Trencrom Hill, although post-Roman finds are lacking from that site. A far more likely identification, although rejected by Thomas, is the sadly mutilated bivallate fort at Carnsew, sited on a 15-metre bluff beside the Hayle estuary, a very likely trading centre. The mid-5th century inscribed stone to the Irishwoman Cunaida, to be detailed later, was found marking a grave directly below this fort's eastern ramparts. Had this fort been held by this Irish clan, their role might not have been hostile at all, but to facilitate trade between West Cornwall and speakers of Q-Celtic in Ireland and South Wales.

It is entirely feasible that a resumption of the Atlantic seaways, this time under Dumnonian control, was the motive behind the migrations to Armorica and Galicia. These two points of colonisation lie at the northwestern tips of Gaul and Iberia, and were the most strategically important points of the entire route. Dumnonian settlers in Armorica took with them their southwestern dialect of British Celtic. This would in time become Breton just as, in Dumnonia itself, it would become Cornish: the two languages remaining the most closely related of the three surviving British languages. The two remained indistinguishable until at least the 8th century. No Celtic language has survived in Galicia, apart from its own name, so it is now impossible to assess the linguistic impact of this colonisation.

Two areas of Armorica, 'facing the sea', soon to be renamed Brittany, 'little Britain', became *Kernev* and *Domnonée* (Kernow and Dumnonia) and there are even indications from the 6th century CE that at least one Dumnonian king had dual kingdoms on either side of the Channel (then called the British Sea). That Armorica had been renamed *Brittania* before the mid 6th century is confirmed by the writer Procopius. A third area of Brittany, Trégor, echoes the Hundred of Trigg, earlier Tricor, in North Cornwall, which included Tintagel.

The British presence in Galicia is confirmed by the Acta of the Councils of Braga which, prior to the year 570, records an *ecclesia Britonensis* among the bishoprics of the area, and a Bishop Mailoc, whose name is British Celtic.

Certainly, by the mid or late 5th century, the old seaways were up and running again, as testified by the copious finds of Mediterranean exotic goods of wine and oil jars from several southwest British sites: Tintagel in particular.

Meanwhile, Cornwall needed little adjustment to the departure of the Romans. It had been one of the least Romanised areas of occupied Britain, and native life simply carried on as normal. The courtyard house settlements of West Penwith would continue in use for another couple of centuries, as would the hundreds of farm estates centred on the enclosed farmsteads known as rounds. However, the fine Roman Samian ware would quickly become impossible to find, and household reliance would again be placed on locally produced pottery.

A few of the pre-Roman hill forts and cliff castles were brought back into use, with some remodelling and renovations, and this may have been triggered by the reopening of the old seaways. Chûn Castle, near Morvah and built astride a major trackway from the tin production areas to ports on both Mount's Bay and St Ives Bay, may have become a distribution centre for the local tin trade. The re-use of Castle Dore, Golant, could well have been intended to replace the export centre function of the Roman fort at Restormel, higher up the river, while the cliff castle at Trevelgue Head, also reused at this time, commands excellent landing beaches. At Hayle, the 5th century Cunaide inscribed stone, to be detailed later, strongly suggests that the Carnsew fort was a trading centre with links to Ireland and South Wales which, by this time, had a significant Irish presence.

The same seaways, particularly those linking Ireland to Wales, to Cornwall and to Brittany, were also about to be well used by men and women practising and spreading a new facet of society: Christianity.

The strange saints that appear on many a Cornish signpost have baffled outsiders for centuries and still do so today for, in many cases those visitors will never have seen those names before. Who were St Teath and St Tudy? St Breock and St Austell? St Buryan and St Levan? Then there is the ubiquitous flag of Cornwall; the white cross on a black field, that is displayed everywhere in the Duchy: the flag of yet another mysterious saint, St Piran. More often than not, the visitor returns home, the question unsolved, and still none the wiser. Having perhaps heard that one of these saints floated here from Ireland on a leaf, and another on a floating millstone, one can forgive their reluctance to delve any further into the subject, but even these apparently absurd details can be reasonably explained.

Christianity had arrived in Britain during the Roman occupation, perhaps in the 2nd, or early 3rd century CE, and developed into its own form, independent of any instruction from, or obedience to, Rome. This became known as the Celtic Church. It embraced several older practices, and never served any king, pope or other head of state. It was never involved in the various intrigues that surrounded the first three centuries of the formation of the Roman church. Instead, and to the annoyance of some, it took its own path. It calculated Easter in a different way from Rome; adopted a different tonsure for its priests, and even its own forms of penance. The Roman church preferred that penance be carried out publicly and with humiliation. The Celtic Church did the exact opposite, encouraging private penance to be carried out in solitary humility. Moreover, priests of the Celtic Church could be women as well as men. Going into 'exile for Christ' was another practice of the Celtic Church that would come to explain the many mysterious and itinerant saints of Cornwall.

Originating in Britain itself, the Celtic Church spread to all corners of the island and into Ireland, with major centres of instruction being set up in Wales, Ireland and eventually, Iona under Colm Cille or St Columba. It soon became strong enough to form its own Council of Bishops, but at the outset, had little in the way of wealth. In 353 CE, the British delegation to the Council of Rimini managed to attend, but needed to beg money from fellow delegates in order to get back home.

By 500 CE, most of Britain's native population had become Christian, and the Celtic Church irked Rome even further when a faction within it embraced the teachings of Pelagius. Apparently a priest of British origin, he rejected St Augustine of Hippo's notion of 'the original sin'; that is, that we were all born to be sinners, inherited from Adam and Eve, requiring divine salvation and absolution. Pelagius taught that we were not born that way at all: but instead that the choice of taking the paths of good or evil lay within the power and will of each individual. This 'Pelagian heresy' had to be stamped out, and Rome sent St Germanus of Auxerre and Lupus, Bishop of Troyes, to Britain in 429 CE to do so. Their efforts in southeastern Britain met with some initial success, but their message failed to get through to the west.

A serious setback for the Celtic Church occurred in the easternmost parts of Britain when Anglo-Saxon colonists began to settle in number from around the middle of the 5th century. There, Christianity severely declined in favour of a pagan Germanic pantheism until the arrival in Kent of St Augustine of Rome in 597 CE, who began spreading Christianity among the Anglo-Saxon peoples. The remainder of Britain, Christian long before St Augustine's visit, remained unaffected until the Archbishopric of Canterbury, solely obedient to Rome, became established.

Celtic priests, and especially those who undertook to take that 'exile for Christ' and travel far from home to spread the Word, sometimes took a 'name in religion', which replaced their own given birth names. Popes in Rome have done this since time out of mind but, in early Christianity, the practice was fairly widespread. In this way a northern Briton, who appears to been named Magonus as a child, was to become St Patrick of Ireland (from the Latin *patricius*, 'patrician, aristocrat'), although Pope Celestine bestowed this name upon him when Patrick visited Rome around the year 433.

From those centres of learning, particularly from St David's in Pembrokeshire, came the missionary priests that would become the Cornish saints. Many were Welsh, some Irish, and a few were home-grown Dumnonians. Several spent time in Dumnonia, founding several churches, and then moved on to Brittany to found more. In time some Breton priests also made the journey north into Cornwall. Winwalo was perhaps the most active of them, setting up several churches from Towednack to Gunwalloe and Landewednack in West Cornwall; and St Winnow and St Winolls in the southeast of the Duchy. One group of priests, both men and women, took a direct route into Cornwall from Ireland, landing in St Ives Bay. The Welsh priest Brychan, apparently of the Irish royal line, was said to have brought 24 saintly children into Cornwall. The likelihood is that these 'children' were actually followers or student priests under his tutilege, and their names also became attached to churches that are mainly concentrated in northeast Cornwall. However, few of the saints that were commemorated in Cornwall, tainted with the 'heresies' of the Celtic Church, would ever be canonised in Rome. From the Vatican's point of view, most Cornish saints remain unofficially sanctified.

They must have presented a strange appearance, clad in simple travel-stained robes, and wearing the peculiar Celtic tonsure. This consisted of shaving the front of the head to a line across the top of the head from one ear to the other, leaving the hair at the back to grow long. Around their necks hung a disc-shaped stone the size of a teaplate, and incised with a cross or the Chi-Rho symbol that featured the first letters of Kristos in Greek lettering. This stone disc was a portable altar, and the origin of the legendary millstone on which St Piran was reputed to have miraculously sailed from Ireland. As for St Ia's voyage from Ireland on her leaf, one only has to observe the leaf-like shape of the ancient Irish leather-hulled boat, the curragh, to see how that legend came about. The curragh was perfectly capable of crossing the Celtic Sea. In 1976-77, the adventurer Tim Severin successfully retraced the legendary voyage of Ireland's St Brendan across the Atlantic to Newfoundland, via the Faeroes and Iceland, sailing a faithfully reconstructed 6th century two-masted curragh.

Those saints who travelled across Cornwall on their way to Brittany, or back again, used two ancient transpeninsular routeways. The first links St Ives Bay with Mount's Bay; the second, known as the Saints' Way, connects the Camel and Fowey estuaries. Most of the saints attracted the writing of 'Lives' which combine historical facts with a liberal smattering of legend.

Over the centuries, Cornwall has had no less than three national saints. The original was St Petroc (now appropriated by Devon). Hailing from south Wales, Petroc had travelled to Cornwall and founded the former great priory at Padstow (itself a contraction of English: Petroc's 'stow' or 'holy place'). He had evidently not been the first priest to found a church there: the town's older Cornish name had been *Lannwedhenek*, 'St Guethenoc's church enclosure.' During the medieval period, St Michael the Archangel replaced Petroc as the Duchy's national saint. Several churches and chapels were dedicated to the Archangel, mostly on high or insular places from Chapel Carn Brea, Britain's 'first and last hill', to St Michael's Mount, Roche Rock, Rough Tor and Looe Island, to name just a few. Further east, his hilltop shrines can be found at places like Brent Tor and Glastonbury Tor.

Eventually, the title of Cornwall's patron saint was handed to St Piran, or Peran, as the name is more commonly spelt. True to the tradition of Cornish saints, Piran himself is something of a mystery for he has never been conclusively identified. The tale is that he was thrown from an Irish

cliff by jealous chieftains, chained to a millstone which then miraculously floated, bearing him safely across the sea to a landfall at
Perranporth. There, in the great expanse of sand dunes beyond the
beach, he built his oratory that is reputed to be the remarkable building
that survives to this day.

The jury is still out as to whether St Piran was the Irish bishop Ciarán
of Saighir (c.501-530); Bishop Ciarán of Clonmacnoise (516-546), whose
father was reputed to have been Cornish, or if he was a native
Dumnonian priest. The initial P replacing C would be a natural adjustment of Ireland's Q-Celtic to Cornwall's P-Celtic. However, Joseph Loth
has argued on philological grounds that Piran could not have been either
of the St Ciaráns. Whoever he was, belief that Piran was of Irish origin
has persisted for at least 700 years.

Because of a legend maintaining that Piran discovered a method of
smelting tin, he became known as the patron saint of tinners, even
though the art of tin smelting was already more than two millennia old.
According to the Calendar of Launceston church, his original feast day
was held on November 17th, but it has long been held on March 5th, an
adjustment to the same date as the feast of Bishop Ciarán of Saighir. The
distinctive national flag of Cornwall, Baner Peran or the flag of St Piran,
is said to represent a cross of white molten tin against the black of the cas-
siterite ore from which it comes. A parallel explanation is that it represents the light of good against the darkness of evil.

The flag received international exposure in 2012 when, on Queen
Elizabeth II's Diamond Jubilee, it flew alongside the flags of the other
constituent nations and states of the United Kingdom on the royal barge
Gloriana at the head of the commemorative Thames flotilla.

St Piran's Oratory, recently re-exposed after several decades of being
buried beneath the sand for its own safety, may or may not have been the
structure that Piran built. No one is quite certain how old it is, except that
it is almost certainly pre-Norman. The recent finding of a cemetery close
by has revealed human remains that date back to the 8th century.

Small early chapels from the centuries prior to the Norman conquest
exist in several places in Cornwall, often in association with a holy well.
These wells were probably venerated long before the advent of
Christianity. Many are reputed to have powers of healing and even of div-
ination. One of the most powerful was at Madron in West Penwith; so

much so that the early Christian priests were careful to site their early chapel a good 100 metres away from it, furnishing the building with an alternative well fed by the same source of water. These pre-Norman chapels, which never became parish churches, are distinguishable by way of their 'double-square' proportions; that is, that their width equals half of their length.

Some early church sites were selected to be within a circular or oval enclosure, known in Cornwall as a *lann*, and place-names with the generic *Lan-* are common. These names are often followed by a personal name, perhaps that of an early founding priest whose cult was later obscured by that of another, more influential person. In this way, Padstow (St Petroc) had been *Lannwedhenek* (the *lann* of an earlier St Guethenoc). Gulval (St Welvela) was also *Lannystli*; and Madron (St Madern) had been *Lanndythi*. It is suspected that, in several cases, an existing enclosure such as an abandoned Iron Age round was reused for this purpose. This was certainly the case at St Buryan, whose oval churchyard was shown by trial excavation to have been an Iron Age enclosure: probably a 'round' or enclosed farmstead. Strangely, St Buryan (Cornish: *Eglosberyan*, 'church of St Beriana') has no recorded Lan-name. On occasion, a religious site that had been founded within a *lann* never progressed to become an established church. These are remembered in names such as Helland, from *hen lann*, 'old church enclosure', and an outstanding example of a preserved *lann* with no church can be seen at Helland, Mabe.

These early religious foundations were not on the grand scale of the parish churches familiar to us today, but rather small chapels accompanied by cells occupied by the priest and his retinue, if he had one. To view a surviving example, one has to travel to the small island of St Helen's in the Isles of Scilly where, within a stone-walled enclosure, are the remains of a tiny 8th century chapel and a circular hut, the cell where the priest himself lived. The chapel was superseded by a similarly tiny 11th century church, built a few metres away from it, and which continued in use until the 15th century. The site is believed to have been founded by a Celtic priest known as St Elidius, or Elyd, and his grave might have been one of the five that were found at the site. A similar arrangement can be found on the neighbouring island of Tean where another tiny 8th century chapel, of which only two walls remain, was associated with three graves

Madron Well Chapel: a lovely example of a pre-Norman Celtic chapel set in a secluded and sheltered spot, close to a holy well famed for its alleged healing and prophetic capabilities.

and a priest known as St Theona. These would have been typical of most early Christian religious sites throughout Cornwall.

Several of these early Celtic monastic sites are clustered around estuaries. The proximity of the sea seems to have been of importance, and perhaps the convenience of nearby landing and embarcation points for travel to and from sister foundations in south Wales and Brittany was the prime consideration.

The early 'saints' of the Celtic church in Cornwall left an indelible mark on Cornish life, and on the Cornish landscape as those visitors who remain utterly bemused by their strange, unfamiliar names on so many signposts, can testify.

Named in stone

A LOW bluff known as Carnsew (*carn du*, 'black crag') at the port of Hayle once carried a circular bivallate fort which in more recent times has been refashioned into a memorial plantation, and bisected by a railway cutting. Its ramparts provide a clear view through the narrow entrance to the Hayle estuary and out into the waters of St Ives Bay. From the Iron Age through to the post-Roman centuries, Carnsew Fort undoubtedly served as a trading centre with ships arriving from, and departing to, South Wales and Ireland and perhaps even further to the north.

In 1843, workmen building the new road of Foundry Lane, below the fort's eastern ramparts, uncovered a slab-lined grave some two metres long, capped with four roof slabs. Filled with sand, charcoal and ashes, it lay under a mound of loose stones, still bearing signs that it had been the site of a funeral pyre.

Lying on the grave was a stone that had once stood proudly at its western end. The height of a tall man, words had been incised into its face in a sort of dog-Latin. Translated, these read: 'Here in peace lately went to rest Cunaida. Here in the grave she lies. She lived years thirty-three.' The lettering style suggests a date between 450 and 475 CE.

This stone heralded the start of a new tradition of early Christian memorial stones, inscribed to remember and honour the dead and, for the first time in Cornish history, names of real people emerge. The granite stone may have been chosen for the purpose because natural veins of tourmaline and quartz form a cross on its surface. The unique reference to her age might be significant, as it equals the age at which Christ is said to have died. The stone occupied a niche in a retaining wall of the Plantation, protected by a translucent sheet, but its inscription is now difficult to read. It is now protected within the nearby Hayle Heritage Centre.

Who was *Cunaida*? The best guess is that she was of high social standing, and a visitor to these shores, for her name is Irish. She was not the only Irish person to visit Cornwall, and to end their days here, in the period between the 5th and 7th centuries. The dating of this stone perfectly matches that of the presence of the Irish *Uí Liatháin* in Cornwall, and perhaps at Carnsew fort, if the *Sanas Cormaic* of c.900 can be believed, and perhaps *Cunaida* had been an important clan member.

On the south side of the isthmus, beside an ancient trackway and once serving as a footbridge over a stream on a parish boundary near Gulval, the mid to late 6th century Bleu Bridge stone (*pluw*, 'parish') commemorates *Quenataucus*, son of *Dinuus*. Both names are latinised Irish. The first has the Irish element *quen*, 'head, chief'; the second is a known Irish name: *Denawas*.

In mid-Cornwall are memorials to more Irishmen. *Olchan*, from *ulkagnas*, 'little wolf' died in the early 6th century near Nanscowe, St Breock although, strangely, his father bore a Roman name, *Severus*. At Lancarffe, near Bodmin, a mid 6th century stone remembers *Dunchad*, 'battle fort', another Irish name latinised to *Dunocatus*, son of *Mescagnas*, the latter name containing a Primitive Irish element meaning 'excitement'. At Welltown, Cardinham, '*Vailathi fili* ('son of') *Vrochani*', who died in the late 6th century, features the Irish names *Faelath*, 'howler' (perhaps 'wolf') and *Frocchan*, 'little heather'.

Near St Endellion, originally at Doyden but now set up at an inland road junction, is the memorial stone of *Brocagnus, son of Nadottus* (or *Radottus*), which also has an early Chi-Rho Christian symbol. *Brocagnus* is the Primitive Irish *broc-agn-as*, 'little badger', a name which appears elsewhere in record as Brychan, also the name of a famous 'saint' or early Celtic priest, and as Brocann, Broccan and Brocan. The origin of the second name on the stone remains unknown.

Further east, in the church at Lewannick, a mid 6th century stone merely records that 'Here lies Ulcagnus', a name identical to the one at Nanscowe: *Olchan*, 'little wolf'. This stone is one of four inscribed stones in Cornwall that also bears the peculiar Irish script known as Ogam, an alphabet of linear marks usually carved into the corner of the stone. Whoever carved this stone committed what must have been an embarrassing error, the original Ogam on the left hand side of the stone reading *Udsagci*, then corrected by a second Ogam on the right-hand side, reading *Ulcagni*.

Strangely, the other three Ogam inscriptions are not on stones bearing Irish names; a riddle that has never been explained, unless these men were priests who had undergone training and instruction at Irish religious centres. Also at Lewannick, in the churchyard, *Ingenvi Memoria*, 'to the memory of Ingenuus', a name of Roman origin, is repeated in Ogam as *Igenawi Memor*. This stone is dated to the early 6th century. In St Kew church, a pillow-shaped stone that could never have stood upright just bears a single name *Iusti*, within a cartouche. Again of Roman origin, Justus, this is accompanied by an Ogam carving: *Usti*.

The third of these lies by a stream at Slaughter Bridge, Worthyvale, near Camelford. *Latinus* lies here, son of *Macarius*; this time two names of Roman origin, but with *Latini* repeated along the edge of the stone in the Irish Ogam script.

There is a fifth stone with an Ogam inscription near the two at Lewannick. Sadly, this is damaged and unreadable, and seemingly on its own without any traceable Latin inscription.

What of the first Cornishmen whose names we know by way of these stones? Many, as expected, have Celtic names: a few have Latin names and were presumably from Romanised families. The most ornately beautiful of all Cornwall's inscribed stones features two men with Celtic names, and is thought to have been commissioned by a widow, as it uniquely begins with the Latin word *vir*, 'man' but here thought to mean 'my man' or 'husband'. Dating from the early 7th century, this stone is now displayed inside Madron church, but probably stood in the circular enclosure, or *lann*, of an early Celtic church enclosure whose shape is still partly preserved by the churchyard wall. Within a cartouche surmounted by an incised leaf-armed cross, the apparent husband was named *Conmael* (appearing in the inscription as *Qonfal*), from *cuno-maglos*, 'princely hound'. As commonly found, the name of the man's father is also there: *Uennorgit*, 'fair slayer'.

Cuno-, 'hound' is a frequent element in these early personal names, and may denote persons of social status, the hunting hound being very much a prestigious possession. It appears again on the moors to the north of Madron, where an impressive stone stands in a field where an ancient trackway divides into two branches. The Men Scryfa, 'stone of writing', has a clearly legible inscription dating to the middle part of the 6th century and names *Rialobran, son of Cunoual* (*rigalo-branos*, 'kingly raven'; *cuno-ualos*, 'worthy hound'). It is a measure of how little the language has changed when considering that, in modern Cornish, these two names would appear as *Rielvran* and *Kenwal*. It is also remarkable how similar the composition of early Celtic personal names was to those of Native American names far away on another continent.

Cuno- also turns up at Cubert, where *Conetocus son of Tigernomalus* is commemorated on a stone of the late 6th century: *cuno-dagos*, 'good hound', and *tigerno-maglos*, 'princely lord'. *Tigernomalus* is the name of a bishop featured in the *Life of St Sampson*, written in the 7th century. St

Samson of Dol himself died somewhere between 560 and 573 CE, so might well have been a contemporary of the *Tigernomalus* of the Cubert church stone. Might the man named on this stone have been this very same bishop?

A further *Cuno-* name features on the mid to late 6th century inscription on the majestic Tristan Stone at the outskirts of Fowey, of which a longer account will be given later in this book. The father of the *Drustan* (perhaps containing *tanos*, 'fire') whose memory is honoured by this mighty pillar stone, *Cunomoros* translates as 'sea hound'.

A seemingly sad memorial is the late 6th century inscribed stone built into an external corner of Cuby church. This is to *Nonnita, Ercilinus, Ricatus*, the three children of *Ercilincus*. Perhaps the three died together in a tragic accident, or as victims of a plague. Nonnita, a feminine name, is the same as the Welsh name Nynnid, also found as a female saint at Pelynt, near Looe (*pluw Nennyd*, 'parish of St Nennyd'). The names of the stricken father and one of his sons contain the element *erci-*, 'grey, speckled', and that of the third son is *rigo-catos*, 'battle-king'.

A stone weighing 0.8 tonnes is now at the Royal Cornwall Museum in Truro, but originally from Rialton near Newquay. This is in *Bonemimori*, 'loving memory' of an unknown man (his name lost through breakage of the stone), the son of *Tribunus*, a Roman name and evidently a member of a Romanised family with pride in that culture 100 years after the last of the Roman army left Britain for the final time. It is dated to the early 6th century.

In general, the inscribed stones of Cornwall were set up at either of two locations; at a site of the early Christian Celtic church; or beside an important early trackway route. The people they commemorate were of high standing in the community, and Christian in faith. Some were noblemen or women; some were perhaps well-established and respected merchants; and some were certainly priests or, in one case at Phillack, near Hayle, maybe a judge or magistrate. This stone is to *Clotuali Mobratti*, 'Cluto-ualos (a name meaning 'worthy of fame'), great of judgement' (*mo-brattos*). One routeside stone, at Redgate, St Cleer, is certainly the memorial of a known Cornish king: Donyarth (perhaps from *dubno-gartos*, 'sleek, dark one'). This stone, also to be mentioned later, is a late 9th century cross-base, with the inscription: *Doniert rogavit pro anima*, 'Donyarth asked (for this memorial) for (the sake of his) soul.

*Men Scryfa, Madron: an early Christian inscribed memorial stone whose
mid 6th century lettering is still clearly legible.*

The *Annales Cambriae*, for the year 875, give the sad entry: *Dungarth rex
Cerniu id est Cornubiae mersus est* ('Donyarth, king of Cornwall, that is
of the Cornish people, is drowned').

Those inscribed stones which also bear Christian symbols, such as the
Chi-Rho symbol, formed from the Greek letters resembling X and P

which begin the name Kristos, 'Christ', or Alpha-Omega Greek letters ('*I am Alpha and Omega, the Beginning and the End*'), are surely the memorials of Celtic priests. These will include the Madron church stone to Conmael (an ornate cross); the stone at Mawgan-in-Meneage to *Cnegumus* (Alpha-Omega symbols and perhaps an M for 'Maria'); St Endellion to *Brocagnus* (Chi-Rho); St Just to *Selus* (Chi-Rho, and an alleged word at the base of the stone: *presbyter*, 'priest'. *Selus* may have been Selyf, later St Selevan, priest and brother to St Just); South Hill, to *Cumrecini* (*com-reginos*, 'very proud one') son of Mauci (Chi-Rho). A late 10th century altar stone now at Camborne parish church, but originally at the tiny and ancient chapel of Fenton Ia (St Ia's well') near Troon, bears the name *Leuiut*. This is Cornish *Lewydh*, and Welsh *Lywydd*, and translates as 'steersman, helmsman, one who directs', an appropriate name for a priest.

The most intriguing of these stands at a crossroads of early trackways on the lonely moor northeast of St Just and on the St Just-Sancreed parish boundary. This is known to stand at the western end of a stone-lined grave found by probing but as yet unexcavated. It bears a cross with expanded ends to its arms and a single name *Taetuera*, below which is what appears to be Alpha and Omega symbols. The name is Celtic *Taithuere*, 'exalter of the journey'. Might this be a name 'taken in religion' and not the man's real name? As mentioned earlier, the practice was common enough. As well as the Magonus-St Patrick of Ireland example, Wynfrith of Wessex became St Boniface and, of course, every Pope in history has done the very same thing and taken a 'name in religion'.

Could the 'exalter of the journey' have been St Just himself? He had churches in the far west of Penwith, and both the west and east sides of the Roseland peninsula at St Just in Roseland and Gorran Haven. Legends claim that he would frequently take himself off to visit St Achebran at St Keverne on the east coast of the Lizard, so journeying seemed to play a large part in the man's life. This stone is simply called the Boslow Stone but, in 1613, it had another name: *Krowze East* (*crows Ust*, 'St Just's cross'). Could this really be the grave and memorial stone of St Just? It is dated to the 600s, which could well be contemporary with the saint himself.

What of late Anglo-Saxon presence on the inscribed stones of Cornwall? These show up on just four, or just possibly five, stones, none of them earlier than the 10th century. One of these, at Lanteglos-by-Camelford and originally from Castle Goff, is the oldest of them. It has a long 10th century inscription which is, unusually, in early English script, saying: *Aelseth 7 Genereth wohte thysne sybstel for Aelwines soul 7 for heysel* (the symbol resembling the figure 7 is used for 'and'). Translated, this is: *Aelseth and Genereth wrought this memorial for Aelwine's soul and for themselves.* All three names are Saxon, but we shall never know who they were.

Now outside the Wharncliffe Arms, Tintagel, but brought there from near Trevillett, is an 11th century flat decorated cross with the single Saxon name *Aelriat*, evidently a priest. The name of another 11th century Saxon priest, *Aegured*, is inscribed on an altar panel in St James's Church, Treslothan. *Alroron*, on the shaft of an 11th century high cross at St Blazey Gate church, but originally from Biscovey, closer to St Austell, may at a stretch be a Saxon name but is more likely to be of Breton origin.

The last of the stones bearing Saxon names is the Penzance Market Cross, now outside the Penlee House Museum and Gallery but once the centrepiece of a manorial cemetery just east of St John's Hall in Penzance on a site now occupied by a large shop and the P.O. Sorting Office. This massive early 11th century cross, with a series of decorated panels, bears two inscriptions. The shorter of them was once believed to have read: *Regis Ricati Crux*, 'cross of King Ricatus', leading to a belief in a very late West Cornish king. However, this reading from the 1940s was mistaken. It in fact reads: *Regisi crux*, 'cross of Raegisi, or Raesige', a Saxon personal name, with additional symbols standing for 'cross of the Lord Christ'. There is also a longer Latin inscription, incomplete due to wear and damage, but reconstructable as: *Procumbent in foris. Quicumque pace venit hic oret*: 'They lie here in the open. Whosoever comes here in peace, let him pray.'

Professor Charles Thomas discovered that longer inscriptions of this age and type are constructed in such a way that they can often cleverly conceal hidden messages. One of these, a chronogram repeated three times in the form MVII, reveal the date of the cross and, presumably the cemetery in which it stood, to have been the year 1007. Another code gives a second Saxon personal name: *Wiweht* (for *Wicgweht*), perhaps that of the sculptor.

Who were these two Saxon men, so far west in a Celtic land? The most likely answer is that they were senior churchmen appointed to Madron church, the mother church of Penzance and of the Manor of Alverton, itself named for another Saxon, *Aluuard*, or *Aelfweard*, who held the estate before 1086 and was probably also a senior priest appointed to Madron by the Roman church presided over by Canterbury.

The lost line: the Tristan Stone

ONE of the most enduring legends is the tragic tale of Tristan and Isolde, first written by the Norman poet Béroul and by Thomas of Britain in the 12th century, further developed by the *Prose Tristan* of 1240, and even became the subject of a Wagnerian opera. Might this legend have been inspired by the most majestic of the Cornish inscribed stones of the post-Roman era?

Today, this 2.8 metre tall granite pillar, on its more recent 2-stage stone base, is known as the Tristan Stone although, in times past, it has simply been referred to as 'The Longstone'. High on its rear face is a Tau cross carved in relief, and hints of a mortice which might have held a cross to cap the stone, leading John Leland in the early 16th century to call it a 'broken crosse'.

The front face of the stone bears a two-line inscription running verti-cally. It is now heavily worn with only parts clearly readable, but it has been confidently read as: DRVSTANVS HIC IACIT CVNOWORI FILIVS: 'Drustan lies here, of Cunomor the son'. Who were these men? Noblemen for certain, of the early Christian faith, and perhaps more than noblemen given the size and splendour of the memorial stone, plus the fact that it must have been dragged more than three miles to its site. This would have involved a strenuous haul up a steep hill from at least the nearest source of granite in the Luxulyan valley. The lettering style dates the inscription to the middle or late 6th century.

Cunomor, 'sea hound' is the same as the name given in early Welsh spelling as Kynvawr, a known king of Dumnonia in the mid 6th century, and said to have also ruled on the far side of the Channel in Brittany, where his contemporary, St Sampson of Dol, encountered a leader named Commorus, perhaps the same man mentioned by Gregory of Tours, another 6th century chronicler, as Chonomor. In the year 884, the Breton monk Wrmonoc, writing the *Life of St Paul Aurelian* (also known as St Pol de Léon, and who died in 575) tells of the king named: '*Marcus,*

who is called by another name, Quonomorius,' who ruled a region of
Brittany settled by British Dumnonians, and named Domnonée. This
account intriguingly tells of a King Marcus, also called Cunomor, 300
years before the formation of a legend that first tells of King Mark of
Cornwall, and 300 years after the name of Cunomor is carved into a
stone in Cornwall.

In later Cornish, Cunomor became Kenvor, a personal name that
features in several places names: Tregenver, 'Kenvor's farm', and Crenver,
earlier *Caergenver*, 'Kenvor's fort', being among them. It is conceivable
that these were estates in the ownership of one man named Cunomor.

The other name on the stone, Drustan, also features in Cornish place-
names. Tredrustan, in the parish of St Breock, is 'Drustan's farm or estate'.
It is also the name from which the Tristan of the legend is derived. The
meaning of the name is not clear, but it may contain the element
-tanos, 'fire'. It is often claimed to be of Pictish origin, as the name, or
variants of it, became popular in Scotland. However, the earliest occurrence there is Drust, son of Domnall, c.663-672. Other men in Scotland
named Drust are mentioned in the 8th and 9th centuries. In 780, there
appears a Drust, son of Talorgan, and Talorgan, son of Drostan, almost
certainly the source of the Trystan, son of Tallwch, found in Welsh
mythology. Even so, the name can hardly be claimed to be of Pictish
origin when its earliest known occurrence is on this Cornish stone, a
century before any of the men named in Pictish records.

Suddenly, this Cornish inscription becomes intriguing. Does it really
name two of the principal characters in the tragic love-story? Can we
dare to interpret the inscription as 'Tristan lies here, of King Mark the
son'? The intrigue does not end there.

John Leland was the self-styled King's Antiquary to Henry VIII, and
who travelled Britain, compiling his Itinerary between 1534 and 1543. At
some point within those years, he visited this area and wrote: 'Casteldour
belongs to the Earl of Sarisbury. A mile off is a broken crosse, thus
inscribed: CONOMOR ET FILIVS CUM DOMINA CLUSILLA.'

Leland failed to see the first line of the inscription naming Drustan. It
was well worn even when Dr William Borlase saw it in the 1750s, and
might only have been legible in certain lights, but Leland saw a third line
which William Borlase did not. His *Clusilla* may have been a misreading
of *Ousilla*, or *Ousilta*, which would be acceptable Latinisations of the

British name *Ad-siltia*, 'to be gazed upon' (the Celtic equivalent of Greek 'Miranda'). This, in turn became Eselt in 10th century Cornish (*hryt eselt*, 'Eselt's ford', is named in a Charter of 967). As French writers had changed Drustan to Tristan (to incorporate their word *triste*, 'sad, sorrowful'); so they altered Eselt to Iseult. The German composer Wagner further changed the name to Isolt.

So, did the Tristan Stone actually name all three of the legend's principal characters? Was its original inscription to be loosely inter- preted as '*Tristan lies here, of (King Marcus) Conomor the son, with the lady Eselt*'? Some are highly sceptical of this, dismissing Leland's reading of the stone as 'simply wrong', but was he wrong? John Leland failed to connect the names he read on the stone with the legend, and never saw the first name at all. He almost certainly knew the legend for, in an account of another location, he wrote: '*Sum say that Conan had a son caullid Tristrame*', but never linked the story with the Tristan Stone. There is no valid reason to doubt that he reported what he observed with all honesty but, if there was a third line of inscription, what happened to it?

The Tristan Stone has suffered in recent centuries. Its original site was a few hundred metres up the hill from its present location, at the Four Turnings crossroads – a meeting point of ancient trackways – and by the gate to Menabilly. One of those trackways was the main cross-peninsula route linking the Camel and Fowey estuaries. Known as The Saints' Way, or *Fordh an Syns*, it was certainly the route travelled by both St Paul Aurelian and by St Sampson of Dol on their journeys from South Wales to Brittany. Also beside the same trackway, 2 km to the north, is the Iron Age hill fort of Castle Dore, also associated in legend with King Mark, and certainly reused in the post-Roman centuries.

The Tristan Stone had been moved from the crossroads to Newtown, about 300 metres to the northwest, about twelve years before Dr Borlase saw it in the 1750s when it lay forlornly in a ditch. Borlase's reading of the inscription was remarkably accurate: CIRVSIVS HIC IACIT CVNOWORI FILIVS. The D of Drustanus is, in fact laterally inverted (as the W of CVNOWORUS is an inverted M, there being no W in the latin alphabet), so that Borlase's reading of it as CI is easily understood; the crossbar of the T is faint and easily missed, hence Borlase's I; and the AN of DRVSTANVS is represented as a ligature – two letters joined together – so that the combined letters look rather like an N leaning heavily to the right.

Borlase did not see a third line, but Leland had seen it clearly. Had a sliver of the stone bearing that line broken off through rough handling during its move from the Four Turnings to Newtown? The stone bears a long downward split from a projecting boss on its opposite side to the right of the inscription. Borlase's drawing shows that boss to have been a good 20cm higher up than at present, and level with the top of the visible inscription, so perhaps the stone suffered breakage on that side during a subsequent move.

When John Blight saw the stone in 1873, it was still at Newtown, but had been set upright. 15 years later, the Ordnance Survey marked it in the same position but its 1907-8 edition marks that site as 'Long Stone (site of)', and also marks the 'Long Stone' after it had been returned to a small grassy island at the centre of the Four Turnings crossroads. There it remained until 1971, when road widening necessitated its removal to the current site.

It will probably never been known if the Tristan Stone is truly linked with the legend. Béroul certainly visited the Cornish sites he featured in his tale and perhaps he saw this majestic stone. Perhaps also, 800 years ago, he could read three names on it, those of two men and a woman, and adopted those to feature as his three main characters. He may also have been aware of the identification of King Mark as Cunomor, as remembered in Breton history, but – for the sake of decorum – wrote of Tristan as the King's nephew, rather than detail an even more shocking adultery between son and stepmother. The tale has become part of the Arthurian mythos but, in reality, the lives of Drustan, Cunomor and Eselt were perhaps half a century or more after the lifetime of any historical Arthur.

Even the possibility that this stone bears testament to one of the great legends of the world cuts no ice with modern bureaucracy. At the time of writing (2016), a heartless decision to grant planning permission for a Wain Homes estate alongside the site means that this most iconic of Cornish monuments is to be moved yet again, to a site that has yet to be decided.

The lost land of Lyonesse

'BACK to the sunset bound of Lyonnesse –
A land of old, upheaven from the abyss
By fire, to sink into the abyss again;
Where fragments of forgotten peoples dwelt,
And the long mountains ended in a coast
Of ever-shifting sand, and far away
The phantom circle of a moaning sea.'

WITH these words in *The Passing of Arthur*, Alfred, Lord Tennyson envisaged Cornwall's mysterious lost land, while standing on a vantage point overlooking Sennen Cove on September 5th, 1860. His *'long mountains'* where *'fragments of forgotten peoples dwelt'* were, in reality, the granite hills of West Penwith. Tennyson, whose *nn* spelling of the name was all his own, is likely to have found this legend, connecting the lost land with the passing of the legendary king, in the Reverend H.J. Whitfeld's *Scilly and its Legends*, published eight years earlier. The powerful story that Whitfeld related is the only version of the Arthurian legend that has the traitor knight Mordred surviving the Battle of Camlann, the last, fateful battle of King Arthur.

Intent on pursuing the remnants of the dying Arthur's soldiers down through the length of Cornwall and into the lost land that was said to have connected Land's End to the distant hills that are now the Isles of Scilly, Mordred contemptuously ignored a cloudy apparition travelling ahead of his host and a hermit's warning that 'the shadow of a mighty one is brooding over thee!' The powerful words of Whitfeld cannot have failed to inspire Tennyson, and the wonderfully graphic final scene deserves to be shared:

'And now Mordred reached the brow of a lofty slope from which, more clearly than he had hitherto been able, he could see his retiring enemies. They were already at a considerable distance upon that winding road which then led across the fertile tract of country called in Cornish 'Lethowsow' or, in after-days, 'the Lionesse.' They were so far in advance that he could only follow their course by catching, at intervals, the gleaming of their arms.

Submerged Iron Age settlement, Isles of Scilly: One of several victims of the slow submergence of the islands, which could provide an explanation of the legend of the Lost Land of Lyonesse.

'Around him was that fair land, now so long lost and forgotten, from the bosom of which men for ages had dug mineral wealth, upon which were seen no fewer than one hundred and forty stately churches, and whose beauty and fruitfulness have been the theme of many a romantic lay. Broken sunlight floated over its soft glades. It never looked so grandly glorious as on that hour of its fate.

'As Mordred pressed on, full of one thought alone, already in imagination hemming in to slaughter, or driving into the waves, his enemies, his attendants and followers began to be sensible of a change in the atmosphere, of a something oppressive and horrible, though he himself perceived it not. Huge battlemented clouds, tinged with lurid red, hung over the horizon. The air became sultry and choking. A tremulous and wavy motion shook the ground at intervals. A low sound, like distant thunder, moaned around. The soldiers of his train drew closer together, awe-struck and terrified. But Mordred heard only the evil voice of his own passions. The war of the elements gave unmistakeable signs of its awaking. But Mordred perceived it not.

'At last, amid a silence that might be felt, so dreadful was it and so dull
– that fearful shade which had hitherto gone before him, and restrained
his madness, suddenly itself stopped. It assumed a definite shape. It was
the form of Merlin, the Enchanter. But it was even more terrible than
Merlin, for it united the unearthly glare of the spectre with the grandeur
of the inspired man. Right in Mordred's path, face to face, did the avenger
stand. They remained for a few seconds, motionless, frowning upon each
other. Neither spake, save with the eye. After those few seconds, the
wizard raised his arm. Then there ensued a confused muttering, a sound,
as though the foundations of the great deep were broken up. Soon, the
voice of the subterranean thunder increased, and the firm soil beneath
their feet began to welk and wave, and fissures appeared upon the
surface, and the rock swelled like the throes of a labouring sea.

'With a wild cry of agony, the band of pursuers became in turn the
pursued. They wheeled and rushed away in headlong flight. But it was in
vain. The earth, rent into a thousand fragments in the grasp of that earth-
quake, upheaved its surface convulsively, gave one brief and conscious
pause, and then, at once, sank down for ever beneath the level of the
deep. In a moment, a continent was submerged, with all its works of art
and piety, with all its living tribes, with all its passions, its hopes and its
fears. The soldiers of Mordred were whirled away in the stream created
by that sudden gulf, which even now flows so violently over its prey
below.

'Last of all, Mordred remained, as it were fascinated and paralysed,
gazing at the phantom with a look in which horror struggled with hate,
and which was stamped with scorn and defiance until the end.

'That morning had dawned upon as bright a scene as ever met the eye.
At evening, there was nought from what was then first termed the
Land's-End to St Martin's Head, but a howling and boiling wilderness of
waves, bearing here and there upon its bosom a fragment from the
perished world beneath, or a corpse tossed upon the billows, over which
sea birds wheeled and screamed.

'The remnant that was preserved reached in safety Cassiteris, called
afterwards Silura, and now Scilly. There, the wicked ceased to trouble,
and the weary were at rest. In their island home, upon which the sea still
encroaches daily, they dwelt securely. From St Martin's height, on their

arrival, they saw the catastrophe that overwhelmed their enemies and, dismounting, knelt upon the turf and thanked God for their deliverance. They never more sought the Britain of their hope and fame. It would have been a changed and melancholy home for them. Arthur was in his tomb at Glastonbury. Guenevere was dead. The Round Table was broken and its best knights perished or dispersed. Their work was done. In the Isles of Scilly, thus miraculously severed from the main land and, as it were, set apart for their sakes, they lived, and there they died.

In after days, their children raised a stately religious house at Tresco, over their bones. But their memory gradually faded away, and was forgotten. Sometimes, on a clear day, there may be seen the remains of walls and buildings under the sea. Sometimes, fishermen bring up relics of other times, and men wonder at them and speculate upon their cause and use. Strangers make pilgrimages to Scilly, and marvel whether it ever exceeded its present limits. But the account of its isolation is remembered only as a confused dream; it is a mystery, an old world tale; a fragment of which, like a portion of a wreck, floats about, here and there, in the visions of the past.

"Such is the legend of the Lionesse."

Powerful stuff indeed, and every bit as spectacular as the legends that apply to the lost lands of the other Brythonic speaking Celtic nations: the Welsh land of Cantre'r Gwaelod in the Bay of Ceredigion off Aberystwyth; and Brittany's Caer Ys which is said to lie off the coast at Douarnenez. Could fact lie behind the legend of Cornwall's Lyonesse, as there is behind many stories that are all too easily dismissed as fantasy?

Certainly, when the original post-Glacial colonists arrived 11,600 years ago, Scilly was still part of the mainland of Britain but, by 8,300 BCE, it had become an island. The seabed between undoubtedly preserves some evidence of Mesolithic activity but so, too, will the seabed around all of Cornwall out to the 30 metre depth contour. Clearly, this event of the rising sea level was too widespread and too long ago to have been the origin of the legend.

Further versions of the legend specify that Mount's Bay was part of the lost land, and this suggests that two other events, three millennia apart, lie behind the legend. The first, and earlier, of the two is located in Mount's Bay.

Remains of forests submerged by rising sea levels in prehistory are known around the Cornish coast and further afield, and these mostly date from the Neolithic period. The Mount's Bay forest is the best known of these for, at extreme low water events which occur periodically, stumps and flattened trunks of ancient trees still become exposed to view. Neolithic Mount's Bay had a very different appearance than today. The iconic pyramidal rock of St Michael's Mount, 70 metres high and surely capped with a tor enclosure, then rose from a low-lying forest that consisted primarily of oak, hazel, beech and alder, and which covered around 20 square kilometres of what is now sea.

By this time, around 2,500 BCE, the relentless rise in sea level was mostly due to the resettling of southern Britain that had been upraised due to the weight of ice that had pressed northern Britain down into the earth's crust; a process that is still taking place, albeit very slowly. Now, at the end of the Neolithic period, the Mount's Bay forest was under constant threat from the sea, exacerbated by periodic storm-surges. The process may have been fairly gradual, but folk memory will recall only the final effect, compressing a slow process into a single catastrophic event. The Mount's Bay forest was doomed, and the Mount itself destined to become the tidal island that it is today and, indeed, had become long before Pytheas the explorer visited in the late 4th century BCE.

Mention of folk memory that dates back to the late Neolithic might seem unfeasible or exaggerated but, in Mount's Bay, it is both real and remarkable. The Cornish name for St Michael's Mount was first recorded in the 16th century and it is: *Carrek Loos yn Coos,* 'grey rock in the wood', which had not been the case for 4,000 years. That a memory so ancient remained in the knowledge of the people of West Cornwall can only be ascribed to a continuity of a tale passed down from parent to child over something in the region of 150 generations.

In that time, the date of the event would have been long forgotten, and brought closer to the present than the reality. One is reminded of the 19th century West Penwith farmer who, when asked the age of a prehistoric site on his land, said: "Et was built a long time back en the time o' they Rawmuns (Romans). About a hun'red year agaw."

A similar contraction of time within folk memory would have occurred with regard to the second element of the historical events that led to the Lyonesse legend. As mentioned earlier, Scilly was separated from the mainland around 10,000 years ago. For a while after that there were separate islands at the Seven Stones, Carn Base and the Cape Cornwall Bank. The Wolf Rock would have been an impressive needle of rare phonolite jutting 20 to 30 metres above the waves, while the Brisons and the Longships were low promontories with jutting and rugged seaward ends.

When Neolithic farmers from the mainland first colonised Scilly around 2,500 BCE, what are now the separate islands of St Mary's, Samson, Bryher, Tresco, St Martin's, the Eastern Isles and several islets in between formed a single landmass. At some time in later antiquity this bore the name Enor, 'mainland' (literally 'the land'), in exactly the same way that the largest islands of the Orkney and Shetland groups are also called 'Mainland'. St Agnes and The Gugh formed a low-necked peninsula to this island, whilst Annet and the Western Rocks formed smaller exposed islands and islets to the southwest.

A considerable part of the main island was wooded, oak, birch and hazel being the predominant species, and it is thought that this provided a habitat for a herd of as many as 150 red deer. Colonisation of the island in the Neolithic-Bronze Age transition period almost surely saw the decimation of both woodland and deer within a relatively short time. Clearance of woodland for farmland, coupled with the need for timber for fences, roof-timbers and boat-building, probably saw very few stands of trees remaining by 2,000 BCE. Deer provided food for the new islanders and the herd may have been rendered extinct in short order, although it is possible that some were kept and domesticated.

The land area of Scilly continued to shrink as sea levels slowly but steadily rose. By the end of the Roman period, around 400 CE, the main island had noticeably decreased in size. St Agnes and The Gugh had together become a separate island. St Agnes is not actually named after any saint, but is likely to be another very old name, perhaps dating from this time. Professor Charles Thomas suggests that it derives from early British *ek-enes*, 'off-island', in similar fashion to the name that Pytheas had heard c.325 BCE for St Michael's Mount, *Iktis*, perhaps a slight mishearing of *ek-tiros*, 'off the land'.

By 400 CE, the low-lying, and increasingly vulnerable, centre of *Enor* was protected from inundation only by the existence of sand-dune ridges, which still exist as submerged sandbars. It was only a matter of time before storm-surges battered their way through and, eventually they did so, and the sea forced its way in to divide Enor into separate islands. It is said, and probably with much truth, that much of what is now sea between St Mary's, Samson, Bryher, Tresco, St Martin's and the Eastern Isles has only been navigable to sea-going ships since Tudor times. Even today, the RMV *Scillonian* can only cross Crow Bar, a major sandbar stretching northward from St Mary's towards Tresco, at high water, which partly explains the ferry's notoriously shallow draught.

The now flooded centre of *Enor* had, for more than a thousand years, been fertile farmland, complete with fields, farmhouses and ancillary buildings. In many places, at low water, lines of boulders set on edge can been seen protruding from the sand and down into the water. These ancient field walls are best seen on the eastern sides of Samson and Bryher, and to the west of St Martin's. Also visible from the air are systems of prehistoric round houses and field systems that show up as dark features against the white sand because seaweeds have fastened to their stone-built walls. The best of these are to the southeast of Tean; around West and East Craggyellis, just east of Tresco's southern end, and between Bryher's southernmost point and Puffin Island.

Here, then, is a truly lost land under the waves, whose buildings and fields can still be discerned. Taken together with the long-abiding memory of the Mount's Bay inundation, the lost land of *Enor* must surely provide a solid basis for the legend of the lost land of Lyonesse.

Where the name Lyonesse comes from is a mystery. The Cornish name for the lost land was *Lethesow*, later to appear as *Lethowsow*. This is actually the Cornish name for the Seven Stones, the deadly reef a little over midway between Land's End and Scilly, marked by an automated lightship, and the last resting place of the notorious *Torrey Canyon*, the supertanker which struck the reef in 1967, resulting in a disastrous oil spill which heavily polluted the Cornish coast for years afterwards. The name *Lethesow* translates into English as 'milky ones', descriptive of incessant white water breaking and swirling on the mostly submerged reef. In the legend, the reef, then a hill, was said to be the site of the lost land's capital, called the City of Lions.

The likeliest explanation lies with the 13th century *Prose Tristan*, a French version of the Tristan and Isolde legend which describes Tristan as being *Léonois*, that is, from Lothian in Scotland (rendered in Latin as

Lodonesia). This may have been from a belief that personal names such as *Drust* and *Drostan* were Pictish, despite the facts that Lothian was never in Pictland, and that the earliest known occurrence of the personal name is *Drustan* on a Cornish inscribed stone dating to a century before any of the Pictish examples. With the story being firmly set in Cornwall, the location of *Léonois* was transferred accordingly, and Tristan is later depicted as having being born in Lyonesse. It was inevitable, therefore, that the lost land would, like Tristan himself, become associated with Arthurian legend, hence the powerful legend recorded by the Rev. Whitfeld.

Certainly the name *Lyonesse* was not quoted by any Cornish writer until Richard Carew in 1602, but John Norden, the cartographer and writer born in Somerset c.1547, knew of coastal inundations and had picked up both *Lioness* and *Lethowsow* nearly 20 years earlier. He wrote (spelling adjusted):

> 'It is left unto this age by tradition that a great part of this promontory is swallowed up by devouring sea, namely, the country of Lioness and other land sometime lying between the present Land's End and the Isles of Scilly some 30 miles distant … And therefore there might be such a Lioness part of this promontory devoured with the sea, being so fiercely beset on either side with violent surges of the merciless ocean. The place where *Lioness* is supposed to have lain is now called of the inhabitants and seafaring men *Lethowsow*; but such is the resolute stoutness of the present sea cliffs, as howsoever they have been heretofore forced to yield, they seem now utterly to deny to give further place unto the threatening billows.'

The legend also features a lone survivor outstripping the flood on a white horse at full gallop, although there is some confusion about who he was, and where he came to safety on the Cornish coast. The favourite is a claimed ancestor of the Trevelyan family, whose coat-of-arms features a white horse rising from the waves and the motto *Tyme Tryeth Troth*. He is said to have come ashore near Perranuthnoe, in Mount's Bay, but a 'Lord of Goonhilly' (Ganilly, Isles of Scilly) is claimed to have landed at Sennen Cove where he founded the ancient Chapel Idne in gratitude for his deliverance. The Vyvyan family of Trelowarren, on the Lizard peninsula, also claims ancestry from a survivor of the Lyonesse disaster. A white horse also features in their family arms and it was said that a white horse was, for many years, kept saddled in a stable at Trelowarren in case of a repeat event.

From royal seat to glorious folly: Tintagel

FOR many, Tintagel is an Arthurian Mecca. Every year, tens of thousands of visitors, some from as far away as the USA and Japan, arrive to gaze at a spectacular drum-shaped headland of slate some 85 metres high. Almost an island, and referred to as such, it is joined to the mainland only by a thin, sway-backed ridge of crumbling rock and scree.

Perched on either side of the abyss are the ruins of a late Norman castle; often called 'King Arthur's Castle' but, in reality, far too late a structure ever to have been linked with the legendary Romano-Celtic hero. Modern tourism locally casts all vestige of good taste to the four winds, with hideous signboards emblazoned with nonsense like 'King Arthur's Car Park' shouting grotesquely at the bewildered visitor. The village of Tintagel, festooned with signs like these or portraying bewhiskered Merlins, has even lost its proper name – Trevena – in favour of the tourism trivia surrounding the castle to which the name properly belongs.

Once the property of the former Earldom of Cornwall, the site and castle ruins have, since 1337, belonged to the Duchy of Cornwall. In recent years, the Duchy has entrusted its management to 'English' Heritage, a move roundly criticised by many Cornish people.

Contrary to popular belief, Tintagel was originally cited by tradition only as the site of Arthur's conception. It did not hold that he was born there, lived there or ruled from there, these notions only dating from the 15th century (Tintagel as his birthplace), or from Victorian fervour inspired by Alfred, Lord Tennyson's epic Arthurian poems *Idylls of the King*. Nonetheless, the public continues to be subject to ill-informed sections of the media speaking of Tintagel as 'Camelot', a claim that no Arthurian scholar would ever voice.

Many popular myths of Tintagel are comparatively recent. The cavern piercing the base of the headland is today proclaimed as 'Merlin's Cave', with tales of it being haunted by the magician's ghost. In Victorian times, this name was unknown, the cave then being known as 'King Arthur's Cave'. A thickly applied veneer of modern hokum has to be stripped away from the site in order to view its fascinating history, as well as its genuinely old heritage of folklore and tradition.

The very earliest traditions of the site associate it with historical Cornish kings of old or, more correctly, the kings of ancient Dumnonia,

Tintagel Castle: Although dominated by a scarcely used late Norman castle, this magnificent headland was almost certainly at least a seasonal or ceremonial seat of the post-Roman Kings of Dumnonia.

the south-western domain of which Cornwall was part. This kingdom certainly existed in Roman and post-Roman times, and may well have dated back into the preceding Iron Age. A deep-seated belief that Tintagel had been a court of these kings found its way into tales of great antiquity, notably that of Tristan. In this, Tintagel is a seat of King Mark of Cornwall, a man who almost certainly existed.

This ancient and intriguing belief lost much of its credibility after C.A. Ralegh Radford's 1933-39 excavation of the site, which announced – wrongly, as it later turned out – that the headland not only contained the late Norman castle but also the remains of a 5th or 6th century monastery of the early Celtic Church, an error still occasionally repeated.

Officialdom and professional sceptics were quick to leap on Radford's claim as providing positive proof that Tintagel had nothing to do with Arthur or the notion of early Cornish kings, but the belief refused to die.

After all, how does one effectively collapse a belief that may be more than a thousand years old?

Geoffrey of Monmouth

THE link between Tintagel and Arthur first saw the light of day in 1136 (or 1139) when the Oxford-based Welsh priest Geoffrey of Monmouth produced his fanciful *History of the Kings of Britain*.

This work has been consistently dismissed by many historians as pure fantasy but, as we will see, what Geoffrey of Monmouth seems to have done was to draw upon a store of very real histories and firmly-rooted traditions, then re-jig them to suit his own purpose. Even when he wrote of King Arthur, especially his forays into Gaul, he had the exploits of a very real person in mind. He often distorted facts to an almost unrecognisable degree, but little of his work was born entirely of his own imagination.

In his *History*, Geoffrey described the lust of King Uther Pendragon for Ygerna (Igraine), wife of Duke Gorlois of Cornwall, and the war resulting from this. While Gorlois fought against the King's troops at the fortress of Dimilioc (a real place: the Iron Age fort which now forms the hilltop churchyard at St Dennis), Uther – disguised as Gorlois by the arts of Merlin – enters the otherwise impregnable fortress of Tintagel, where Ygerna had been placed for her own safety. Gorlois dies in battle that same night, and the end result of the subterfuge is the adulterous conception of the future King Arthur.

This early 12th century work is the first appearance of the name Tintagel (as *Tintagol*). Both the place-name and the tale of Arthur's conception have been dismissed by some as 'invented', but these are hasty conclusions. Geoffrey seemed pretty incapable of outright invention, even if he did wildly distort, and it is almost certain that he gleaned these tales from somewhere. Did he draw upon genuine local memory?

It is not known where he found the place-name. It could equally be Cornish (*din tagell*, 'fort of the constriction', in reference to the headland's narrow neck), or Norman-French. The authors of *Arthurian Sites in the West* (University of Exeter 1975) refer to a similarly spectacular site on the Channel Island of Sark, now called *Tintageu*, but earlier *Tente d'Agel*. This, they claim, is interpreted in the local patois as 'Castle of the Devil'. However, no trace of the name Tintagel for the Cornish site can be found prior to Geoffrey's work, written in the Norman period, and so the latter derivation is the more likely. The name appears in no pre-12th century record, including Domesday, which mentions only Bossiney (as *Botcinii*), the manor in which Tintagel was situated.

It has yet to be explained why Geoffrey of Monmouth made the decision to feature this geographically obscure site, unless a strong tradition already existed. Certainly, belief in an undying Arthur predated his work as illustrated by the incident in Bodmin in 1113, in reaction to ridicule of local belief that King Arthur still lived. What seems likely is that Geoffrey heard a long-standing belief that this remote headland was the place where Arthur had been conceived. Also, that it had been the seat of kings, demoted by Geoffrey to dukes. After all, even the fiercely partisan Welsh of medieval times (and Geoffrey himself was a Welshman), who might be expected to claim Arthur purely as their own, conceded in their *Triads* and the *Mabinogion* that Arthur's home was in Cornwall: not Tintagel, but an unlocated fortress called Kelliwic. Even in their eyes, Arthur was a native Dumnonian.

Due to the misapprehensions engendered by Radford's excavations, it has been claimed that Geoffrey placed his scene at Tintagel out of deference to the contemporary Earl of Cornwall whose castle, it was then said, was newly built at the time he wrote his *History*. However, it is now known that no such castle existed on the headland until the following century.

The castle

UNTIL fairly recently, it was assumed that Tintagel Castle had been built c.1140 by Reginald de Dunstanville, Earl of Cornwall and bastard son of Henry I. Not until new archaeological work in the 1980s and 1990s did a whole new picture emerge: proving beyond all doubt that nothing of the castle itself predates the 13th century.

In Earl Reginald's time, the castle of Bossiney Manor was not at Tintagel, but at the hamlet of Bossiney itself. This was a small ringwork, perhaps topped by a timber palisade and containing a few buildings. The remains of this, known as Bossiney Mound, still stand beside the former chapel at Bossiney.

In the 13th century, the sub-tenant of Bossiney, Robert de Hornicote, was styling himself '*Robert de Tintaioel*' and, in 1233, he and his son

Gervase formally handed over to Richard, Earl of Cornwall, 'my island of Tyntagel and the castle of Richard', implying that the Earl had already begun its construction.

Richard, second son of King John, dreamed of being proclaimed as Holy Roman Emperor. His building of a castle at Tintagel, in an old-fashioned style, was clearly intended to exploit the deep-seated popular belief in the royal status of the site which dated back to Roman times at least; a status not only remembered by the people of Cornwall but now, through Geoffrey of Monmouth, of international repute. To revive the ancient seat of the Cornish kings, with links to Arthur himself, would undoubtedly elevate Earl Richard's own standing among the populace, and give a boost to his ambitions.

Strategically, the castle was utterly useless. By the 13th century, it lay far from any major route through Cornwall unlike other castles of the Earldom such as Launceston and Restormel. As Professor Charles Thomas has pointed out: 'a whole war could have raged up and down the peninsula without a Tintagel garrison being aware of it'. Cornwall's political centre was then at Launceston, to be superseded by Restormel and nearby Lostwithiel at the creation of the Duchy in 1337. Tintagel, then, had no practical standing or use at all, other than its almost deified associations with the distant past.

In short, Tintagel Castle was little more than a glorious folly, designed to boost Earl Richard's ambition which was finally realised at Aachen in 1257 when he was crowned 'King of the Romans', and became the richest man in the world, although he would never attain his ultimate ambition: the title of Holy Roman Emperor. Richard's only known use of the castle was when he controversially sheltered Dafydd ap Llywelyn there in 1245; a Welsh rebel and nephew to both himself and his elder brother King Henry III (in doing this, Richard knowingly acted against the King's interests, and was himself risking execution). Later, it briefly acted as a prison for two high-ranking captives, Thomas, Earl of Warwick in 1308 and John de Northampton, Lord Mayor of London in 1385. In 1337, a survey for the newly created Duchy of Cornwall found that the roof timbers of the castle's main hall had been dismantled a few years earlier by John of Eltham, the sixth Earl of Cornwall. By Tudor times, the castle was a total ruin.

The ruins of 'King Arthur's Castle' then, have nothing directly to do with the figure of King Arthur who, if historically genuine, would have lived some 700 years before its construction but Arthur had been, in part, a reason for it being built.

Earlier remains

RADFORD'S work on Tintagel Island in the 1930s turned up several complexes of small rectangular buildings (his Sites A to E), which were apparently associated with a huge quantity of post-Roman exotic ware, imported from the Mediterranean. For some reason, he saw this as evidence that these buildings represented the remains of a 5th or 6th century Celtic monastery of major importance, perhaps the lost site of the *Rosnant* mentioned in Irish annals.

The work that commenced in the 1980s reached very different conclusions. On the evidence that then began to emerge, Professor Thomas argued that no one would now consider Tintagel to have been a monastic site for three main reasons:

1) Tintagel had no religious continuity of tradition, unlike other Cornish pre-Norman monasteries;
2) The buildings and layout were quite unlike any found at monastic sites of the period;
3) The site, as a religious foundation, appears in no records.

There had to be a more feasible explanation for the sheer amount of imported Mediterranean pottery found at Tintagel – more than had been found at all excavated post-Roman sites in Britain put together. The ware consisted mainly of olive-oil jars, dishes and metre-high jars, perhaps once containing fine wines, all from trade with the Mediterranean via the Atlantic trading route. The goods had been despatched from the Middle East, Asia Minor, Eastern Greece and North Africa.

Professor Thomas has suggested a typical trade visit from a merchant ship, delivering its wares of oil and wine in exchange for, chiefly, tin, to high-status sites like Carnsew fort on the Hayle estuary. Then it would move on to Tintagel where it could berth in the cove below the later medieval postern gate known as Porth Hern (Cornish: *porth horn*, 'iron gate'), even with the sea level being more than three metres below its present level. A likely mooring site, with the natural rock artificially shaped for the purpose, has recently been found by marine archaeologists at this location. At Tintagel, the bulk of the cargo was offloaded before the remainder was taken up the Bristol Channel to end up at sites like South Cadbury Castle, Somerset (often known as Cadbury-Camelot) and Dinas Powys in South Wales. Why was so much of it being delivered to Tintagel unless the site was of exceptional importance: a major centre of power? More evidence was to follow.

In 1983, an intense surface fire reduced the soil on a third of the headland's flat top to powdered ash, revealing the foundation courses of an astonishing number of buildings. A detailed survey of the rest of the headland found that not only its top, but even cliff-side ledges, were covered with up to a hundred rectilinear buildings. Some, like Radford's Sites A to E, were probably from Earl Richard's time, perhaps to house the construction team who were building his castle. The bulk were far older than that. Even more Mediterranean ware was found, suggesting that post-Roman buildings even lay underneath the 13th century ones.

Sections dug through the castle's Inner Ward on Tintagel Island found that it had been built on artificially filled ground. Underneath, the former land surface had been terraced, and yielded still more imported ware, leading to a firm belief that the centre of the post-Roman complex lay there, beneath the present castle ruins in what had been a sheltered, sunlit hollow.

Such evidence, reinforced by the traditional association of the site with Dumnonian kings, has led to the current interpretation of Tintagel as a major royal seat. The limitations of its natural resources, even though there are six fresh water springs and collection pits on the headland, points to it having been either a seasonal seat, or one used for regal ceremonies such as coronations, dynastic funerals and weddings.

On a natural rock overlooking the southern cliff, and on the highest point of the headland, is a feature known as 'King Arthur's Footprint'. Victorian guides used to tell visitors that Arthur stepped from here to Glebe Cliff in a single stride (and, as detailed below, there is an intriguing link between the two locations). The carved hollow in the upper surface of a natural outcrop is largely artificial and fits a size-ten foot pretty well. It also echoes similar features at other British high status sites of the period, notably at Dunadd, Scotland, one of the chief seats of the kings of Dalriada. There, a newly crowned king would place his foot into the 'footprint' to symbolise his rule over the land, and unity with it. It would follow that this might have been the case at Tintagel, too.

Could High Kings of Britain have been crowned here, too? Professor Thomas emphatically says: '*Arthur, never ...*' But, if an historical Arthur had ever been High King, whyever not? If he had been conceived at Tintagel or even born there (as first suggested by William of Worcester in 1480), and if he had been the King of the Britons recorded by 6th century Gaulish historians as *Riotamus* ('over-king') – who was almost certainly the principal person on whom Geoffrey of Monmouth based his Arthur figure – might he not have chosen that very place for his own corona- tion? It was also a place of established power, with links to the eastern Mediterranean and with Byzantium itself. Such a connection with the seat of the senior Roman emperor would have been highly symbolic, for a late 5th or 6th century King of the Britons, albeit a Britain independent of Rome and Byzantium, was still the Champion of Romanitas, the prin- ciples of Roman civilisation in Britain and in Europe.

The high status settlement at Tintagel has been dated to a period from c.450 to c.700 CE, during which time its mainland approach was defended by a massive ditch and rampart following a natural fault line, and restricting that approach to a three-metre width ('...*three armed soldiers can hold it against you*', wrote Geoffrey of Monmouth). This same ditch was used by Earl Richard to protect the Lower Ward of his castle. In post-Roman times, the now crumbling neck of the headland would have been a high, grassy and gently sloping saddle just a few metres wide at its top. The ditch has been dated to the post-Roman era but, although hard evidence has yet to be found for Iron Age occupation of the site, it is hard to imagine the Celtic chieftains of that era passing up such a superb site for a cliff castle like the many that they built around the Cornish coast.

Notwithstanding the present lack of Iron Age evidence, the post- Roman kings of Dumnonia might well have been perpetuating an earlier importance of the site, just as Earl Richard sought to revive memories of its ancient status in order to enhance his own. Late Roman ware and coins have, significantly, also turned up at Tintagel, and an incomplete inscription on a piece of incised slate (to be detailed later) may be to Honorius, who was Emperor at the time of the Roman withdrawal from Britain in 410 CE. Two Roman 'milestones' are also known in the immediate area: one at Tintagel church (dedicated to Caesar Gaius

Valerius Licinius 308-324 CE), and the other at Trethevey less than 3 kilometres to the north-east (to the Caesars Gallus and Volusianus 251 CE), these pointing to the existence an overland trade route passing very close to Tintagel.

This would certainly be the route featured in the *Ravenna Cosmography*, an itinerary of British and European routes complied c.700 CE from sources of about 400 CE. This route begins at Exeter (*Isca Dumnoniorum*) and led westwards. Its place-names are badly corrupt but have been largely deciphered in recent years. Crossing the upper reaches of the River Tamar at *Tamaris*, a name similar to the *Tamari fluvii* featured by Ptolemy in the 2nd century, its western limit is named as *Pilais*. This is probably for *P(ortus) Alaunus*, a lost late Roman port on the east bank of the Camel estuary, somewhere between Polzeath and Rock. A former name of the Camel River was the Alan.

Between *Tamaris* and *Portus Alaunus*, the itinerary lists *Purocoronavis*, correctly *Durocornovion*, 'fortress of the Cornovii, or Cornish', and containing (as *Cornou*) the oldest known reference to Cornwall's native name: Kernow. What better candidate can there be for this fortress than Tintagel, which might then have been an official station or tribute centre?

Tintagel Churchyard

THE Norman church of St Materiana stands in magnificent isolation on the top of Glebe Cliff well away from Tintagel village, and half a kilometre south of Tintagel Island and Castle. It contains the 4th century Roman 'milestone', or waymark, mentioned above, and the older, western part of the churchyard overlies an earlier earthwork enclosure that was once seen by some as a possible Roman signal station. Recent work has reinterpreted this earthwork as the enclosing bank of an early cemetery contemporary with the post-Roman royal seat on Tintagel Island, and closely linked with it.

Within the enclosed area are a number of grassy mounds and a stubby standing stone. One of these mounds, originally opened in 1942, was reopened for more detailed study in 1990 and 1991. At least three graves were found, two of which had been slate-lined. A socketed stone, which might have held ritual libations, stood at the end of an inner mound that may cover further burials. Elsewhere in the parent mound were slates marked with compass-drawn patterns, and sherds of the same

Mediterranean amphorae that had been found in abundance on Tintagel Island.

These burials were certainly early Christian and appeared to date from the same broad horizon as the royal stronghold on Tintagel Island. It would seem that many more burials await discovery in the adjacent mounds. Were these the graves of Dumnonian royalty and nobility?

The granite standing stone (the nearest source of granite is 8 kilometres away to the south east) may once have been inscribed like so many others of the period in Cornwall. Sadly and frustratingly, close examination has revealed no surviving traces of an inscription.

Historical sequence of Tintagel

IRON AGE use of the headland as a cliff castle, from c.300 BCE, is strongly suspected but remains unproven. Placing that aside, the historical sequence of site is as follows:

PERIOD 1 (3rd–4th century CE): Tintagel may have been the site of an official station overseen by Roman administration, perhaps connected with mineral extraction and trade, and probably named *Durocornovion*.

PERIOD 2 (c.450–c.700 CE): The site became a major stronghold and seat of the Dumnonian kings, perhaps only used seasonally and/or for special royal events. It had trading links with the eastern Mediterranean and North Africa, and its enclosed cemetery was located on Glebe Cliff nearby.

PERIOD 3 (c.1000–c.1200 CE): After several centuries of disuse and neglect, the headland became the site of the chapel of St Juliot (Julitte), perhaps built by the monks of Bodmin Priory. In the latter half of this period, Tintagel first became featured in writing, and so named by Geoffrey of Monmouth in his History of the Kings of Britain (c.1136).

PERIOD 4 (c.1233–1337): Richard, Earl of Cornwall built his castle as a symbol of personal ambition, rather than to play any part in practical strategy. Useless to anyone else, it became disused and was partially dismantled before the creation of the Duchy in 1337.

The 'Arthur' Slate

In 1998, excavations by the University of Glasgow, headed by Professor Chris Morris, were studying a small terrace below Ralegh Radford's Site C when a piece of trimmed-down and re-used slate was found. Measuring 35cm by 20cm, it had been used as a drain cover c.600 CE, but lettering of two earlier periods were seen to have been roughly incised on its surface.

At the top of the stone are parts of four large Roman capitals, incised with something like a bradawl, and of a style consistent with a date of c.400 CE. These have been tentatively interpreted as H AVG, perhaps for Honorius Augustus, Western Roman Emperor from 393 to 423 CE. He had been the very man who, in response to pleas from British councils for military aid in 410 after final withdrawal of Roman troops from Britain, had told them to look to their own defence.

Below these letters were words in a lettering style datable to c.550 CE. The surviving lines read: PATERNI…/COLI AVI FICIT / ARTOGNOV / COL (O AVI?)… FICIT. The letters appear to have been scratched into the slate by a knifepoint.

What this actually means is unclear and it may be nothing more than 6th century graffiti. *Paterni* could translate as 'father of', or be a personal name derived from this Latin word, as with the Welsh name *Padarn*. *Coll* is a Celtic (Brythonic) man's name, translating as 'hazel', and which features as a character's name in the *Mabinogion*. *Avi* is believed to mean 'ancestor, forebear of', while *ficit* is the Latin word *fecit*, 'has made, has built'.

The name on the third line: *Artognou*, created great excitement leading to media hype of the worst possible kind. The excavator, Professor Morris, and Professor Charles Thomas who authenticated the find, admitted to their hearts sinking when they saw the letters ARTO-, fearing what would certainly follow.

The resultant media hysteria was shamelessly stage-managed by the site managers, 'English' Heritage who, with enhanced entrance fee receipts firmly uppermost in mind, suppressed news of the find until the start of the peak holiday season. The major newspapers then trumpeted the find to an astonished nation on August 7th that year.

'English' Heritage's chief archaeologist, Dr Geoffrey Wainwright, delivered to the Press the statement that *Artognou* was a Latin spelling of the British name *Arthnou*, then absurdly claimed that this meant 'Arthur'.

Understandably, pandemonium took over.

Wainwright went even further. 'It proves for the first time, ' he enthused, 'that the name existed at that time, and that the stone belonged to a person of status. I hope it will put some meat on the historical figure. He is one of the great British heroes, a tough, rough leader of men.'

'This is the find of a lifetime,' he added, now well into his stride. 'It is remarkable that a stone has been discovered with the name *Arthnou* inscribed on it at Tintagel, a place with which King Arthur has long been associated.' He went on to state that inscribed stones had never before been found on a secular site, an astonishing thing for any professional archaeologist to claim when one bears in mind that a high proportion of Cornwall's post-Roman inscribed stones occupy sites unconnected with religion: Men Scryfa, the Tristan Stone, the Slaughter Bridge stone and the Boslow Stone being just four outstanding examples of many.

All in all, the press conference gleefully arranged by 'English' Heritage was, as Professor Thomas neatly remarked: 'Hot on commerce, decidedly weak on fact and scholarship, and simply cheapens one of Cornwall's greatest sites.' He was far from being the only person to be appalled by this shameless display of irresponsibility and blatant profiteering by a supposedly professional agency.

Predictably, the idiocy spawned by 'English' Heritage soon attracted more of it. A Plymouth man contacted the Press and claimed that he had carved the stone when a child, copying the inscription from the back cover of a book about King Arthur. No such book cover has ever existed and, in any case, the man's claim was impossible. Archaeologists of the highest calibre had found the stone in a layer of soil that had been clearly undisturbed since the 7th century and, of course, no comparable inscription exists from which this could ever have been copied.

The name *Artognou* is indeed British Celtic, consisting of *arto-*, 'bear', and *-gnou*, 'known as' (or, possibly, from *-geno-s*, 'born'). Other British names in *Arto-* are also known: *Arthyen* being one such. *Artognou* does not, and cannot, represent Arthur, a Celtic form of the Latin name *Artorius*. At least two individuals carried this name during the Roman occupation: Artorius Justus (3rd century CE) and Lucius Artorius Castus, (fl. 185 CE). As Professor Thomas acidly remarked: 'The names Artognou and Arthur are as closely related as Gerald and Geronimo!'

The hysteria, of course, swamped the true importance of the find. This suggests that Tintagel was in use during the reign of Honorius and confirms that, in the mid 6th century, men called Coll, Artognou and, possibly, Paternus, were at Tintagel, the first residents of the site to be authentically named.

Other traditions of Tintagel

OTHER LEGENDS and works of fancy feature Tintagel, all of them coined since the building of Earl Richard's castle. The 13th century *Perlesvaus*, translated by Sebastian Evans as *The High History of the Holy Grail*, reflects the site's geography, and even offers an explanation for the erosion of the headland's narrow neck.

This account has Arthur, accompanied by Gawain and Lancelot, riding into unfamiliar territory and coming across the ruins of a castle, part of which had fallen away into an abyss. Above the Great Hall is a chapel from which emerges an old, bald-headed priest. Arthur asks which castle this is, and is told that he has come to the fabled Tintagel. He then asks why the ground has fallen away. Not yet knowing the visitors' identities, the priest tells them of King Uther Pendragon's lust for Ygerna, the death of her husband Gorlois, and how Uther, aided by Merlin's trickery, had entered the castle disguised as Duke Gorlois to lie with Ygerna.

> 'And so,' said the priest, 'was begat King Arthur in a great hall that was next to this enclosure where this abysm is. And for this sin has the ground sunken away in this wise.'

Beside the chapel, the priest indicates a lordly tomb which had been that of Merlin, who had commanded that he not be interred inside the chapel. The priest tells them that Merlin's body is no longer in the tomb. 'So soon as it was set therein, it was taken out and snatched away, either on God's behalf or the Enemy's, but which we know not.' He finishes by saying: 'In such manner I tell you was King Arthur conceived in sin that is now the best king in the world.'

Other legends, purely local, are that the castle was built by giants, was finished in a blue and green chequered pattern and that, on two nights of the year at the Midsummer and Midwinter solstices, it vanishes completely.

The true impregnability of this fortress of the kings of Dumnonia was best described by Geoffrey of Monmouth, who ascribed these words to Ulfin of Ridcaradoch (modern Rosecraddock, St Cleer) as he advises

Uther Pendragon: 'The castle is built high above the sea which surrounds it on all sides, and there is no other way in except that offered by a narrow ridge of rock. Three armed soldiers could hold it against you, even if you stood there with the whole kingdom of Britain at your side.'

Even in the light of Tintagel's 5th to 8th century royal status, historians still insist that the site has nothing to do with the figure of Arthur, real or legendary. It is sometimes hinted that the available evidence refutes the ancient tradition but, invariably, without qualification. In direct contrast to their engineered hysteria after the 1998 discovery of the Artognou Stone, 'English' Heritage's site material has told the visitor that it is unlikely that Arthur ever came to Tintagel, a statement that was perhaps ill-considered.

True, there is no direct evidence of Arthur's presence at Tintagel but what evidence there is in fact enhances and supports the likelihood of truth behind the tradition. It provides the ideal scenario for the conception and, perhaps, birth of Arthur, and maybe even his coronation as High King. Tradition has always claimed that the site was a royal seat at that precise time, a claim that was rubbished for decades by the very profession whose work has now confirmed it. There is no earthly reason why an historical Arthur could not have been conceived there, as the legends have claimed for centuries. Tintagel remains the only claimant to be the location of this event, and Geoffrey of Monmouth is unlikely to have simply made it up. He almost certainly acted upon a story he had heard and in view of what else has been borne out in recent years, that is sufficient for others to cast a rather less sceptical, and more questioning, eye over his claim.

A man called Arthur

'NYNS YW MAROW ARTHOR RUW' – King Arthur is not dead. Such has been the enduring Celtic belief of an historically elusive hero who will one day return to rid the land of its oppressors, and the belief is older than Geoffrey of Monmouth who first brought Arthur to a wide audience in his *History of the Kings of Britain*, written in either 1136 or 1139.

Two decades earlier, in 1113, nine monks from Laon in France, and on a visit to Bodmin, scoffed at a townsman's insistence that King Arthur still lived, and provoked a near riot, but who was this King? This is a subject that is deftly avoided by nearly all mainstream historians who might provide better service if they took the subject seriously. After all, an enduring myth such as Arthur's must surely have some basis in truth, and not be so readily cast aside.

There is, in fact, more documentary evidence for the existence of a British warleader named Arthur than exists for several characters that are readily accepted as historical fact. Several pre-Norman writings feature him, among the earliest being the poem *Y Gododdin* from the early 7th century. In this the valour of a warrior is praised, but this adds: 'Although he was no Arthur.' *The Song of the Graves*, dating from about the same time, lists the final resting places of several noted warriors but, in the Old Welsh of the original: *Anoeth bid bet y Arthur* – 'A mystery to the world is the grave of Arthur.'

The *Annales Cambriae*, or Welsh Easter Annals, list many accepted events, and two of its entries mention Arthur himself. The given years of its earlier entries are debatably inaccurate, but for Year 72 (518 CE) it states: 'Battle of Badon in which Arthur carried the Cross of Our Lord Jesus Christ on his shoulders (or shield) for three days and nights and the Britons were the victors'. 21 years later, it lists: 'The strife of Camlann in which Arthur and Medraut perished.' Already we see the beginnings of the legend: the decisive battle against the Saxons, then the tragic last battle at which Arthur fell, along with a warrior who later becomes the traitor Mordred (although the Annales entry rather suggests that the original fought alongside Arthur).

Throwing what seems to be fairly conclusive evidence into doubt, the 6th century priest Gildas wrote a critical lament called *De Excidio et Conquestu Britanniae*, 'On the Ruin and Conquest of Britain.' This bemoaned the state of the island, following the withdrawal of the Romans and the Saxon advent, lambasting several contemporary British kings along the way, including Dumnonia's Constantine. He made no mention of Arthur, but of a predecessor: Ambrosius Aurelianus, who had gained notable victories. Gildas followed this with: 'From that time forth, sometimes the Britons were victorious, sometimes the enemy, up to the year of the siege of Mount Badon, which was almost the most recent, but not the least, slaughter of the gallows-crew' (i.e. the Saxons).

The 9th century Welsh monk Nennius restores Arthur as the victor in this resounding victory that, from his mention of hot springs, would appear to have been near Bath. 'Then, in those days, Arthur fought against them (the Saxons) alongside the kings of the Britons, but he himself was Dux Bellorum.' This title translates as 'duke or leader of battles', but can be summed up as 'commander-in-chief.' Nennius then goes on to list twelve battles that Arthur had led and won. Some were in Lincolnshire, one was certainly on the Scottish borders, but: 'The twelfth battle was on Badon Hill, in which 960 men fell in one day from a single charge of Arthur, and he alone overthrew them. In all the battles he stood as victor.'

The background to the story lies in the decades following the final withdrawal of Roman troops from Britain in 410 CE. A good deal of this is as much legend as history, and it is difficult to sort one from the other.

A British king named as Vortigern (*uor-tigernos*, 'over-lord') had invited Jutes from across the North Sea at some time after 429 CE as a mercenary force to help his own troops resist Pictish and Saxon raids. He handed them a large part of Kent, without consulting the local British king Gwrangon, but the Jutes demanded more and got it through treachery. This was the notorious (and original) 'Night of the Long Knives' when British leaders met the Jutish ones to discuss a treaty. The Jutes had concealed daggers up their sleeves and, on a given signal, each stabbed to death the British leader sitting next to him. Only Vortigern was spared and effectively became in thrall to the Jutes, who then teamed up with Angles and Saxons in an attempt to take over Britain.

Two of Vortigern's own sons turned against their father and a series of battles against the incursors commenced. Both sons, Vortimer and Catigern, died during these battles, which appear to have taken place in the early 450s. Vortigern himself was probably dead by 455, apparently at the hands of a new leader, the same Ambrosius Aurelianus mentioned by Gildas, and who had first appeared in 437, in a battle waged in Hampshire against another British leader Vitolinus. Was this Vortigern's real name, as the given one appears to be a title equating to the *superbus tyrannus* mentioned by Gildas, seemingly in reference to Vortigern himself? Vortigern's grandfather had borne the name Vitolinus, while his father had been named Vitalus.

The door lay open to further Germanic expansion in Britain and, with Ambrosius either ageing or dead, a new leader of a British resistance was in demand. This, it appears, was Arthur. The widespread locations of his battles as listed by Nennius suggests that his strength lay in a fast-moving cavalry force, very like those employed by the Romans and, indeed by the *Comes Brittaniorum* mentioned in 405, and whose title 'Count of Britain' is somewhat reminiscent of that given by Nennius to Arthur: 'Duke of Battles.'

The name Arthur is a Celtic form of a Roman name, *Artorius*, and at least two men of this name had been in Roman Britain. Lucius Artorius Castus held a command at *Eboracum* (York) and, in 184, took a legion from there across the Channel into *Armorica* (Brittany) to quell an uprising. In the late 5th century, a British king was to do something very similar, as shall be seen. An Artorius Justus also served Rome in Britain in the 3rd century.

With an Artorius succeeding a man with another Roman name, it is tempting to imagine him as a younger member of the same family of Romanised Britons; could his full name have been Artorius Aurelianus? If so, then any confusion between what he and Ambrosius achieved could be better understood.

The historical background is broadly credible, but how did the legend develop from it? The real birth of the legend is down to Geoffrey of Monmouth and it was his early 12th century account that gave rise to all that followed, through continental writers to Sir Thomas Malory and even to Tennyson. Geoffrey's account has often been written off as fiction but the scholar Geoffrey Ashe has noted that what he actually did was to weave a largely fictional story around real events and several real people. Geoffrey of Monmouth had a real man in mind when he wrote of King Arthur. Whether that man was really Arthur is the chief argument, but there was a real British king who, in the late 460s, was the only man who did what Geoffrey claimed for Arthur.

As is often frustratingly the case, given dates create a problem. If Geoffrey's man was indeed Arthur, then he may have lived too early to have been at the Battle of Mount Badon. The *Annales Cambriae* dates may be wildly out, but Gildas provides a cryptic clue to it, by linking Badon with a 43 year term related to either his own birth date, or to the rise of Vortigern. No one has ever determined exactly what Gildas's ambiguous Latin really tells us in this particular phrase. Gildas was writing in the 530s. If he meant that his birth date and the battle were in the same year then we come to a date around 490, still too late. However, if he meant that the battle took place 43 years after Vortigern's rise to power in 429, then it would date Badon to 468. Another possibility is that Gildas was saying that Badon took place 43 years before he was born, which would also put us close to 468. This date would connect well with the man who seems to have been the model for Geoffrey of Monmouth's Arthur. However, to find him, we are reliant on 6th century Gaulish chronicles, as he is not to be found in what remains of contemporary British record.

Rome had long departed but for many of Britain's citizens, especially among the aristocracy, the island still stood on the side of *Romanitas*, the ideals of Roman civilisation. Therefore, it is not remarkable that, in the 460s, Gallo-Romans in Gaul should seek aid from Britain in their own considerable problems and this they did when threatened by advances by the Visigoths from the territories they held in Aquitaine, largely thanks to the disastrous ambitions of the Briton Constantine in 411. Syagrius, commander of the Gallo-Romans, had a case that Britain owed them the help he was now asking for.

In 469 or 470, a British king only recorded historically as Riotamus (an apparent title meaning 'over-king') took 12,000 troops over to Gaul. Some have argued that he was a British leader based in Brittany, but the Breton colonisation from Dumnonia was in its infancy and could not have provided any meaningful force, let alone one that numbered so many. Nor would any Breton leader have taken those troops 'by way of Ocean' as recorded, as he would have already have been on the Gaulish mainland. The number of the British troops has also been questioned as being unrealistically high, but it pales into insignificance when compared with the 100,000 that had been led by Queen Boudica in the 1st century CE, or the 30,000 Caledonian Celts that had opposed Agricola.

The 6th century Gaulish writer Jourdanes wrote:

> 'Now Euric, king of the Visigoths, perceived the frequent changes of of Roman emperors and strove to hold Gaul in his own right. The (western) emperor Anthemius heard of it and asked the Britons for aid. Their king Riotimus came with twelve thousand men into the state of the Bituriges by way of Ocean, and was received as he disembarked from his ships.'

The British under the command of Riotamus appear to have first helped Syagrius to clear out a Saxon pirate base in the Loire estuary; no mean feat when considering that its leader, Odovacer, was within a few short years, in 476, to become the first Germanic king of Rome. Indeed, a major battle in this campaign at *Andegavum* (Angers) could well have been one of the battles won by Arthur and listed by Nennius as Agned. This might well have meant *Andeg(avum)*.

The British forces then moved inland and southeastwards to *Avaricum* (Bourges) as a vanguard force to await the advance of King Euric's Visigoths. While in this area, Riotamus was the recipient of a letter from the prolific writer Sidonius Apollinaris, Bishop of *Nemossus* (Clermont-Ferrand), and which still survives. It appears that British officers had been luring slaves away from the servants of local landowners who had then asked the Bishop to intervene. From the letter it seems that the two men had already met, and the man that the Bishop describes is every inch a king:

> 'I am a direct witness of your remarkable integrity which causes you to suffer embarrassment for the wrongdoing of others. The bearer of this letter is humble and obscure, so unimportant as to invite exploitation of his harmless helplessness. He complains that his slaves have been taken away, enticed by the Britons. I have no idea if his plea is well-founded but, if you will hear both sides impartially, I fancy the poor man can uphold his case; that is, if amongst a crowd of keenwitted, armed and boisterous men, united in their courage, comradeship and sheer force of numbers, there can be a possibility for a single unarmed man, a humble rustic, a stranger of little means, to achieve justice and a fair hearing. Farewell.' The outcome of the hearing is not known.

What happened next wrote its way into Geoffrey of Monmouth's manipulated account of Arthur, and the legend that endured thereafter.

Geoffrey had his Arthur fighting against the Romans in Gaul when the man he had selected as his model for the king had actually gone to their aid. Geoffrey then had Arthur betrayed to the enemy during his absence by his deputy ruler at home, Mordred – the Medraut of the Annales Cambriae – leading to the fateful last battle at Camlann, and Arthur's departure to Avalon.

In similar fashion, Riotamus was also the subject of a betrayal to the enemy by a deputy ruler. This enemy was not the Saxons, nor was the betrayer Mordred. Instead, it was a man named Arvandus, Imperial Prefect of Gaul and deputy to the Emperor Anthemius in Rome, and who was in league with Euric, king of the Germanic Visigoths, in a plot to partition Gaul and wrest the throne of the Western Roman Empire from Anthemius. Recognising the considerable threat of the British forces at Bourges, and that they were temporarily isolated from Syagrius's main army, Arvandus wrote a letter to Euric urging him not to make peace with 'this Greek emperor' (Anthemius) but, instead to 'attack the British beyond the Loire '.

Euric launched a surprise attack with a massive force, and we have two 6th century Gaulish historians to thank for accounts of what happened. Gregory of Tours wrote that: 'The British were driven from Bourges by the Goths after the killing of so many of them at Bourg de Déols.' Jordanes gave a longer account: 'Euric, king of the Visigoths, came against them (the British) with an innumerable army and, after a long fight, he routed Riotamus, King of the Britons, before the Romans (i.e. Syagrius) could reach him. When he lost the greater part of his army, he fled with all the men he could muster and came to the Burgundians, a neighbouring tribe friendly to the Romans.'

At that point, Riotamus becomes lost from history and may not have survived. Nonetheless, one further detail slots rather startlingly into the legends that followed. His northeastward retreat from Bourges into friendly Burgundian territory would have brought him and the tattered remnants of his army to a town with a Celtic name that the Romans wrote as *Aballone*. Its medieval and modern name is ... Avallon. The year was 470 CE.

Riotamus was almost certainly the man that Geoffrey of Monmouth had in mind when formulating his King Arthur, and he would be the definitive model for the king as featured by every Arthurian writer since then. Was his name really Artorius, or was Riotamus simply remembered as 'another Artorius' after Lucius Artorius Castus and his armed venture into Gaul 300 years earlier?

In recent years, one writer after another has attempted to identify Arthur with other historical characters but, to be frank, none of them hold water. Each identification is that of an obscure individual whose achievements are even more obscure: hardly the stuff from which enduring legends are born. However, a man like Riotamus, a soldier-king sought out to be the last torch-bearer of hope for a doomed and dying Empire even if he did fail through betrayal, is many times more likely to have been proposed as a model for such a powerful legend that, for fifteen centuries, has lasted, grown and spread across the entire world.

How connected was Arthur to Cornwall and Dumnonia? Certainly, there are many local legends of him: from his alleged conception at Tintagel, to his hunting lodge at Castle-an-Dinas, St Columb, to battles in the far west of Cornwall and to the lost land of Lyonesse, where Great and Little Arthur are names of islands in the Scillonian archipelago. Often, he has been linked with Wales and even Scotland. The very earliest records of him are from Welsh and southern Scottish sources and, if Nennius's list of his battles are to be believed, then he certainly fought as far north as the Scottish borders.

If *Badon* was Bath, then its location implies a spearhead movement of the Saxons westward, threatening an approach to Dumnonia's borders. A century or so later, a similar movement led to the decisive Saxon victory at the Battle of Dyrham, just a few miles away, in 577 CE. South of the Somerset Levels, then an expanse of water and swamp, and visible from Glastonbury where Arthur is said to have been buried, is the magnificent and impressive hill fort of South Cadbury Castle, first built during the Iron Age. This has long been associated with King Arthur and claimed to be the site of Camelot, but it was also heavily refortified in the Arthurian period, and on a scale unmatched by any other refortified Iron Age site. South Cadbury also stands close to a Roman route heading into Dumnonia and its massive presence also stands before the Dumnonian border as though daring any invading force to make the attempt to get past it.

The Welsh cycle of myth known as *The Mabinogion* specifically gives Arthur a Cornish home at a fortress called *Celli Wig*, or *Kelliwic*, implying that he was not only Dumnonian, but Cornish. There are two main candidates for this location: the Iron Age hill fort of Castle Killibury, or Kelly Rounds, a few miles west of Wadebridge; and the huge hill fort of Castle Canyke on the east side of Bodmin, close to a place called Callywith, and to the main trans-peninsular route linking the Camel and Fowey estuaries and known today as the Saint's Way. It was also in Bodmin that the incident in 1113, involving a local belief in the undying King, took place.

The arguments will doubtless rage on but, at least, we do have something truly historical to go on regarding King Arthur, even if the mystery has yet be fully solved.

The Battle of Vellan-druchar

THE LEGEND runs that the 'Sea Kings' or 'Danes' were taken to landing at Gwenver beach, Sennen, and pillaging the hamlet of Escalls. Noting that their raids were unopposed, they landed a larger force to range further inland and raid the larger, wealthier settlements which they believed to be unprotected. Heavy surf delayed their landing, giving local people time to send out the alarm.

That night, the beacon was lit on Chapel Carn Brea. Another blazed out on Castle-an-dinas and then on Trencrom. Carn Brea responded, and another shone out from St Agnes Beacon. More fires were lit on Belowda Beacon, the Great Stone (Roche Rock?), St Bellarmine's Tor, Rough Tor, Bronn Weneli (Brown Willy) and Cadon Barrow (Condolden Barrow), high above Tintagel.

There, Prince Arthur, as the legend calls him, responded immediately, taking the war-hosts of nine kings westward. The journey took them two days while the Danes were doing their worst. The legend says that the invading force avoided high ground and crossed the peninsula 'down through the bottoms' to the sea on the northern side, suggesting they had got as far as Marazion Marsh then forced their way up to the Hayle estuary.

Arthur's forces caught up with them at a place called *Vellan-druchar*, as they were on their way back to their ships. So terrible was the carnage that the nearby millwheel was being turned by the flow of blood rather than water. Not a single Dane escaped with his life.

Those who been left to guard the ships at Gwenver attempted to escape but a local wise-woman raised a spell to 'bring home the west wind' by emptying the holy well against the hill, and sweeping the church from door to altar. The west wind duly obliged, driving the invaders' ships onto the rocks, or high up on the beach to be stranded. This coincided with a particularly high spring tide, so that the ships rotted on the sands for years afterwards. Arthur's forces quickly despatched the remaining guards, and the victory was complete. Arthur and the nine kings reconfirmed their mutual loyalty in the water from St Senan's Well, gave thanks for the victory in the nearby chapel, and held their victory feast on the Table-Maen, a tabular block of granite that still exists at Mayon.

There, Merlin appeared, and intoned one of his customarily gloomy prophecies:

'The Northmen wild once more shall land,
And leave their bones on Escalls' sand.
The soil of Vellan-druchar's plain
Again shall take a sanguine stain,
And o'er the millwheel roll a flood
Of Danish mixed with Cornish blood.
When thus the vanquished find no tomb,
Expect the dreadful day of doom.'

This is, of course, legend, and the figure of King, or Prince, Arthur has yet to be confirmed as truly historical, but could this story have had a basis in truth?

The Arthurian connection points us to the late 5th and early 6th century, far too early for Danes to have been involved, but not too early for the invaders to have been Saxons, whose homeland was not far to the south of the Danish peninsula.

In the later part of the 5th century, a Saxon force is known to have founded a pirate base on islands in the Loire estuary, on the Biscay coast of France, under leaders named as Corsold and his successor Odovacer, who later became the first Germanic ruler of Italy. A Visigothic admiral wrote of his own ships, based in the territories they then held in Aquitaine and Northern Spain, being constantly on the lookout in the Bay of Biscay for 'the curved ships of the Saxons'. In 471, Irish Annals recorded a 'second Saxon raid on Ireland', and the most likely starting point for this and the earlier, undated, raid, would have been the Saxon base on the Loire.

Any sea voyage from there to Ireland would have passed the 'halfway house' of the Penwith peninsula, and it is inconceivable that Saxon pirates would simply pass it by without stopping to plunder it. Raids with little or no opposition might well have led to a more concerted assault and, suddenly, the Vellan-druchar scenario becomes a very realistic possibility.

Arthur's nine kings and warhosts are also of interest, as it suggests a magical exaggeration. In Celtic lore, the number three is of mystic significance; nine, or three times three, was regarded as being extremely powerful. This further suggests that the nine kings (troop-commanders?) of the legend may only have been three in number. Tintagel, from whence they started out, was in the old division, or *keverang* of Cornwall known as Trigg. In the 7th century, this was called *Pagus Tricurius*, 'land of the Tricorii', a British word meaning 'three war-hosts'. That the legend is based upon a real event becomes just that bit more likely. Were three war-hosts from Trigg involved, perhaps not led by Arthur, but by the King of Dumnonia himself who, given the likely period of the battle, may have been Gwrwawr, Tudwawl or Kynwawr.

The site of Vellan-druchar exists in reality, and lies just to the northeast of St Buryan, and just south of the B3283 road, which may well follow an ancient routeway. In tangled, swampy willows in the valley bottom are the ruins of Vellan-druchar Cottage, near which was once a mill recorded in 1609 as *Mellen Trucke* (*melin droghya*, 'tucking, or fulling, mill'). Interestingly, local legend also claims that Arthur was in ownership of the great cliff castle at Treryn Dinas, built in the Iron Age, but only three miles southwest of the *Vellan-druchar* battle site.

Kings of Dumnonia and Cornwall

ONE PROBLEM faced by historians looking into the post-Roman centuries is not so much the lack of historical record, but the scarcity of information in what does survive from that period, or soon after it. Another is how to distinguish and separate legend from history; an onerous task at best. Both problems emerge when it comes to compiling information about the kings ruling Dumnonia and Cornwall during that period.

Often, Cornish 'kings' are implied as having been factual but, in fact, they mostly derive from Geoffrey of Monmouth's highly fanciful *History of the Kings of Britain*, written in the 1130s. Geoffrey has a whole list of these, supposedly dating from c.1100 BCE to 600 CE: Corineus; Gwendolen (a queen); Henwinus; Cunedagius; Cloten; Dunvallo Molmutius; Belinus; Tenvantius; Thanor; Asclepiodotus; Caradocus; Dionotus. This initial sequence ends c.390 BCE. A later sequence quoted by Geoffrey starts c. 510 CE and gives: Gorlois (as Duke); Cador (as Duke and King); Constantine (as Duke and later, King of Britain); and Blederic, current when St Augustine arrives in Kent in 597 CE. One or two of these may have been real people.

Some of these names are genuinely Celtic, implying at least some measure of authenticity. However, several do not appear in any other record and to ascribe genuine existence and status to them is highly inadvisable. One suspects, for example, that Geoffrey's Queen Gwendolen was gleaned by him from Gwenddoleu ap Ceidiaw, a real person (and a man), a northern British chieftain who died at the Battle of Arfderydd (Cumbria) in 573 CE, and whose death was lamented by his friend, the poet Myrddin – the original Merlin – who is said to have suffered temporary insanity as a result of the battle's savagery and the death of his close friend and lord, and then lived wild for a time in the Caledonian Forest. Other names in the list, such as Asclepiodotus, a Greek name, and Thanor, apparently Germanic, are neither the Celtic nor adopted Latin names to be expected in early and post-Roman Britain, and best to be discounted.

Another source, the 13th century *Prose Tristan*, adds two more to this list: Felix, in the late 5th century CE; and Mark of Cornwall, from the early 6th century CE. These appear to immediately precede Gorlois in Geoffrey's sequence. As both sources contain so many names that are otherwise unconfirmable, then we have to look elsewhere for threads of reliability. There are two such sources, from the 12th and 13th century but the form of a few names they contain show them to have been drawn or copied from earlier material.

The first, at Oxford University, is simply known as Jesus College MS 20, and contains a list of Dumnonian kings which reads backwards in time: a daughter of Judhael, then Theudu, son of Peredur, son of Cado, son of Gereint, son of Erbin, son of Kynwawr, son of Tudwawl, son of Gwrwawr, son of Gadeon, son of Cynan, son of Eudaf Hen.

The second document is *Bonedd y Saint* (Lineage of the Saints) which mentions: Kybi, son of Selyf, son of Gereint, son of Erbin, son of Custennin Gorneu. The last seems to slot between the Erbin and Kynwawr of the first list.

Some of these names, several given in Old Welsh form, are known elsewhere. One or two are even roughly datable, and it would seem that at least part of these lists might be reliable. In particular, a sequence from Gwrwawr to Theudu can be reconstructed with some measure of confidence, and would cover a period from the mid 5th century CE to the late 7th century; the same approximate period of Tintagel's use as a seasonal or ceremonial royal seat.

The following is as reliable a sequence as can possibly be achieved of the Kings of Dumnonia and Cornwall from the mid 5th century onwards; kings that, regrettably are neither named nor detailed by the current management at Tintagel.

GWRWAWR, perhaps son of Gadeon: No details are known about this king, whose name is derived from British: *uiro-maro-s*, 'great man'. In early Cornish, his name would probably be represented as: *Gorvaur*. His period would seem to have been around the third quarter of the 5th century CE.

TUDWAWL, son of Gwrwawr: Perhaps flourishing in the last quarter of the 5th century, this king's name is from British: *toto-ualo-s*, 'worthy of the people', later *Tudwal*, but nothing more is known about him. His name is known elsewhere; for example, a Bishop Tudwal flourished in 6th century Wales. The same name appears in a place-name, Treluswell (*Tredutual* 1296), 'Tudwal's farm/settlement'.

KYNWAWR, son of Tudwawl: Cornish: *Kenvor*, and from British *cuno-moro-s*, 'hound of the sea'. This king is mentioned in the *Life of St Paul Aurelian*, and largely associated with the peninsula between St Austell Bay and the Fowey estuary. The name occurs in at least five Cornish place-names, such as Tregenver, Falmouth ('Kenvor's settlement/farm') and Crenver, near Crowan (*Caergenver* 1301, 'Kenvor's fort'). Were these named after different men bearing the same name, or a single man of importance with extensive land ownerships?

The Breton monk Wrmonoc, in his 9th century *Life of St Paul Aurelian*, would seem to equate this king with another famous Cornish king. His text reads that, while crossing Cornwall, St Paul's fame: '...reached the ears of Marcus, whom men call by another name, Quonomorius, a powerful monarch under whose rule dwelt the people of four different languages. This ruler desired to firmly and lastingly set the foundations of a Christian faith in this land into which it had but lately arrived, and to unite all his subjects in adherence to it'. Quonomorius is identical to *cuno-moro-s*, whereas Marcus could be the Latin name, or a Latinisation of the British name *marko-s*, 'horse' (Cornish: *margh*). One legend claimed that King Mark of Cornwall had horse's ears, an obvious play on the name, and a theme stolen from the Greek legend of King Midas.

St Paul Aurelian was said by Wrmonoc to have spent some time in Cornwall, setting up his church at Paul, near Penzance, close to where his sister Sativola (Exeter's St Sidwell) dwelt for a while and, while serving as King Mark's chaplain, presented the king with a set of handbells. Mark wanted him to stay and set up a bishopric in Cornwall, but St Paul respectfully declined, being set upon founding a monastery in Brittany. Mark gave in to his wishes and, before leaving, St Paul asked the king for one of the bells as a memento of his stay. To this day, a Celtic handbell dated to the 6th century is preserved in the saint's Breton cathedral of St Pol de Leon.

Was Kynwawr the well-known King Mark? Wrmonoc's account would strongly suggest so, but this is still not conclusive. Cornish tradition certainly links Mark with Tintagel and with the hill fort of Castle Dore, Golant, while the 1501 Cornish miracle play *Beunans Meriasek*, (Life of St Meriasek), features him as '*mytern margh ryel*' (royal King Mark).

Another itinerant priest who was said to have encountered King Mark in Cornwall was St Sampson, to whom the founding of the church of St Sampson, at Golant on the Fowey estuary, and at the king's request, is ascribed. Sampson also went on to Brittany where he founded the monastery of Dol in 521. Taken with the dating of St Paul Aurelian's death at an advanced age in 575, this would suggest that Sampson met a king who was still a young man.

The mention of Marcus Quonomorius ruling over 'four different languages' is intriguing. A man called Chonomor is mentioned in the *History of the Franks*, written by Gregory, Bishop of Tours in 594, as ruling as 'Count' in Brittany, while Breton tradition remembers a 'Count' called Commore or Commorus. With a substantial British Dumnonian presence in Brittany, did Kynwawr seek and gain a dual kingdom on both sides of the Channel? Were the four languages British and Irish (or Latin) in Cornwall, and Gaulish and Frankish in Brittany? It is significant that, to this day, three regions of the Breton peninsula are named Domnonée, Kernev and Trégor (Dumnonia, Kernow and Trigg).

Breton legend claims a rather darker side to his character, as a usurper and murderer, but such tales may well have been spread abroad by the Church after he fell out with St Sampson, who was displeased by him overthrowing a local chieftain named Judual. It was during a rebellion by the same Judual that Kynwawr died, apparently in the year 554, and his grave is said to be the massive cairn on the 330-metre hill of Menez-Hom, to the northeast of Douarnenez.

Breton place-names recall him, not as Commore or Chonomor, but as Mark. One of his castles was said to be at Plomarc'h, just east of Douarnenez where an offshore island is the Ile Tristan, while the king's ghost appears in storms off the headland of Penmarc'h, riding a winged horse in the teeth of the gale.

Perhaps the most significant Cornish monument recording Cunomorus as the name of an important man stands where tradition firmly places the king himself and, like the Breton place-names, associates him closely with a man called Tristan. The regal, 2.8 metre tall Tristan Stone stands at the approaches to Fowey, and as well as bearing a Tau cross in relief high on its rear face, has a worn inscription to: DRVSTANVS IC IACIT CVNOMORI FILIVS ('Drustan lies here, of Cunomoros the son'). The lettering style dates the inscription to the middle third of the 6th century CE, entirely consistent with the dates implied elsewhere for the rule of Kynwawr. Much more about the Tristan Stone appears elsewhere in this book.

CONSTANTINE *Custennin Gorneu*, 'Constantine of Cornwall', an early mention of the Duchy's native name of Kernow, which can be traced back to least 400 CE. Named in honour of Constantine the Great (c.272-337 CE), the first Roman Emperor to convert to Christianity, we owe confirmation of his existence to the lamentations of the priest Gildas, who wrote of him c.540 CE in his work bemoaning the state of a Britain under invasive pressure from the Germanic Anglo-Saxons, and called *De Excidio et Conquestu Britanniae*, 'Of the Downfall and Conquest of the Britons'. In this, Gildas, never a man to mince his words, lays into five contemporary British kings, lambasting Constantine as the 'tyrannical whelp of the unclean lioness of Damnonia'. Gildas goes on to accuse him of breaking oaths against deceit and tyranny, of various adulteries after casting off his own wife, and of disguising himself as an abbot to murder two royal youths praying at an altar. Gildas ends by imploring Constantine to repent his sins lest he be damned.

It would appear that he did so. *The Life of St Petroc* describes how, near to Little Petherick, the saint protects a stag from being hunted down by a wealthy man called Constantine, who is then converted to Christianity by the saint. Constantine becomes a monk, giving St Petroc an ivory horn which becomes one of the saint's most treasured relics, and co-founds St Petroc's monastery at Bodmin. *The Life of St David* mentions that King Constantine of Cornwall gave up his crown to enter the priest-hood at the monastery of St David at *Menavia* (Mynyw) in Pembrokeshire. He became remembered as St Constantine, with churches dedicated to him at Constantine Bay (*Egloscostentin*) and the village of Constantine (*Lanngostentin*) near the head of the Helford River. Later he is said to become a hermit at Cosmeston (earlier: *Costyneston*) near Cardiff.

Other claims are perhaps less reliable, but nonetheless interesting. Bishop Richard Challoner's *Brittania Sancta* (1745) has Constantine being sent to Ireland and the monastery of St Carthag at Rathene, where he worked in the foundation's mill for 4 years. His identity was only uncovered after being overheard muttering to himself that no one would ever believe that this humble miller had once been the king of Cornwall.

Later, St Columba sent him to convert the people of Galloway, but at an advanced age, he was killed at Kintyre during a pirate raid on 11th March 590 (another source gives the date of his martyrdom as 9th March 576). His shrine is at Govan. However, it may well be that St Constantine of Cornwall and St Davids, and the St Constantine of Govan were two different men.

If the Dumnonian king-list and the evidence suggested by the Tristan Stone can be reconciled, then Constantine may have been the elder, or surviving, brother to Drustan, the Tristan of legend.

Several sources mention a *Bledric map Custennin*, described by the *Llyfr Baglan* as *Dux Cornubiae*, 'Duke of Cornwall'; almost certainly a genuine original for Geoffrey of Monmouth's 'Blederic', who he places in 597. Bledric is stated by Caradoc of Llancarfan to have been killed in a battle against Ethelfrith of Northumbria at Bangor-on-Dee, c.600. The time-scale, when compared with that of Constantine, and of Ethelfrith, who did fight a battle near Chester and who died in 606, is realistic. Unfortunately the *Llyfr Baglan* then somewhat muddles the issue by stating that Bledric was brother to Dumnonia's King Gerent I, rather than being his uncle as the king-lists would suggest.

ERBIN, son of Constantine: The king-lists appear to name Erbin as succeeding Constantine as King of Dumnonia, but little is known about him. The name is a Celtic form of the Latin name Urbanus, and appears in the Cornish place-name Treverbyn, of which there are four examples (*trev Erbyn*, 'Erbin's farm/settlement'). Although some surviving genealogies have him as the son of Gereint others, in line with the traditions, weights the evidence in favour of him having been Gereint's father.

GEREINT, or GERENT I, son of Erbin: *The Welsh White Book of*

Rhydderch and *Red Book of Hergest* both contain the romantic tale of *Gereint and Enid*, in which the hero is specified as the son of Erbin, King of Dumnonia. *A Gereint rac Deheu*, 'Gerent for the South' is named as a hero of the Battle of Catraeth (Catterick, Yorkshire), which took place in 597 CE, in the Welsh poem *Y Gododdin*, attributed to the bard Aneirin. The battle date would be consistent with that of this Dumnonian king. A further poem, *Gereint ap Erbin*, also called *Lament for Gereint*, laments his death at an undated Battle of Llongborth, probably Langport in Somerset, right on the Dumnonian border. His cavalry force is described as '*men of Diwneint*', the Old Welsh form of the name Dumnonia. This poem, probably of 10th or 11th century composition, appears in the *Black Book of Carmarthen*, although the poet may have confused this Gerent with a later King Gerent of Dumnonia who may well have died at Langport in the early 8th century.

Legend associates Gerent I with the Roseland peninsula of Cornwall, where a church is dedicated to St Gerens (at Gerrans). The nearby Iron Age fort of Dingerein Castle (*din Gerens*, 'fortress of Gerent') has only been so named and associated with the king since Victorian times. Just up the coast, on a high eminence overlooking Gerrans Bay, is the colossal Bronze Age barrow of Carne Beacon, under which the king's body was said to have been laid to rest after being borne across the bay in a golden ship with silver oars, and which is said to have been buried with him. Sadly, a 19th century excavation of the barrow failed to find either.

Ancient genealogies give this Gerent two sons who became priests: Yestin (St Just) and Selyf (St Selevan), the latter being the father of St Kybi (St Cuby), known at Cuby church at the higher end of Tregony, and as far north as Anglesey where Holyhead's Welsh name is Caergybi, 'fort of St Kybi'. That a priest of this era could be a father is acceptable; celibacy among the lower orders of priesthood was not required by the Catholic Church until the 12th century and, in any case, the Celtic church was at this time largely independent of Rome. The Jesus College MS 20 list gives Gerent I a third son: Cado, who succeeded him as king of Dumnonia.

CADO, son of Gerent: Nothing other than their inclusion in the king-list is known of the real Cado, or his named successors Peredur and Theudu. Cado was almost certainly the man chosen by Geoffrey of Monmouth for his Cador, Duke of Cornwall and son of Gorlois, before confusing matters further by naming Cador's son as Constantine.

PEREDUR, son of Cado: The existence of a Dumnonian king of this name might have inspired the Peredur of a romantic tale in *The Mabinogion*, which is an early form of the Grail quest legend. Geoffrey of Monmouth's *Vita Merlini*, 'Life of Merlin', based on the real life Myrddin Wyllt, has a Peredur allied with Merlin and King Rhydderch against another king, Gwenddolau, in the late 6th century, but this is set in the north of Cumbria and the western Scottish border region, and may have no connection with a Dumnonian king of the same name.

THEUDU, son of Peredur: This king might have inspired the villainous King Teudar who appears in the Tudor period Cornish plays of *Beunans Meriasek*, 'Life of St Meriasek', and *Beunans Ke*, 'Life of St Kea'; the name perhaps being respelt in a satirical swipe at the Tudor dynasty itself, thinly disguising contemporary Tudor monarchs in the role of a malevolent Cornish one. The satirical target in the earlier play was undoubtedly Henry VII, as it was written just four years after the Cornish campaign against him in 1497. The second play was composed just after the vicious uprising of 1549, in the brief reign of the boy-king Edward VI, which saw an estimated 11% of Cornwall's male population killed by English forces loyal to the Tudor dynasty. *Beunans Ke* was also written not long after the destruction of Glasney Collegiate Church, Penryn, a major seat of learning, in Henry VIII's Dissolution of the Monasteries, and where most of the surviving Cornish language plays had been written since the 14th century. The clerical playwrights had, therefore, little cause to love the Tudors, and the existence of a real King Theudu during the general 'Age of the Saints' might well have given them the perfect opportunity to lampoon, ridicule and defame the reigning dynasty, and get away with it if challenged.

From this point in history, the surviving king-lists, or those parts that might be considered reliable, peter out, leaving a frustrating gap in the sequence and knowledge of Dumnonian kings until records produce a second King Gerent, at around 700 CE.

GERENT II is first mentioned at around the year 705, when a meeting of the churches of Wessex requested a newly installed Aldhelm, first bishop of Sherborne Abbey, to write to him in an attempt to persuade the Celtic Church in his realm to conform to the doctrines and practices of the Church as laid down by Rome. Aldhelm wrote his letter to '*Gerontius Rex*', later mentioning his kingdom as *Domnonia*, almost the last time that the original kingdom's name was recorded and 700 years after the name's first recorded appearance.

Aldhelm and Gerent appear to have known each other well. The letter is at all times respectful of the Celtic king and friendly in tone. Aldhelm wrote elsewhere of travelling into *Domnonia* and on into *Cornubia*, a visit that may have predated the letter, and was almost certainly approved by the king who may have received him in person. There was nothing unusual about such an inter-ethnic friendship; the later Saxon King Alfred of Wessex had as his own close friend and biographer the Welsh bishop Asser.

It is clear from the letter that Aldhelm considered his relationship with Gerent to be firm enough to offer criticism of the king's Cornish bishops, and their refusal to conform to Roman practices. These included an alternative computation for the date of Easter, and their continuing to apply the Celtic tonsure. This consisted of shaving the front part of the head, leaving the rest of the hair to grow long, in contrast to the Roman practice of shaving an area of the pate, and cutting the hair short in the fashion that many would associate with Friar Tuck.

It is doubtful that Gerent had a great deal of influence over his bishops, who, after all, would have considered themselves subjects of a rather higher and Heavenly authority than him. Two centuries later, in 905, King Eadwulf of Wessex instructed Bishop Eadwulf of Sherborne to annually visit: 'the land of the Cornish race, to stamp out their errors for, previously, as much as they could, they resisted the truth and did not obey Papal decrees'. Aldhelm's approach on behalf of the Roman Church, had palpably failed and, in fact, Cornwall was the last of the Celtic nations to hold out against obedience to Rome.

Nonetheless, the friendship between Gerent II and Bishop Aldhelm had two major effects. Firstly, it was strong enough for Gerent to gift land in the Rame Peninsula to Aldhelm's Sherborne Abbey; initially 5 hides of land at *Macuir* (Maker). He may well have later added up to 13 hides more land from that estate in his gifts to Sherborne Abbey, and another areas at *Ros*, seemingly close by in the Rame Peninsula. It is very likely that, after Aldhelm's death, Sherborne Abbey quietly passed ownership of those lands to Ine, king of the West Saxons, doubtless in exchange for favour.

The second effect was that, as Aldhelm had the ear of both Gerent and the West Saxon king Ine, he was able to use his influence and divine appointment to keep them from each other's throats. Only after Aldhelm's death in 709 were the two kings again at war.

In 710, Ine of Wessex, with his kinsman Nunna, launched an attack against the borders of Dumnonia. It is not known for certain where this took place, but it is likely that Ine planned well and took a numerous army. The *Anglo-Saxon Chronicle* only records that: 'Ine and Nunna his kinsman fought against Gerent.' Roger of Wendover, writing 500 years later, is adamant that the West Saxons were the victors: 'Ine, king of the West Saxons, fought against Gerent, king of the Welsh (*Wallensium*) and, in the beginning of the battle, Duke Higebald was slain; but at last the Welsh king (*rex Wallensis*) fled, leaving his arms and spoils to the *Angliae* (Anglis).'

If the 10th or 11th century *Lament for Geraint* poem confused Gerent I with this king, then a defeat would be confirmed, and the retreat mentioned by Roger of Wendover could possibly have been an effect of Gerent's death in this battle. The poem states that: 'after raucous battle-cry came retreat,' and goes on to say: 'At Llongborth was not Geraint slain, and brave men from the land of Dumnonia (*Diwnaint*); even though they were killed, they did their share of killing.'

The Battle of Hehil in 722, a victory for the Cornish, may have been close to the site of Llongborth, gaining back territory lost to West Saxon control in 710, but fought by Gerent's successor. The frustration is that we have no idea who that man was. After Gerent II, the record of Dumnonian and Cornish kings is blank until the late 9th century. During this period of a century and a half, Dumnonia as a named entity also vanishes from the record, leaving only the land referred to in *Celtic* as *Cerniu*, and in Latin as *Cornubia*: today's *Kernow*. The datings returned from excavation firmly suggest that Gerent II was the last of the Dumnonian kings to utilise Tintagel. There is now a long gap in the records, and next historically confirmed king that we hear of is:

DONYARTH: A sustained period of peace between the West Saxons and the Celts of the far southwest appears to have reigned from the 760s until 815, when Ecgberht of Wessex resumed hostilities between the latter date and a year before his own death in 839. On the available evidence, Ecgberht seems to have been the first to break into Dumnonian territory, seizing east and north Devon in the process, while Cornwall, Dartmoor and the South Hams remained under Cornish control and rule. After that, peace and stability reigned again between the two kingdoms, and the Cornish king during at least part of that period was Donyarth.

The peace seems to have been firm enough for Donyarth to allow the teenage prince Alfred, heir to the throne of Wessex, to mount a hunting expedition on Cornish soil (which still extended as far east as the Exe estuary). According to Alfred's own chronicler, the Welsh bishop Asser, this took place between 863 and 868 CE, Alfred not gaining the throne of Wessex until 871, at the age of 22.

A period of peace sadly means a lack of record, so little else is known of King Donyarth until 875 when the Welsh Easter Annals, or *Annales Cambriae*, recorded that: '*Dungarth rex Cerniu, id est Cornubiae, mersus est*' (Donyarth, king of Cornwall, that is, of the Cornish people, is drowned').

At Redgate in the parish of St Cleer, stands an ornate Celtic cross base, bearing carved knotwork, and part of the shaft of another, unrelated and decorated cross, which was set up beside it in 1849. The cross-base bears a clear inscription, with lettering dated to the second half of the 9th century, which reads: '*Doniert rogavit pro anima*' (Donyarth asked [for this memorial] for [the sake of] his soul). How King Donyarth met his tragic death is not known. However, the proximity of the memorial to the series of rapids on the River Fowey known as Golitha Falls has led to a credible theory that he may have fallen victim to a hunting accident in a swollen, fast-flowing river.

There is no reason to believe that the cross base, inscription and carved knotwork are anything but native Cornish; however, the University of London has in recent years quite shockingly circulated educational sheets to schools that describe it as 'Anglo-Saxon'. The name Donyarth is certainly Celtic, and may derive from British *dubno-garto-s*, 'sleek, dark one', while the script used for the inscription is one that is known to have originated in Ireland, and later adopted in Britain.

After the sad demise of Donyarth, there is again a gap in the records in which one, perhaps two, more kings of Cornwall might have reigned before we hear of the next one.

HUWAL: Arguments continue to rage over whether the record of this king refers to a Cornish king, or a Welsh one. *The Anglo-Saxon Chronicle* for the year 927 records that King Athelstan of Wessex: 'had power over all the kings that were in this island; first Huwal, king of the West Welsh

(*Westwala*), then Constantine, king of the Scots; Uwen, king of the people of Gwent; and Ealdred, son of Eadwulf from Bamburgh (*Bebbanbyrig*). With pledge and with oaths they fastened a peace in the place called Eamont Bridge (*Eamotum*) (Cumbria) on July 12th, and renounced all idol-worship, and from there turned away in peace'.

Roger of Wendover's somewhat embellished version of this, written c.1235, was that : 'He (Athelstan) next conquered in battle and defeated all the inferior kings of the island, to wit, Hunwal (*sic*), king of the Britons, Constantine, king of the Scots, Wulferth, king of the Wenti; he also expelled Alfred, son of Eadulf, from the castle of Bamburgh. On which they all, with the kings of the other provinces, seeing that they were not a match for his prowess, came together unto him and requested peace and, renouncing idolatry, they made a lasting league with him.'

The word in the Anglo-Saxon Chronicle that fixes Huwal as the Cornish king is *Westwala*, 'West Welsh'. This term appears several times in earlier entries, and is only ever applied to the Dumnonians or Cornish. Never is it used to describe the Welsh, who were referred to as *Northwalas*. Nonetheless, the opposite argument is that this referred to Hywel, known as Hywel Dda (Hywel the Good, c.880-950) king of Deheubarth, South Wales. However, Hywel had already signed a similar treaty at Tamworth with Athelstan's father, Edward of Wessex, in 918, and the further treaty with Athelstan at Hereford, immediately after the Eamont Bridge event and also signed by another Welsh king, Owain of Glywysing and Gwent, agreed the Wye as the western border of Athelstan's realm. He is most unlikely to have signed yet another treaty, so soon afterwards, at Eamont Bridge and, therefore the Eamont signatory must have been a king of similar name but of the *Westwalas*, and not of a kingdom among the *Northwalas*.

Legends that Huwal fought a battle against Athelstan at Boleigh, in West Penwith, and that the English king then sailed to conquer Scilly, are of late coinage and almost certainly false. There is no reliable record of Athelstan ever setting foot on Cornish soil, and the legend appears to have been concocted to lend credibility for the alleged Charter granted to St Buryan by Athelstan, and which is almost certainly a medieval forgery. Place-names mentioned in this purported charter show assibilated forms, a process that did not occur in the Cornish language until c.1200, nearly three centuries later. Also, the date of the alleged signing of this charter at Kingston-on-Thames, by Athelstan and witnesses is given as 943, three years after Athelstan's recorded death on October 27th, 940.

Was Huwal the last of the Cornish kings? William of Worcester, writing in the 15th century, and followed by several others, included an intriguing reference to one CADOC (also Condor or Candorus), who he states to have been the last of the Cornish royal line at the time of the Norman Conquest, and briefly appointed by William I to be the first Eorl (Earl) of Cornwall. Cadoc's descendants are said to have lived on in the areas of Pydar Hundred and in Bodmin. The Bodmin lawyer Thomas Flamank, one of the leaders of the Cornish uprising against Henry VII in 1497, firmly claimed direct descent from Cadoc, whose name translates as 'man of battle'. As Flamanks still flourish in Cornwall and among the Cornish diaspora, it is not wholly beyond the realms of possibility that the Cornish royal bloodline might not yet be extinguished.

Chapter 4

Commotion times

The Saxons are coming!

THERE IS a degree of uncertainty about when Germanic people first began to colonise Britain. Certainly many had been serving Roman legionaries and officers, but had most likely left during various military withdrawals from the island. Roman recorders and geographers found no place-names of Germanic origin in Britain, the majority being of native Celtic origin, apart from those coined by the Romans themselves in their Latin tongue.

There have been one or two recent attempts to establish that Germanic languages were spoken in eastern Britain before the Roman occupation, although it has to be said that these arguments are heavily flawed on account of the fact that the questioners are not themselves linguists, nor toponymists. Their hypothesis fails against a study of place-names and tribal names recorded by Roman geographers and commentators.

The standard work on this subject, which examines the opinions of established linguistic experts, is *The Place-Names of Roman Britain*, by A.L.F. Rivet and Colin Smith (1979). Examination of 83 identifiable place-names east of a line drawn from the Dorset-Hampshire boundary to the Humber shows that 68 of them are derived from Brythonic Celtic; 14 are Latin, with one of uncertain derivation. 25 tribal names occurred in that same area: all are Brythonic Celtic. None of these names show any Germanic influence, which would have been present, if not dominant, had that language been spoken in the area at that time.

The same applies to the personal names of Britons encountered by the Romans: Commios, Cunobelinos, Cartimandua, Caratacos, Prasutagos,

Boudica, and so on. Every one of those names is British Celtic. On the strength of such overwhelming evidence to the contrary, the question of Germanic languages being commonly spoken in eastern Britain prior to the mid 5th century CE can be safely rejected.

In the post-Roman era, most Celtic place-names in eastern Britain were replaced by new ones coined in the Germanic language spoken by new settlers from the mid 5th century onwards. Some Celtic names were retained but respelt to suit the orthography and structure of those Germanic languages that would eventually become English.

It is possible, or even probable, that some Germanic entrepreneurs had set themselves up on this side of the North Sea for trading purposes with their homelands, around the Roman 'Saxon Shore' forts set up around 300 CE from Norfolk to Hampshire. Many believe that these forts were trade centres, adding a precautionary and deterrent measure of homeland security by way of their impressive show of strength. Such entrepreneurs would certainly have gained extensive knowledge of the hinterland that they could pass on to their compatriots, and it was along that same stretch of coastline that the first Germanic colonists were to arrive.

Legend claims that the Celtic king Vortigern unwittingly began the process by inviting Jutish forces into Kent as mercenary aid, and it is generally agreed that major Germanic colonisation began at around that time: the mid 5th century CE; perhaps a generation after the final Roman withdrawal from Britain in 410 CE.

There were four groups of people who ventured across the North Sea into eastern Britain: Jutes from the southern part of the Danish peninsula; Angles and Saxons from the northern German regions of Angeln and Saxony; and Frisians from northwest Germany and the eastern Low Countries. For convenience rather than accuracy, these have been given the umbrella terms of Anglo-Saxon, then Saxon and, finally, English (after the Angles).

Recent studies find that initial influxes of Germanic peoples into east and south-eastern Britain were relatively small, probably not much greater than 200,000. Just how did these manage to become so dominant in an island populated by an estimated 2.5 million Celtic natives?

The most Romanised and populous area of Britain lay southeastward of a line drawn from Dorset to the Humber. By 400 CE, many of the native British in much of that area had themselves become culturally Roman. Their leaders often preferred to live in Roman-style villas and many even spoke Latin in preference to their own tongue. Their craftsmen manufactured goods that were in the Roman style and, unlike their contemporaries in less Romanised areas of Britain including Dumnonia, had adopted a system of currency.

After the Roman withdrawal from Britain, that same area of the island was that in which the Anglo-Saxon colonisation was concentrated and, over the following century, the effect in that area was enormous. The local languages, both Celtic British and Latin, ceased to be spoken. No records were kept for a long while. Place-names were, more often than not, replaced with ones in the Germanic Anglo-Saxon tongue, or remodelled in accordance with the conventions of that language. Christianity disappeared, agriculture radically altered in character, and the sophisticated products of pottery and metalware vanished into thin air. For the native Britons, this was both catastrophic and utterly chaotic, but not so for the Anglo-Saxons who were not accustomed to Roman sophistication, and were better suited to societies that worked on a smaller scale.

How exactly did this Germanic dominance take place? The recent genetic study showed that wholesale slaughter of the Britons in the south and east of the island simply did not occur; nor was there any appreciable or forced migration of native people from there into the western parts of Britain. Conflicts and isolated acts of slaughter certainly took place, but not to the extent suggested by the writings of Gildas c.530, and nowhere near enough to replace one population with another. However, the evidence does suggest that the native population halved in number, perhaps due to plague events getting into that area of Britain from the Continent, especially in the first half of the 6th century. The *Annales Cambriae* record two distinct and deadly bubonic plagues in Britain during 537 and 547. The second, known as the Justinian plague, had originated in Constantinople, and spread northwestward through Europe like wildfire, eventually getting into southeastern Britain via the trading links which by-passed the Anglo-Saxon homelands. It killed Maelgwn, king of Gwynedd, who had been lambasted by Gildas, and, if it did indeed kill half the native population of Britain, then such a weakening would have made Saxon colonisation a far easier task.

There is good evidence to show that this situation was exacerbated by several years of worsened weather and low crop yields due to dust-laden skies caused by major volcanic events in Indonesia.

The genetic evidence cannot be judged with any great accuracy, but in the areas that the Anglo-Saxons colonised, about half of the population remained of British stock. In the opinion of participating archaeologist Mark Robinson, it would only have taken 400 Anglo-Saxons arriving annually over a 75 year period to inject 25% of their DNA into the population, although the actual figure may be nearer to 40%. Meanwhile, in Dumnonia, the kingdoms of Wales and the northern regions of Britain, life simply carried on as before, and unaffected by what was happening further east or south.

Studies by Professor Mark Thomas, Professor Michael Stumpf and Dr Heinrich Harke in 2006 have come up with a new angle on what was happening in southern and eastern Britain at the time: that the Anglo-Saxon colonists were operating a social structure based upon apartheid.

This took two main forms. Firstly, a far greater value was placed upon the life of an Anglo-Saxon than on that of a native Briton: according to the Laws of Ine and of Ethelbert, from twice to five times more valuable. This sum was weregild, or blood money, and was payable to the family of the deceased to head off the likelihood of blood feuds. This had the effect of reducing the native Britons to second-class citizens in Anglo-Saxon occupied areas, and treating them accordingly.

The second form taken by this process of discrimination was an embargo placed upon interbreeding, with an emphasis on producing large families. In effect, and within those occupied areas, Anglo-Saxon families greatly outbred the native ones, to the extent that their own genetic, cultural and linguistic group became greatly more dominant and numerous within a mere handful of generations.

This system of apartheid seemed to be common among Germanic peoples. In Gaul, the Franks operated a similar policy, as did Euric, king of the Visigoths, in the lands that he held in northern Spain and Aquitaine.

According to Professor Mark Thomas: 'The native Britons were genetically and culturally absorbed by the Anglo-Saxons over a period as little as a few hundred years. An initially small invading Anglo-Saxon elite appears to have quickly established itself by having more children who survived to adulthood, thanks to their military power and economic advantage. We believe that they also prevented the native British genes from getting into the Anglo-Saxon population by restricting intermarriage in a system of apartheid that left the country culturally and genetically Germanised. This is exactly what we see today (in England) – a population of a sizable Germanic genetic origin, speaking a principally Germanic language.'

This conclusion relates solely to the bulk of what is today called England. It did not occur in Cornwall, Wales or Scotland, none of which were conquered or settled in anything greater than a very minor extent by Anglo-Saxons. The current and startlingly different genetic distinctions of these three areas have been highlighted by the extensive genetic survey of Britain that has been carried out recently by the University of Oxford under Sir Walter Bodmer.

Over time, Anglo-Saxon colonisation and dominance spread across much of what is now England, leading to new kingdoms and the Heptarchy of Anglo-Saxon realms. For Cornwall and Dumnonia, the threat of Anglo-Saxon advance towards them would come from the new kingdom of Wessex, allegedly founded by Cerdic in the early 6th century CE: a semi-legendary Anglo-Saxon leader with an oddly Celtic name, as had his son Cynric. However, this took a long time to occur.

Celtic Dumnonia was not the easiest place for the West Saxons to advance upon. Landward approach was restricted to a width of less than 20 miles, due to the vast expanses of open water, lagoons and treacherous marshes of the area now known as the Somerset Levels, and it took West Saxon ambition a very long time indeed to batter at Dumnonia's door.

Nor were these West Saxons the somewhat barbarous people who had originally forced themselves on Britain's North Sea and eastern Channel coasts. By the time they began to threaten Dumnonia's border they were no longer the people who had worshipped Woden and Thunor, but Christians who had embraced the beliefs and doctrines of Rome, and the improved level of civilisation and literacy that came with it.

The first indication of westward advance by Wessex was in 577 CE, and the Battle of *Deorham* (Dyrham, which lies to the east of Bristol). This major Anglo-Saxon victory, in which no less than three Celtic kings were killed, Conmail, Condidan and Farinmail, drove a wedge between the Celts of Wales and those of Dumnonia, restricting the two to maritime contact. This battle took place close to the Fosse Way, the major

Roman route linking *Aquae Sulis* (Bath) and *Corinium Dubonnorum* (Cirencester). Those two cities, along with *Glevum* (Gloucester), were taken by the West Saxons who were led by Ceawlin and his son Cuthwine. The *Deorham* victory was later to be consolidated by Cenwealh of Wessex when, in 652 at Bradford on Avon and in an apparent southward push, he achieved a breakthrough against the Britons which also breached the great defensive earthwork known as the Wansdyke.

The long established Roman routes were, without doubt, the key to West Saxon expansion, giving easy routes westward into unknown territory. The next West Saxon victories that we hear of appear to have consolidated their hold on the former Durotrigian territory approximating to modern Dorset.

Beandune, most likely Bindon above East Lulworth, and the first of these victories in 614 CE, was led by the West Saxon king Cynegils and his son Cwichelm, whose army is claimed to have slain 2,046 of the 'Welsh' (*walas*). Hosking's suggestion of a site near Axmouth in East Devon is much too far west to have been feasible at this time.

The next was *Peonnum* in 658 CE, under Cenwealh's command of the West Saxons. The two leading contenders for this battle site are Penselwood, on the Somerset-Wiltshire border near Zeals; and Penn, Yeovil. The latter would appear to be the more logical site for opening the way to the Dumnonian border, and lies on the route of the Fosse Way as it traces its path westward towards Exeter. Cenwealh is said by the *Anglo-Saxon Chronicle* to have pursued the 'Welsh' (*walas*) to the river Parrett (*Pedridan*) after the battle. *Pedridan* is a Celtic name, meaning 'four fords', and is also found in Cornwall in place-names such as Perdredda, Patrieda and Pathada. The fact Cenwealh could go no further than the Parrett, whose line formed part of the Dumnonian border, indicates that the borders of the Celtic kingdom had yet to be breached by West Saxon advance.

If *Posentesbyrig*, a further West Saxon victory led by Cenwealh in 661 CE, was involved with westward expansion of Wessex at all, then Poundbury, a fort just outside *Durnovaria* (Dorchester) would be by far the best candidate for effectively securing the whole of Durotrigian territory for the kingdom of Wessex. This site also lay on a Roman route leading west towards distant Exeter. Hosking and Stevenson have suggested Posbury near Crediton for the site of *Posentesbyrig* but, once again, this is much too far west for a campaign to absorb Dumnonia; never an easy task, and one that was bound to have taken a considerable number of years to achieve. In fact, no West Saxon king is known to have ventured as far west as Crediton prior to Ecgberht in the early 9th century.

However, *Posentesbyrig* is far more likely not to have been a southern battle site at all, but part of a conflict between Wessex and the Midlands Saxon kingdom of Mercia, which undoubtedly deflected West Saxon attention from their south western plans. The *Anglo-Saxon Chronicle* seems to link Wessex and Mercia in the battle, and adds that Wulfhere, King of Mercia and son of Penda, then pursued Cenwealh across country as far as Ashdown in Sussex. In this case, the Shropshire site of Pontesbury is by far the most likely identification, and entirely unconnected with West Saxon intentions regarding Dumnonia.

In 682 CE, King Centwine of Wessex 'pursued the Britons (*Bretwealas*) to the sea', according to the *Anglo-Saxon Chronicle* but, without reference to either location or the provenance of these Britons, this is far too vague a reference from which to form any conclusions or link it with an advance upon Dumnonia. However, a period of peace certainly reigned for several decades, allowing the Dumnonian king Gerent II to strike up a cordial friendship with the Saxon priest Aldhelm, Abbot of Malmesbury and later Bishop of Sherborne Abbey.

It is not known for certain when Bishop Aldhelm wrote his famous letter to *Gerontius Rex*, but it was most certainly between the years 680 when Aldhelm was Abbot of Malmesbury and 705 when he was promoted to Bishop at Sherborne, and most likely the latter given his more senior position. The contents of the letter show glimpses of this friendly relationship as the Saxon bishop addresses Gerent with respect throughout, and yet feels comfortable enough with the Dumnonian king to offer sharp criticism of the Celtic bishops within Gerent's realm for their often hostile attitude towards the Roman Church which the West Saxons themselves had only begun to adopt a century earlier, with the arrival of St Augustine in Kent (597 CE). The Celtic Church was, of course, considerably older.

The aim of Aldhelm's letter was to persuade the conversion of the Celtic Church in Dumnonia to the Roman Catholicism practised by the

West Saxons. He was not successful, presumably because the Cornish priesthood considered themselves subjects of a rather higher king than their mortal one. Aldhelm also wrote that he had travelled within Dumnonia (*Domnonia*) and Cornwall (*Cornubia*) and been given the safe passage he had also enjoyed in Dyfed and Ireland, and the likelihood that he and Gerent actually met in person is strong.

As previously mentioned, it is likely that Gerent granted lands at Maker (*Macuir*) to Sherborne Abbey around 705 CE, as a gift of friend-ship to Aldhelm, and mentions of another area in the same region a century later hint that he may have added to that gift. Little did Gerent suspect where that would lead.

What now seems most likely is that Aldhelm, a highly educated churchman greatly respected by Saxon and Celt alike, played a highly influential role in keeping King Ine of Wessex off the backs of Gerent and Dumnonia for several years. Bishop Aldhelm died in 709. Within a year, and freed from the Bishop's restraints, Ine launched a major attack upon Gerent in an attempt to break into Dumnonia.

The *Anglo-Saxon Chronicle* does not mention where this took place, merely stating that: 'Ine and Nun his kinsman fought against Gerent (*Gerente*), king of the British (*Wala, Weala*)'. Roger of Wendover, writing in the 13th century, claimed that: 'Ine, king of the West Saxons, fought against Gerent, king of the Welsh (*Wallensium*) and, in the beginning of the battle, the duke Higebald (a Saxon) was slain; but at last the Welsh king (*rex Wallensis*) retreated, leaving his arms and spoils to the Angliae'.

Gerent might well have been of advanced years at this battle, and it is likely that age might have contributed to his death in battle. The Welsh poem, 'Lament for Geraint', contained in *The Black Book of Carmarthen* laments the king's death in a battle fought by Dumnonians. The poem does not mention any Celtic victory but rather hints at defeat, with the line: 'and after raucous battle-cry came retreat' echoing part of Roger of Wendover's account.

This battle was at a place named in the poem as *Llongborth*, a Welsh name translating as 'ship haven'. 'At Llongborth was not Geraint slain and brave men from the land of Dumnonia (*Diwnaint*): even though they were killed, they did their share of killing.'

The outstanding location for this event is the Somerset town of Langport. When looking at modern maps, this might raise an eyebrow,

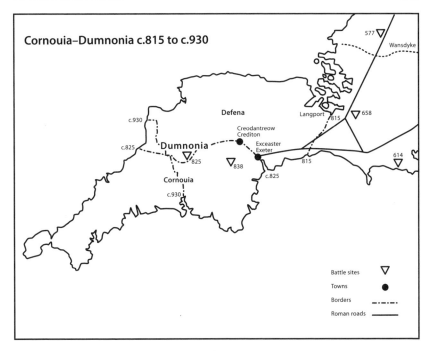

Cornouia-Dumnonia under military pressure from Wessex.

as the town is 15 miles inland from the Bristol Channel and 20 miles from the south coast. However, in 710, it lay near the southern end of a vast inlet of water and marsh now known as the Somerset Levels. It is also on the River Parrett, the Dumnonian border itself, which remains tidal as far as Langport. It may easily have been a 'ship haven'. Langport is also located at a handy crossing point where opposing spurs of higher land form a pinch-point between the lagoons and marshes to the north, and further treacherous marshland extending to the south.

The sole sticking point of this argument is the name of the place. Is it the Old English 'long market place' (*Longport*, 10th century), or is it an Anglicisation of the Celtic *Llongborth*? If the latter, which is just as likely as the former, then Langport is indeed a prime candidate for Gerent's final, fatal battle.

We do not know the name of Gerent's successor to the throne of Dumnonia, but it is clear that he fought back to regain the border, and maybe to wrest back control of the very same border crossing. The *Anglo-Saxon Chronicle* is loathe to mention any Saxon defeat until finally coming clean in the 9th century when mentioning losses to to the Danish Vikings, so do not mention the Battle of Hehil in 722. The *Annales Cambriae* do so, and state that it was 'among the Cornish (*apud Cornuenses*)' and confirming that the British were the victors.

Hehil is unlocated but, again, must be close to the Parrett-Axe border of Dumnonia and Wessex. Suggested locations far to the west of there are wholly unrealistic, as the West Saxons had yet to breach Dumnonia's borders. If, as is generally believed, this is an early representation of the Cornish word *heyl*, then we are looking for an estuary with extensive tidal flats, which *heyl* alludes to, in contrast to the deep-water estuaries and rias of the south coast, where the Cornish term used is *logh*. Would this also have been Langport? The description would fit. Were *Llongborth* and *Hehil* one and the same place, and the location of two successive battles, the second to regain native control of the border crossing that had been lost to the West Saxons a few years earlier?

After *Hehil*, the record hints at sporadic events of West Saxon conflict but not necessarily against the Dumnonians. In 743, and again in 753, Cuthred, king of Wessex, 'fought against the British', but against which British faction and where, are left unspecified. Cuthred's successor, Cynewulf, also 'often fought against the British in great fights'; a record that is, once more, far too vague to be helpful. However, around the year 766, we find Cynewulf granting land in Somerset to Wells church, his stated reason for the grant being: 'for love of God, for atonement of my sins and also ... for certain harassment of our enemies, the race of the Cornish (*Cornubiorum gentis*).' Nonetheless, there is no indication that Cynewulf or any of his predecessors made any inroad westward across the Dumnonian border. The Anglo-Saxon Chronicle is silent on this, when any breakthrough would surely have been announced.

After this, the record falls silent, and it would seem that Dumnonia remained free from further West Saxon aggression for half a century, its original border and territory remaining more or less intact. That would radically change after Ecgberht came to the throne of Wessex at the beginning of the 9th century.

There is much uncertainty about the status of kings and society in general in Dumnonia after the death of Gerent II, after whose reign there is a large gap in surviving records which record no kings until Donyarth in the later 9th century, as king of a much reduced region. Cessation of direct trade with the Byzantine Empire, the abandonment of Tintagel, and the demise of Gerent II all seem to have coincided, belatedly plunging Dumnonia and Cornwall into the leanness of a Dark Age. The centre of Atlantic seaway trading shifted south to Vigo in Galicia, where a British colony persisted (a bishopric named Bretana was still recorded there in 830). It may be that this loss of status reflected on the region's kings who became regarded in a far lesser light and seriously weakening their influence. Certainly the quality of local produce equally suffered, and the last gasp of Dumnonia was an uncanny echo of the degeneration that had been seen in the Late Bronze Age. Even so, it would not be until Ecgberht of Wessex that Saxon eyes would see the weakened Dumnonia as ripe for the picking.

The ravages of Ecgberht

HALF a century of non-aggression from Wessex almost certainly led to a false sense of security and a degree of laxity in a Dumnonia that had lost its way. It is also likely that Dumnonia did not possess a standing army. Instead, its defence depended upon the summoning of warhosts from each of its *keverangow* (later called 'Hundreds'); a process that necessarily took time to mobilise.

When Ecgberht succeeded to the throne of Wessex in 802 CE, thoughts of succeeding in Dumnonia where his predecessors had failed was surely uppermost in his mind. Intelligence of what was happening – or not happening – in that Celtic kingdom was by then readily available to him by way of the Saxon clergy being increasingly appointed to Dumnonian churches by Canterbury. Armed with a flow of such information from the far southwest, he could afford to bide his time and wait for the right moment to strike. The record shows that, when it came to military strategy, Ecgberht of Wessex was no slouch.

That long period of peace between Cornwall/Dumnonia and Wessex came to a shuddering halt with the sudden events of 815. It must have come out of the blue for the Dumnonians, who were given no prior warning of his intentions to push the territory of Wessex much further west than it had ever been.

Ecgberht was a committed expansionist, not only striving to push the boundaries of Wessex westward into Dumnonian territory, but also northward into Mercia. Against Mercia, he certainly gained a notable success but, against Dumnonia, this was only partial. However, aided by William of Malmesbury's 12th century query as to whether Ecgberht's campaign was sufficient to subjugate and conquer Cornwall, some historians have been quick to seize upon the scanty surviving evidence to claim that it was: a mighty leap of faith at best, for closer examination tells a very different story.

The *Anglo-Saxon Chronicle* tells us that, in 815, 'King Ecgberht ravaged from east to west against the West British (*Westwalas*)', but what did this actually mean?

It is often forgotten that the eastern border of the Cornish and Dumnonian kingdom (otherwise known as the West British and Westwalas) was not then at the Tamar as now, but considerably further to the east. All indications are that, when Ecgberht acceded to the throne of Wessex, the border stubbornly remained in its ancient place: the line of the Axe and Parrett rivers, or the narrow pinch-point between the marshes south of the Somerset Levels and the south coast of Devon near Seaton. His early intention of adding as much of Dumnonia as he could to his own kingdom would require well planned but lightning strategy: to break in along the convenient routeways, effectively seizing the eastern half of Devon as far as the Exe and, if possible, to make a show of strength even further to the west.

This is what he seems to have achieved or, at least in part. In one bold move, made without warning, Ecgberht could easily have taken a poorly defended and ill-prepared eastern Devon and its principal routeways in short order. Isolated Dumnonians to the north of those routes, in the areas on and around Exmoor and the Quantocks most probably had no idea that, in a matter of days, they had become subjects of Wessex, or that the border had now been effectively pushed westward to the line of the Taw and Exe rivers.

It was also surely the moment when the name Dumnonia ceased to exist. Henceforth, records would only show that of Cornwall (as *Cerniu* or *Cornubia*). By now, what remained of the Celtic kingdom would have been alerted, with a military force assembled in haste and probably making for the old Roman capital at Exeter.

Subsequent history suggests that Ecgberht pushed even further westward but, if he did, it could only have been an in-and-out raid designed to be a statement of intent, and a demonstration to the Cornish of his military power.

Progression westward from the Taw-Exe line would prove difficult for any West Saxon force. Firstly, they would face the forbidding and, to them, unexplored, massif of Dartmoor. This was surely not to be considered. The West Saxons would never before have seen such a forbidding landscape, with bare, soaring slopes rising abruptly to weirdly-shaped towers of granite on the peaks, often sheathed in swirling mists that spoke of unimaginable threat to minds that were steeped in superstition. Many would have heard widespread tales of Wild Hunts, Wish Hounds and worse, and most would have regarded it as a secret realm of ancient and vengeful gods and supernatural forces unknown to them. Even if Ecgberht himself had been bold enough to risk a foray onto Dartmoor, it is doubtful that many in his army would have had the courage to follow.

To take a southward route through the South Hams was also inadvisable. Intelligence would have informed Ecgberht of the deep estuaries of the Teign, Dart, and Yeolm, with more at Salcombe, Bigbury and Holbeton. Each had steep-sided valleys leading back to the abrupt southern rise of Dartmoor, and would have rang alarm bells in the reasoned mind of any experienced campaigner and strategist. To be caught between any of those estuaries would be potentially disastrous if set upon by Cornish forces, with retreat made unfeasibly difficult. Moreover, he would also have known from Saxon mariners that an even larger obstacle lay beyond them all: the expanse of Plymouth Sound and the great width of the lower Tamar. Clearly, the southern route was not an option to be considered, especially if Cornish forces were to move into Exeter and, therefore, behind them.

This left the West Saxon king with a single option that was further facilitated by the existence of an ancient route westward from Exeter that the Romans had used and listed in their itineraries. This crossed the Culm Measures of northern Devon, keeping to the north of the dreaded wilderness of Dartmoor, and crossing a gentle undulating landscape far more suited to what he might have had in mind: a lightning raid into Cornish territory.

If he did so, it is highly unlikely that he went any further than the long stretch of coast running due north-south from Widemouth Bay to Hartland, despite some unfounded claims to the contrary. The old, easily followed route would have taken him via North Tawton to the Tamar, crossing it near Bridgerule and emerging at the coast near Bude. This would certainly make sense of the reference to Ecgberht ravaging 'from east to west'. It is unthinkable that Ecgberht could then have led his troops through another 80 miles of totally unknown enemy territory, and it is highly unlikely that he ever considered it. Again, the unknown terrain would have presented barriers, with deep river valleys and the granite massif of Bodmin Moor being every bit as formidable and forbidding as Dartmoor.

F.E. Halliday, in 1959, went so far as to write that, after or during this raid, Ecgberht compelled the Cornish kings to pay him homage. This is not fact, but entirely a figment of Halliday's own imagination. What Egcberht might have achieved was hinted at by the 13th century chronicler Roger of Wendover, who wrote of this incident that: 'Egbert, king of the West Saxons attacked that region called Cornubia and added it to his kingdom, after many had been slain on either side.' This should not be taken literally, especially as the Tamar was not then the border, but probably meant that his raid placed what is now north Devon, and perhaps Cornwall north of the Ottery, under Ecgberht's control. That the Cornish still resisted to the west of Crediton was to be suggested just ten years later, but only the two records survive of Ecgberht's opening gambit.

The Battle of Gafulforda

THE RECORD is silent for a further ten years before the *Anglo-Saxon Chronicle* records another southwestern conflict: 'The Weala (Cornish) fought the Defena (Devonians) at Gafulforda'. The only known record of this incident, it is a stark statement giving us little in the way of fact.

Nonetheless, it has given rise to further claims that are totally unjustified given the paucity of evidence. Malcolm Todd, in 1987, turned this single record into: 'A rebellion by the Cornish in 825 failed when they were defeated by Ecgberht at Gafulford', a wild assumption which is quite unjustifiable.

The record says nothing of 'rebellion' or Ecgberht, and even fails to give the result of the battle. Furthermore, under strict rules of definition, one kingdom can scarcely 'rebel' against another. The Collins Gem *Kings and Queens of Britain* even states that Ecgberht was at *Gafulforda* in person, but again the record says no such thing. The *Anglo-Saxon Chronicle* does record his presence that same year in a battle against Beornwulf, king of Mercia at *Ellandun* (Wroughton, Wiltshire), but not at *Gafulforda*. Williams, Smith and Kirby, in *A Biographical Dictionary of Dark Age Britain* (1991) stray even further into fantasy when, without a shred of evidence, they claim that: 'In the south west, he (Ecgberht) accomplished the final conquest of the Cornish Britons, whose kingdom was permanently incorporated into Wessex.' On such a wild claim that seems to be based on little more than wishful thinking, the *Anglo-Saxon Chronicle* is very silent indeed when it would surely have shouted any such significant conquest from the rooftops and, of course, Cornish kings were continuing to rule at dates long after Ecgberht's demise.

However, Ecgberht does seem to have been in the region of the new Taw-Exe Cornish border in 825. A charter granting 5 hides of land at Martyr Worthy, Hampshire, to the Minster of SS Peter and Paul, Winchester, was signed by him at a place called *Creodantreow* (presumably somewhere near Crediton) in August of that year. This states that: 'the beginning of this document is written among the 'hostes' when Ecgberht, king of the Gewissei, moved against the Britons.' (Sawyer: *Anglo-Saxon Charters* S 273). *Hostes* is a frustratingly ambiguous word as it can mean both 'army' and 'enemy'. If he was writing 'among the enemy', then he was in disputed border territory on that Taw-Exe line, but this is a long way from Gafulforda, if the favoured identification of that site as Galford, near Lydford in modern Devon, is correct. On the other hand, Galford is close to territory where Ecgberht, or his army, were likely to have been ten years earlier. If Ecgberht's 'move against the Britons' was at Galford, then the fact that he was back on the border at Crediton suggests that it did not go well for him.

It is impossible to make much of the *Gafulforda* entry, but the battle may have been a reaction by the Cornish against a second attempt by Ecgberht to penetrate the wide corridor of undemanding terrain to the north of Dartmoor, perhaps to locate a lower fordable crossing of the Tamar. Such an area would have been worth securing, and the likelihood is strong that Ecgberht eventually did so, perhaps even as far as the Ottery on the western side of the Tamar. This would certainly explain his grandson Alfred (r. 871-899) being able to establish his westernmost *burh* at Lydford, not far from Galford, and the opening-up of North Devon and the area north of the Ottery for later Saxon settlement, even though no Saxon presence in the latter can be shown to pre-date the 10th century.

It is therefore both reasonable and logical to accept that Ecgberht did succeed in assuming control of North Devon and, perhaps the northern-most corner of Cornwall (this only remaining under West Saxon control for a single century) by about 830, whilst Dartmoor and the South Hams remained as Cornish territory until the coming of Athelstan, a century later. Ecgberht made no further inroads westward, and peace ensued for at least a while until the Cornish found an opportunity to hit back.

The Battle of Hengestesdun

EVEN THOUGH the *Anglo-Saxon Chronicle* deals with the event in two sentences, its record for 838 CE remains one of the most intriguing episodes in early Cornish history:

> 'There came a great army of ships to the Westwalas (Cornish) where they were joined by the people who commenced war against Ecgberht, the West Saxon king. When he heard this, he went with his army against them and fought with them at Hengestesdun, where he put to flight both the Walas and the Danes'.

Roger of Wendover, writing at around 1235, was to be a little more verbose: 'In the year of Our Lord 835 (for 838) the Wallenses (Welsh) and the Danis (Danes) with united forces invaded the kingdom of Egbert with fire and sword, seeking to demolish his castles and towns; on hearing of which, King Egbert went to meet the enemy with a numerous army and, after making an enormous slaughter of his enemies, he at length put the Welsh and Danes to rout with much loss and freed his country from the hostile irruption.'

In anyone's language, this is a fascinating event of history. Why an alliance of such diverse and distant cultures as the Cornish and the Danes? How did it ever come about? How did they communicate? That the Danes had, by then, been eyeing Britain for more than 45 years is well known and it could be that, among their number, or among the Cornish, were some who had become bilingual through previous trading contact.

An attractive possibility emerges from the few facts that are actually available: were the Cornish offering their own harbours as safe havens from which the Vikings could launch raids and attacks against the ports of their common West Saxon enemies? Just two years previously, Ecgberht is said to have fought against 25 ship companies at *Carrum* (Carhampton, Somerset) and, for the first time in its pages, the *Anglo-*

Saxon Chronicle makes the rare admission that the West Saxons were the losers.

Being on the Somerset coast, it might be too much to expect a Viking fleet of 25 ships to have sailed there all the way from Denmark, down the Channel, around Land's End and up to Somerset, and still have its warriors fresh enough to take on a determined West Saxon force, let alone be victorious. A closer base, and shorter sail, is far more likely. This could well have been in Ireland or south Wales, but a Cornish one is also perfectly feasible. In the case of Carhampton, a north coast base, such as Padstow and the Camel estuary, would have been convenient, and from where the ships could hug the coast and find suitable places of shelter en route if weather conditions turned sour. Such a base would also be convenient for intelligence filtering down from further east. Certainly the Danes (albeit 150 years later) well knew how to find Padstow and its Canterbury-controlled priory.

In 838, and for a planned advance on Ecgberht, a south coast port is the more likely, and the outstanding candidate is Plymouth Sound, then still deep within Cornish territory. The West Saxon king himself would still have been unlikely to have based himself any further west than Crediton or Exeter, and intelligence of the Danish arrival, and of their alarming alliance with the Cornish, would have taken time to reach him, perhaps by sea. It is clear that the Cornu-Danish force was already well on the march before he could have a chance to react, and this raises a new question: Where was *Hengestesdun*?

Until quite recently, it has always been assumed that the site of the battle was Hingston Down, the eastern spur of Kit Hill, between Callington and Gunnislake, the place-name alone being accepted without question as sole evidence for the identification. Is this slim evidence sufficient, and how feasible a location is it?

The Cornish Hingston Down, as a location for this battle, presents several serious problems that render it untenable. Firstly, it lies just 2 miles west of the Tamar valley at Gunnislake, at which point the river is wide, deep and flows strongly through a deep, wooded and almost ravine-like valley where a concealed Cornish army could have lain in wait; scarcely a wise place for a 9th century Saxon army to cross. It is conceivable that Ecgberht might have looked to cross much further upstream, then to turn south, but would he really have considered such a

Hingston Down, Moretonhampstead: The likeliest location of the battle in 838 CE between a Cornu-Danish alliance and Ecgberht of Wessex.

move, deep into unexplored enemy territory, with a river between himself and safety which was deepening, widening and flowing into a valley with precipitous sides? To take any such route would have been to invite disaster, with an ever-increasing risk of being cut off and advancing further into the deepest possible danger. It is impossible to believe that such an experienced campaigner and wily tactician as Ecgberht would ever have entertained such a foolhardy undertaking.

When the wording of the two existing accounts is considered, the likelihood of the Cornish site as the battle location becomes even more unlikely. This conclusion is compounded by the fact that, in the time that intelligence of the Cornu-Danish alliance and intent took to travel at least 45 miles to reach Ecgberht (on receipt of which he then gathers his army and marches a minimum of another 45 miles westward), the Cornish and the Danes have marched only a few miles inland and in a direction that takes them nowhere near Ecgberht's territory. It simply does not stack up. So, if the Cornish Hingston Down was not the battle site, where was it? Was there another Hingston Down within 9th century

Cornish territory, and much closer to Saxon-held land at that time?

The answer to this is yes, and when identified, its location fits perfectly. It has to be considered that the Cornu-Danish army would be looking to inflict considerable damage on West Saxon gains, and to select a route that would be unexplored by the West Saxons. A goal of retaking Exeter, Crediton or both would have grievously damaged Ecgberht, and this appears to be what Roger of Wendover was indicating. We need to be looking for a site that is on course for those destinations, and ideally within easy reach of them.

A further clue to this location is the place-name given in the Anglo-Saxon Chronicle. *Hengestesdun* is a Saxon name, 'stallion's hill' (or perhaps after a man named Hengest), and it is extremely unlikely that a Saxon name would have been given, in 838, to a site deep within Celtic territory as yet unexplored by the West Saxons, and on the far side of the forbidding heights of Dartmoor. Such a name could, however, have been given to a place that could readily be seen from Saxon-held land, and such a place exists.

This is Hingston Down, Moretonhampstead, on the eastern fringes of the Dartmoor massif, and within 10 miles of both Exeter and Crediton. It also lies at the northeastern end of a very ancient trackway route from Plymouth Sound, and across the wilds of the high moor, where the West Saxons still feared to venture; but a perfect and familiar route for the Cornish to guide their allies along, and to take. Doubtless, the Danes would also have regarded the weirdness of Dartmoor with trepidation, but have been encouraged by relaxed Cornish indifference to a familiar landscape.

The ancient route is still largely preserved today, being followed for the most part by the B3212 Yelverton to Moretonhampstead road. This Hingston Down has a similar place-name history as the site to the west of the Tamar. Both were cited as *Hengesdon* in 1333. Lying to the east of Moretonhampstead, this site overlooks the deep, wooded valley of the Teign.

This *Hengestesdun* is not a good place for a battle, but it is a wonderful choice of site for a well-planned ambush that Ecgberht would have had ample time to plan. Had he placed his forces in the dense woods of the Teign valley, or those of the tributary valley that wraps around the hill's northern side, an opposing force, oblivious to their concealed presence and descending the slopes, would not have stood an earthly chance once the trap was sprung. Moreover, the northern valley would have provided a concealed route for a detachment of Ecgberht's forces to move in behind the Cornu-Danes, cutting off all hope of retreat. Had it gone wrong for him, then Ecgberht was only 10 miles from safety in his own territory. It would, indeed, have been a slaughter, and probably only with light casualties to the West Saxons.

Although still unproven, this site, and its approaches from both directions, provides the perfect scenario for the Battle of *Hengestesdun*, and with none of the significant weaknesses that reject the western site near Callington.

It is clear from that facts we have at hand, and from the probable location of this last battle site, that Ecgberht achieved nothing that could remotely justify claims that he then 'subjugated' or 'conquered' Cornwall, except maybe to consolidate his hold on north Devon and the very northern corner of Cornwall, and open them up for later Saxon colonisation, if he had not already done so.

Had he conquered Cornwall in reality, and added it to his expanding realm of Wessex, the *Anglo-Saxon Chronicle* would not only have mentioned it, but blazed it up in lights. After all, Cornwall was the only place left in southern Britain that was still not under Saxon rule. However, this fails to prevent some from making further unjustifiable claims. Malcolm Todd again: 'This victory (Hengestesdun) marked the end of an independent British kingdom in the far west,' he wrote, adding that subsequent Cornish kings: 'can only have been dependents of Wessex, reigning as vassals in a conquered land'. Yet no early source makes any such claim and, indeed, why would it be necessary for a Cornish king, if already reduced to a vassal status, to sign a treaty with Athelstan in the following century?

Less than 40 years later, in 875, the *Annales Cambriae* recorded the death by drowning of Donyarth, described as '*rex Cerniu*' (king of Cornwall). Would Ecgberht, after a supposed conquest, have allowed native kings to continue, even if nothing more than 'vassal'figureheads? He did not do so in Mercia, for the short time that he held it, and it is highly unlikely that he would have behaved any differently in the case of Cornwall.

At *Hengestesdun*, Ecgberht merely faced down and defeated an alarming threat to his own recent additions to his own realm. He was given no chance to follow up on that victory, as there were far more pressing matters on his mind. Viking raids and attacks on Wessex were on the increase, and he was obliged to turn back towards the east and deal with those. After all, there was little point in attempting to add Cornwall to his own kingdom if his realm was only to fall to the Danes. Within a year of *Hengestesdun*, Ecgberht was dead, with Cornwall remaining a free and unconquered kingdom, with the probable exception of the corner to the north of the river Ottery, but still retaining Dartmoor and the South Hams within its own territory.

A period of peace

THE BATTLE of *Hengestesdun* was the last conflict that Cornwall had with Wessex until Athelstan 88 years later. Ecgberht's successor, his only son Aethelwulf, never came near the Cornish border. In the mid 860s, Aethelwulf's teenage son, Alfred (later to become Alfred the Great) was even permitted to enter Cornish territory on a hunting trip.

The young Alfred suffered from a debilitating condition that some believe to have been Crohn's disease, and had allegedly sought healing in Ireland. The account of his hunting trip on Cornish soil, provided by his biographer and friend, the Welsh bishop Asser, states that he visited a church dedicated to an otherwise unknown Saint Gueriir, to pray for healing. This has often been taken to have been the church of St Neot, purely on the strength of Asser's statement that Alfred visited a church: 'in which Sanctus Gueriir lies in peace (and now Sanctus Niot lies there as well)'. However, others believe this church to have been somewhere in the South Hams, which had remained Cornish territory at this time.

For this to take place, Aethelwulf must have negotiated peace with the Cornish kingdom, although the surviving record does not say so. Wessex was under constant attack from Viking forces and the last thing Aethelwulf needed was a repeat of the Hengestesdun affair, and assaults upon his western border. The same applied to his short-reigning successors Aethelbald (r.858-60), Aethelbert (r. 860-65) and Aethelred (r. 865-71).

When Alfred succeeded to the throne of Wessex in 871, the Viking threat was as great as ever, and the peace with Cornwall remained in place. The Cornish king at the time of Alfred's succession was Donyarth who was to die from drowning just 4 years later. It is not known if the two ever met.

In the meantime, the Church was recognising no borders, and had included Cornwall in the Diocese of Exeter. Bishop Asser, a Welshman, wrote that, around 884, King Alfred: 'gave me Exeter, with all the territory which belonged to it in Saxonia and Cornubia'. This was probably a shrewd move on Alfred's part, to appoint a Celtic bishop to a diocese that included the Celtic kingdom, and which would keep the Cornish happy.

In 891, according to the *Anglo-Saxon Chronicle*, three Irishmen, adrift in a boat without oars, came ashore: 'among the Cornish (*Cornwalum*) and then went immediately to King Alfred.' It is not known where this landfall occurred, but it may well have been in the Bude-Stratton area of North Cornwall, where Alfred is known to have held lands. This entry is also remarkable for being the first time that the name of Cornwall becomes linguistically hybridised with elements of its Cornish and Saxon renditions.

During the brief reign of Alfred's brother Aethelred, c.868, a hoard of valuable objects was carefully hidden at a spot a mile or so south of St Austell. The Trewhiddle Hoard was discovered 17 feet below ground by tinstreamers in 1774. 114 Anglo-Saxon coins, a silver chalice, and other gold and silver objects were found, including a 4-tailed scourge made from tiny silver chainwork and strands of silver wire. The circumstances of this hoard remain a mystery. Some have thought it a panic conceal-ment to keep it out of the hands of the Vikings, but there was no hostile Viking activity in Cornwall at this time. On the other hand, the chalice and particularly the scourge attest that these had been church property.

It bears all the hallmarks of having been the proceeds of a robbery from a Canterbury-controlled and English-dominated church, perhaps carried out by Cornishmen disgruntled by the increasing amount of West Saxon clerical presence and influence in their ancient Celtic land. Two of the items in the hoard are the sole surviving examples of their kind anywhere in pre-Norman Christian Europe. Perhaps their rarity became realised by the robbers; that the goods were far too hot to handle, let alone sell, and so they buried them. If they could not benefit from them, nor would the Church do so.

Much of Alfred's reign was spent in conflict with the Danes, and he set up a network throughout the Wessex region of fortified settlements, known as *burhs*, as a means of defence against their frequent incursions. In the old region of Dumnonia, these were established at Watchet, Langport, Bridport, Exeter and Lydford, the last being within that area of Devon, to the north of the Dartmoor massif, that Ecgberht had taken during the 820s. No Saxon burh was ever established to the west of the Tamar, beyond Alfred's realm.

Alfred of Wessex died in 899. From a Cornish perspective, his Will is of great interest in specifying what land the king of Wessex actually held in a peninsula that, according to some opinions, had been conquered by Ecgberht and absorbed into Wessex.

'To Edward, my elder son, the land at Straetneat in Triconscire (and other lands outside Cornwall) ... to my youngest son the land ... and at Liwtune and the lands that hereto belong; which are all that I in the Wealcynne have, except in Triconscire.'

Straetneat is Stratton, close to Bude, and the Old Cornish name, *Stradneth* ('valley of the river Neet') is respelt here in accordance with Saxon orthography. Stratton lay in the northern part of Trigg, formerly *Trigordh*, '(region of) three war hosts'; one of six ancient divisions of Cornwall known as *keverangow* (of which more later) to which Alfred intriguingly attached the Saxon word *scire*, 'shire'. *Liwtune* is generally accepted as being Lifton, Devon, close to the Tamar and east of the Cornish town of Launceston, while the word *Wealcynne* translates as 'British-kind', i.e. the Celtic people of Cornwall.

So, in the whole of Cornish territory, which still included Dartmoor and the South Hams, all that Alfred possessed was a small part of the area north of the Ottery, today dominated by English language place-names; and another parcel near Lifton, on the east side of the Tamar, and within the same area that his grandfather had almost certainly seized 70 years or so earlier. Had Cornwall been conquered and absorbed in its entirety, as some are overly keen to claim, one would expect the king of Wessex to have possessed a great deal more than that. On the strength of the evidence that is available, the only part of Cornwall within its present boundaries that ever became annexed to Wessex was that corner to the north of the river Ottery. Its inclusion in Wessex would only last for a century, as Cornwall was to have it returned only three decades or so after Alfred's death.

Influence by stealth

As ALFRED of Wessex's Will had stated, all that he owned that lay west of the River Tamar was land at Stratton. This, of course, lay within that area north of the River Ottery that Ecgberht of Wessex had probably gained earlier that century, yet at some time between 815 and 839, King Ecgberht of Wessex is said to have given several Cornish estates to Sherborne Abbey, firstly at *Kelk*, *Ros* and *Macor*, then *Polltun*, *Caellwic* and *Landwithan*. How did he come to acquire land that, at first glance, he should not have had?

The first three are all alongside the Tamar: Kilkhampton in the far north of Cornwall is the first-named and within the area that Ecgberht had seized. The other two are on the Rame peninsula. *Macor* is the village of Maker, while the name *Ros* is preserved in the place-name Eglarooze (*eglos*, 'church' + regional name *Ros*, 'promontory'). These look suspiciously like the lands that the Dumnonian King Gerent II had gifted to Bishop Aldhelm at Sherborne Abbey at around 705 CE. The Church had then quietly passed them onto King Ine of Wessex and, presumably, they had remained in the hands of the Kings of Wessex right up to the time of Ecgberht's succession.

The second list consists of *Polltun*, Pawton, near Wadebridge and *Landwithan*, Lawhitton near Launceston. *Caellwic* remains unidentified but is thought to be an estate close to Pawton, perhaps Kelly, near Wadebridge, or Callywith, to the northeast of Bodmin. As it is clear that Ecgberht of Wessex had not secured any conquest of Cornwall, or even ventured greatly to the west of the Tamar, then how could he be granting lands that did not appear to be his to give? The clue lies with the transfer of the lands at *Ros* and *Macor*.

This question has vexed historians for decades, and prompted others to make claims of a conquest that remains completely unconfirmed by historical record. The answer to this mystery is blindingly simple and, in fact, was hinted at by Cornish historian Charles Henderson (1900-1933). Ecgberht and subsequent West Saxon kings did not acquire these estates by conquest, but by stealth, and through the increasingly Canterbury-controlled church.

The astute Henderson, who remains in the highest regard, packed more historical and archaeological research into his tragically short life than most could have achieved in three lifetimes. His conclusion about this enigma, missed by almost every other historian, explains how it was done. He wrote that, while Ecgberht's political arrangements are unrecorded, 'with the ability of a statesman, he made religious penetration by Saxon ecclesiastics a possibility'.

In fact, and in collusion with Canterbury, controller of the Roman faith in Britain, Ecgberht had secured an increasing number of Saxon clerical appointments into Cornish churches. These had taken control of church lands, which they then gifted to the West Saxon king for him to pass onto the nearest Episcopal See to Cornwall at Sherborne. Later, in 909 when Edward the Elder had established a new bishopric at Crediton, *Polltun*, *Landwithan* and *Caellwic* were handed to the new bishop, Eadulf, in order that he might 'from them each year visit the Cornish people to eradicate their errors, for in times past, as far as possible, they resisted the truth and were not obedient to Papal decrees.'

This, of course, alluded to the Roman church's entreaties to the Cornish king Gerent II, 200 years earlier, that the Celtic (Columban) Church in Cornwall should cease its accustomed practices and conform to those of Rome. Although the Roman church, through the increasing appointment of priests appointed by Canterbury, had made significant inroads into Cornish centres of religion, many places still held to the old practices.

Between 981 and 988, Archbishop Dunstan wrote to King Athelred of Wessex advising that the same three estates should be handed to the Bishop of St Germans, a new Cornish bishopric, but not diocese, having been set up under Bishop Conan (a Celtic name) at around 930. This does not seem to have happened and the three estates ended up with Exeter, when the See of Crediton was moved to there in 1050.

It would seem, therefore, that the acquisition of land that was then granted to others by Saxon kings was not achieved by military means, or by conquest, but stealthily by way of the Church. Of course, Canterbury and Rome held allegiance to a rather higher king than any earthly one, but Canterbury and the churches it increasingly controlled would hold Saxon kings in far greater esteem and favour than ever it would for Cornish rulers far away, whose realm had long resisted obedience to Rome.

The real architect of enforcing obedience to Rome and extending the power of the Church beyond the world of spiritual practice was

Archbishop Theodore of Canterbury, in office from 668 to 690. In 705, King Ine's kingdom of Wessex had been divided into two bishoprics, centred in Winchester and Sherborne, and it was from Sherborne that Bishop Aldhelm unsuccessfully approached Dumnonia's King Gerent II about the insistence of his bishops on maintaining the practices of the Celtic Church.

Aldhelm played this cleverly, building up a cordial friendship with Gerent to the degree that the Dumnonian king felt spiritually obliged to gift him lands in the southeastern corner of Cornwall that were soon passed onto Ine himself. In this way, Saxon Wessex had gained a foothold in Celtic Dumnonia without a single West Saxon soldier having to step onto its soil and, after Ecgberht's army finally broke into Dumnonia, the West Saxon bishops at Sherborne had effective control over the Church in the far southwestern peninsula.

It was still far from plain sailing as the practices of the Celtic Church in Cornwall still held out in many places. Between the years 833 and 870, the Celtic Bishop Kenstec in 'Cornubia and the place which in the British tongue is called Dinuurin', the Priory of St Petroc and ecclesiastical centre at Bodmin, felt it necessary to write to Archbishop Ceolnoth at Canterbury reminding him of the monastic nature and different traditions of the Church in Dumnonia. Nonetheless, the rule of Canterbury and Rome was being reluctantly acknowledged at about this time, although the older practices were still observed in places. One such unorthodoxy is recorded as having been carried out at this time by the bishop of the Cornish monastery of Lanaled (St Germans) and, while such pockets of resistance persisted, Cornwall's right to its own diocese remained denied.

Although, for some centuries, a large number of small monastic foundations had been set up throughout Cornwall, its two major religious houses were those at *Lanaled*, the Priory of St Germans which dated back to at least the 7th century; and *Dinuurin*, the Priory of St Petroc at Bodmin. The initial Priory founded by St Petroc himself had been located at *Lannwedhenek*, later Petrocstow (now Padstow), with that at Bodmin having been set up by St Guron. Lannwedhenek had been founded in the 5th century by a priest born in south Wales named Guethenoc, a brother of St Winwalo and who went on to become Bishop Guethenoc of Vannes in Brittany. It is said that St Petroc, having established himself at Padstow, then negotiated with St Guron with a view to establishing a larger foundation at *Dinuurin*. Guron, who appears to have been in advancing years, agreed and moved on to found another religious house at Gorran. The Bodmin foundation retained the name *Dinuurin*, 'fortress of St Guron', at least into the mid 9th century, and grew to become a major landowner in Cornwall.

Cornwall was the last of the Celtic nations to hold out against submitting to practising obedience to Rome. The Breton churches had been the first to do so, closely followed by southern Ireland in the 620s, and the northern parts of Ireland in 692. Scotland's churches submitted to Rome in the early 8th century; the Manx churches at about the same time, followed by Wales later in the same century.

Meanwhile, Cornish lands continued to end up in the hands of English kings. Around the year 900, Bishop Asser of Sherborne, who had been King Alfred's biographer, gifted church-owned lands at Plympton (still Cornish territory) to Edward the Elder, and doubtless many other estates similarly came under English control in this way, including the large estate of Tywarnhayle, comprising much of Perranzabuloe parish, but which had been owned by the Priory of St Petroc at Bodmin. In 909, a new western diocese was formed, with its centre at Crediton, but Cornwall continued to be denied its own regional bishop until around 930. This was a native Cornish priest, Conan, followed by other countrymen: Daniel and Cemoyre, the latter of whom appeared to have been obliged to take a Saxon forename. However, these appointments still fell far short of a separate Cornish diocese.

In one manumission entry, for the freeing of slaves at Bodmin, this bishop Cemoyre appears with both his English and Celtic names: *These are the names of those women whom Wulfsige Cemoyre freed: Rum, Addalburg and Ogurcen, before these beholding witnesses: Osian the priest, Cantgueithen the deacon, Leucum the clerk.* His consecration lists him only as Wulfsige, but in other manumissions he sometimes appears as Wulfsige, and sometimes as Cemoyre or Cemuyre. This name is reminiscent of the Breton record of a leader named Commore or Chonomor who appears to have the known British name Cunomoros, also that of a known Cornish king in the 6th century.

This strange practice of men having one Saxon name and one Celtic name occurs in the names of three other men in the later 10th century.

One record has lands in the Meneage district of the Lizard peninsula being granted to *Wulfnoth Rumoncant*. *Wunsie Cenmonoc* is a priest who, in the Bodmin Manumissions, frees three slaves, then appears elsewhere in the same manumissions as a witness, but under the single Saxon name *Wunsi(g)e*, and finally as a manumitter but with just the Celtic name *Cenmonoc* being recorded. The final part of this name might be *managh*, 'monk'. Then, in 969, lands near Probus and Lamorran are gifted to *Aelfeah Gerent* and his wife *Noruurei*. Again this man has names in two languages, the Celtic one always appearing last. Two of these four men were certainly churchmen, and the other two must also have been so. That one had a wife is not remarkable: celibacy had yet to be demanded of the lower orders of the priesthood.

The practice of Cornish priests being obliged to take a second Saxon name would appear to have been a short-lived one under the bishopric of Crediton, and does not occur again after 994, when Cornwall was finally given its own separate diocese, with its see located at St Germans. Not that Cornwall had everything its own way. From 981, after Wulfsige Cemoyre, all its appointed bishops were English, as was the first to be appointed to the new Cornish diocese, Ealdred. Appointments of English bishops to the new Cornish diocese would continue to be the case until 1050 when it ceased to exist.

The Bodmin Manumissions are a stark reminder of the reality of slavery in our past. Written as margin notes in an older book of gospels, these record the freeing of people, both male and female, from serfdom before the altar of St Petroc, Bodmin, between the years 940 and 1050. They also provide a whole list of contemporary personal names: Cornish, English and some of biblical or Latin origin. Of the people with demonstrably Cornish names, 68 had been enslaved, 37 were witnesses and 11 had been slave owners. 15 English people had been slaves, 35 witnesses and 21 had owned slaves. Of the latter, several appear to have been churchmen. No one can be sure how long the practice of serfdom or slavery had been part of society. Classical Roman writers from the late Iron Age and Roman occupation periods suggest that it was in existence in Britain in their own time, while thralldom or serfdom was a feature of early Anglo-Saxon life as well.

If one sets aside kings and clerics named in the Bodmin Manumissions, eight of the slave-owners are given secular titles. Of these, the Saxons Aethelweard and Ordgar, both described as Dux, were Ealdormen of their own respective territories within Wessex, and probably present to represent the interests of Sherborne and Tavistock Abbeys. Of the remaining, four of the titled men have Celtic names: *Maccos centurionis* ('Hundred-reeve'); *Tethion consul*; with *Cufure* and *Ylcaerthon* both described as *praepositus*, 'reeve'. Also, when the same slave-owning churchmen and kings are removed from the list, it becomes clear that the majority of secular slave-owners were, in fact, Cornishmen.

None of this paints a picture of a conquered or subjugated land. Cornish religious houses, mining, fishing and vast areas of Cornish territory were paying no tax into any Saxon exchequer. It must have been going somewhere, and that can only have been into a Cornish dynastic exchequer. As Michael Wood wrote in *Domesday* (1980), the fixing of the border at the Tamar c.930 had left the Cornish distinct from England, retaining their own dynastic ruler and observing their own laws and customs, similar in many ways to the Indian princedoms under the Raj.

Although, by the 10th century, there was a greater Saxon presence in Cornwall, chiefly by way of the Church but also by settlement in the far northeastern corner and the Tamarside parishes south of Launceston, it is clear that Cornwall did not undergo a Saxon period as most of England did. Nothing of the practices carried out in Saxon societies appeared in Cornwall. No *burh* had been set up west of the Tamar; no villages on the Saxon pattern had been founded. It is therefore disappointing to find that a published report of the native Cornish settlement of Mawgan Porth by English Heritage describes it as being of a ' late Saxon period' that Cornwall never underwent.

The Mawgan Porth settlement was founded at around 850 CE and was occupied for roughly 200 years. Three clusters of houses were found during excavations in the 1950s; a fourth is believed to have existed. The largest cluster consisted of four rectangular buildings clustered around a central courtyard. Apart from the shapes, this was reminiscent of the arrangement found in the West Penwith courtyard houses of eight centuries earlier, although there is almost certainly no connection between the two. With stone walls 0.7 metres thick, the largest building was a forerunner of the medieval longhouses that were yet to come. The inhabitants were native Cornish farmers and fishermen, undoubtedly speaking an early form of Cornish that would not have been unlike the Welsh and Breton of the same period. They kept sheep, goats, horses and oxen, as well as dogs, cats and poultry.

Upslope from the houses was a cemetery of slate-lined graves, the western part of which had been set aside for the burial of children. The ratio of child interments to those of adults was unusually high, suggesting a tragic level of infant mortality.

The pottery they used was of a type known as 'bar-lug'. This style originated in northern Europe and may have been widely distributed by Frisian traders. In Cornwall, local people began to manufacture it themselves, developing a distinctively Cornish style found throughout the region during this period. Over a thousand sherds were discovered on the Mawgan Porth site alone but, curiously, metal implements were lacking. One single coin of Aethelred II, datable to the period 990-995, was also found. The coin could have been dropped there by a visiting priest or merchant, but it was enough for some to deny the undoubted Cornish nature of the settlement, and to deplorably redesignate the whole site as 'late Saxon'. The coin appears to have been minted at Lydford, Devon, although a limited mint was also in operation at St Stephens, Launceston at this time.

Few Cornish settlements of this date have been examined, but those that have show the houses to have been generally rectangular, with walls built of turf as well as of stone.

Earlier Cornish pottery of the post-Roman centuries varied over the years. In the immediate sub-Roman years, Gwithian ware was basically an inferior form of the native ware common to the area during the Roman occupation. Grass-marked pottery became popular in the 6th and 7th centuries. Largely consisting of platters and cooking pots, their name comes from the imprints of chopped grass or straw on which the vessel had been stood to prevent it from adhering to the drying slab, prior to its being fired. At the same time, eastern Mediterranean amphorae, containing wine and oils, continued to be imported, along with reddish dishes and bowls shipped in from Asia Minor and North Africa. Kitchenware manufactured in Brittany was also being brought in between the 6th and 8th centuries.

The fashion of bar-lug pottery was replaced by Sandy Lane style 1 pottery in the 11th century, particularly in West Cornwall, where many

The Giant's Grave, Ludgvan: The last remnant of a linear earthwork that might once have crossed the isthmus of Penwith between Mount's Bay and St Ives Bay.

examples of these wheel-made cooking pots again show grass mark imprints on the base.

The tin industry continued to flourish throughout the early medieval centuries, as those between the Roman departure and Norman invasion are now referred to. A streamwork at Boscarne on Bodmin Moor was exploited between 635 and 1000 CE, a tinners' shovel fashioned from oak being found there and dated to that period. Ingots of tin found at Praa Sands have been dated to the 7th century.

Cornwall also has three linear earthworks that are tentatively assigned to the post-Roman centuries, and which appear to define distinct territories. An old rhyme states that: 'One day the Devil, having nothing to do, built a great hedge from Lerryn to Looe' (although another version and its current name say that it was a local giant who had time on his hands). The Giant's Hedge forms a boundary to a large area of land between the Fowey and Looe estuaries and can be most easily seen near Lanreath. Some link this with a post-Roman occupation of the Castle Dore hill fort, but this is sited on the opposite side of the Fowey estuary. Close examination of another hill fort, Hall Rings near Pelynt, might establish a more relevant link.

The Bolster Bank originally ran from Trevaunance Cove at St Agnes to Chapel Porth, cutting off an area that includes the isolated hill of St Agnes Beacon (or Carn Breanek), and St Agnes Head. This area contains a wealth of minerals that have been extensively mined over an extremely long period of time. The bank, which is quite impressive in places, and with hints of its external ditch remaining, may have been constructed to protect this valuable asset. The bank is named after a farm about halfway along its length, whose name was spelt *Bothlester* in 1398. This literally translates as 'boat hump'. The bank is breached in two places close by, and the isolated length of bank between the breaches does indeed resemble an upturned boat. In turn, the feature lent its name to the giant Bolster who was said to have built it, and who is annually celebrated by the people of St Agnes today.

The third linear earthwork is much less known and again recalls the legendary giants of Cornwall. The Giant's Grave is now just a short length of bank, with traces of a seaward facing ditch near the Newtown roundabout between Long Rock and Crowlas. It is considered to be all that is left of an earthwork that may have cut off the entire Penwith peninsula; much of its course is now followed by the A30 trunk road, which has obliterated most of it.

The Cornish Hundreds

ALFRED of Wessex's mention of *Triconscire* (Trigg) introduces a further detail of pre-Norman Cornwall: the existence of internal divisions. Only those to the west of the river Tamar remain known and these were originally six in number.

It has been claimed that these were the same as the 'Hundreds' into which Anglo-Saxon shires were divided. However, the *Keverangow* of Cornwall are older than these, as confirmed by the mention of one of them in Alfred's Will, which is dated to around 880 CE, and while the major part of Cornwall west of the Tamar remained as part of an independent Celtic kingdom, outside of Saxon rule. The same *keverang*, Trigg, has an even earlier reference from the 7th century. Several of the *keverangow* themselves became referred to as 'shires'.

The closest equivalent to the Cornish *Keverangow* are the *Cantrefi* of

Wales, a word meaning 'one hundred settlements', into which each of the ancient Welsh kingdoms were divided.

The meaning of the singular term *keverang* is 'district from which a military unit can be raised', and finds cognates in the Welsh *cyfrang*, 'meeting, encounter, battle' and Middle Breton *cuuranc*, 'military assembly'. They may have been minor kingdoms within the overall kingdom of Dumnonia, and the later kingdom of Cornwall. If they paralleled the Welsh *cantrefi*, then each had its own adminstrative legal court. In a Welsh *cantref*, this took the form of an assembly of *uchelwyr*, 'high men, nobility' the main landowners (a Cornish language equivalent would be: *ughelwer*). Often presided over by the king (presumably the minor king overseeing each *cantref*) or his appointed representative, this court had judges, a clerk, ushers and often two professional pleaders. Matters over which this court presided were crimes and disputes over boundaries and inheritances. It is highly likely that similar practices applied to each Cornish *keverang*, and the High King (of Dumnonia or Cornwall) could summon a war host from each to comprise his own army should the need arise.

The original six Cornish *keverangow* were as follows:

PENWITH (*pennwydh*, 'end-district, furthest end') covered the westernmost part of Cornwall from Land's End to Scorrier. Named as early as the 10th century, it was one of only two keverangow to retain its name in the local government reorganisation of 1974, even though the modern borders differed from the originals. That has now been rendered redundant by the formation of a unitary authority for Cornwall. The westernmost part, The Land's End peninsula west of the Hayle-Marazion isthmus, is still referred to as West Penwith.

KERRIER (*keryer*, 'place of forts'). From a northern point at Scorrier, Kerrier covered an area from Praa Sands to Falmouth, and included the whole of the Lizard peninsula. This was the second of the *keverangow* to retain its name after 1974.

POWDER (*pow ereder*, 'ploughland region') consisted of an area of south Cornwall from the Roseland peninsula to the Fowey estuary. It included Truro and extended as far north as St Allen and Lostwithiel.

Middle English *scire*, 'shire' was added to the name from 1187 to 1331.

PYDAR (Old Cornish *pedera*, 'fourth [region]') lay immediately north of Powder, and included the north coast from St Agnes to the Camel estuary. This was also suffixed by English *scire*, 'shire', from 1130 to 1539.

TRIGG (*trigordh*, 'three war-hosts'). The northeastern part of Cornwall from the Camel estuary to the Tamar. This has the oldest reference of the six keverangow, the 7th century *Life of St Sampson* naming it as *Pagus Tricurius*. This also had English 'shire' added to its name from Alfred's mention of it c.880. At around 1200, Trigg was divided into three, adding two further *keverangow* to the list. Trigg was retained as the name of the western part; the central division was Lesnewth (*lys nowydh*, 'new court/administrative centre), and the eastern one was Stratton. Similar names appeared in Celtic-speaking Gaul; *Tricorii* and *Tricurium* meaning the same as Trigg; and *Petrucorii*, meaning 'people of four war-hosts,' whilst Trégor remains a northern Breton district.

WIVELSHIRE (Middle English: *twifealdscire*, 'two-fold shire'). This southeastern keverang, spanning south Cornwall from the Fowey estuary to the Tamar, with a tongue of land extending northward to include Launceston, completes the list. Its Cornish name is lost, replaced by one in Middle English, and it had been split into two halves by 1185 when first mentioned by name: West and East Wivelshire. The two halves were also referred to in Domesday by the names of their principal manors: Fawiton (West) and Rialton (East). These Cornish names, with Saxon *tun*, 'settlement' attached, are *Fawi* (also a river-name meaning 'beech-trees river'), and *Riel*, 'royal'.

For the purposes of the Domesday survey in 1086, the names of other Hundreds were also replaced by those of their principal manors: Penwith became Connerton; Kerrier was renamed Winnianton; Pydar was Pawton; Powder took the name Tybesta; and the re-amalgamated trio of Trigg, Lesnewth and Stratton was simply Stratton.

King Athelstan is coming!

THROUGHOUT the reign of Alfred in Wessex, and his son Edward the Elder (reigned 899-924), there was peace between the Cornish and the

West Saxons, who continued to have their hands full with Danish raiders and settlers elsewhere. Nonetheless, this did not prevent Edward from proclaiming pre-eminence over all peoples south of the Clyde-Forth line: the Gaels, Danes, Cumbrians, Welsh, English and Cornish. One might suspect that consent from those peoples was somewhat lacking, although Hywel Dda, king of Deheubarth in South Wales, did sign a treaty with Edward in 918 and, in 927, had agreed the River Wye as the western border of Athelstan's kingdom.

It was Edward who created the short-lived Diocese of Crediton but otherwise his reign had little effect on the Cornish and their way of life. His son Athelstan, who succeeded to the Wessex throne in 924, and at the age of 28, had rather more ambition against the native Britons of the far southwest.

Much has been claimed about King Athelstan and Cornwall, but sources such as the *Anglo-Saxon Chronicle* are silent about most of it. The Chronicle does record the treaty signed at Eamont Bridge between Athelstan and several kings, including Huwal of the Westwalas, but it was left to William of Malmesbury in 1125 to fill in the gaps:

> 'He (Athelstan) turned towards the Western British who are called the Cornwallish because, situated in the west of Britain, they are opposite to the extremity of Gaul. Fiercely attacking, he obliged them to retreat from Exeter which, till that time, they had inhabited with equal privileges with the Angles, fixing the boundary of their province on the left bank of the river Tamar, just as he had appointed the river Wye to the North Britons. This city then, which he had cleansed by purging it of its contaminating race, he fortified with towers and surrounded with a wall of squared stone.'

Placing this record alongside historical and place-name evidence, it would appear that Athelstan took Exeter, the South Hams and Dartmoor into his realm of Wessex, to be lost by Cornwall for evermore. In fixing his own kingdom's western border at the east bank of the Tamar, this restored the area north of the River Ottery, that Ecgberht seems to have gained a century earlier, to Cornish ownership.

Harder to pin down is the date at which this occurred. If William of Malmesbury's account can be accepted, as many do, then it followed Athelstan's meeting with Welsh kings Hywel Dda and Owein at Hereford, at which the Wye was fixed as the border between the Welsh kingdoms and Athelstan's own. This took place soon after the event at Eamont Bridge, near Penrith in Cumbria, on 12th July 927, at which several British kings signed a treaty with Athelstan. Of this, the Anglo-Saxon Chronicle states that Athelstan: 'had power over all the kings that were in this island; first Huwal king of the Westwala; Constantine, king of the Scots; Uwen, king of the Wenta, and Ealdred, son of Ealdulf from Bamburgh. With pledges and oaths they fastened a peace in the place called Eamont Bridge, on July 12th, renounced all idolatry and, from there, turned away in peace.'

Roger of Wendover's slightly different account, written c.1235, says that Athelstan: 'next conquered in battle and defeated all the inferior kings of the island, to wit: Hunwal (sic), king of the Britons; Constantine, king of the Scots; Wulferth, king of the Wenti; he also expelled Alfred, son of Eadulf, from the castle at Bamburgh. On which they all, with the kings of the other provinces, seeing that they were not a match for his prowess, came together unto him and requested peace and, renouncing idolatry, they made a lasting league with him.'

As much of Athelstan's reign was taken up with fighting the Danes in the north and east of the country, a date for the Exeter event, and the fixing of the Tamar border, of between 927 and 931 is about as near as can be achieved. The latter date is the likelier, as it was within a year or so of then that Athelstan instructed the Church to appoint a Cornish bishop, Conan, with a seat at St German's. Conan was signing charters in his role as bishop from 931.

The setting of the Tamar's east bank as the boundary between Cornwall and the English region of Wessex bears all the hallmarks of a territorial agreement, just as the previous setting-out of the Welsh boundary was. That Cornwall should receive its own Canterbury-approved bishop would seem a likely ingredient of such an agreement that would have been made between Athelstan and Huwal, even if it would not have its own separate diocese for another sixty years or so. It would also seem that the Cornish had not been completely cleared out of Exeter, but continued to occupy the area inside the northwestern corner of the walled city, and which was known as *Bretayne* well into the 12th century. The east bank of the Tamar remains the legal boundary of Cornwall to this day, being enshrined within the Duchy Charters of 1337-8, with the territorial Duchy of Cornwall continuing to own the bed and waters of the Tamar as confirmed within the Tamar Bridge Act of 1998.

A good deal of fantasy has been written, and oft-repeated, about Athelstan and Cornwall. Chiefly to blame for this was John Leland, the early 16th century writer to whom King Athelstan was very much a hero-figure. Much of what is claimed about Athelstan and Cornwall is purely down to Leland's fertile imagination; in particular the baseless claim that he conquered the length of Cornwall, then the Isles of Scilly, after which he allegedly founded the collegiate church of St Buryan in thanks for his victory. These claims also led to a false belief that Athelstan defeated Huwal, king of Cornwall, in a battle at Boleigh, where the Bronze Age pair of menhirs known as the Pipers, near the Merry Maidens stone circle, are said to mark where the two kings faced other. Of course, all historical sources remain totally silent about any of these purported events. Athelstan's traditional link with Probus church is also a likely invention.

Leland also falsely claimed that Athelstan 'refounded' the Priory of St Petroc at Bodmin, and that he made grants of privilege to that Priory and St Petroc's original site at Padstow. To this end, he respelled *Aldestowe* (Middle English: *ald stow*, 'old holy place', and an alternative English name for *Petrocstow*, which became shortened to Padstow) as *Adelstowe*, in order to imply that the name translated as 'Athelstan's holy place'.

Also false are the two charters that Athelstan issued with regard to two Cornish churches: St Buryan and St Petroc's at Bodmin. The latter has been described by experts as 'spurious' and the former as 'dubious', with only a single historian accepting it as genuine. Both are almost certainly forgeries drawn up several centuries after Athelstan's death.

In the case of St Buryan's purported 'charter', the forger had little knowledge of the development of the Cornish language which, at around 1200, underwent a process known as assibilation: a softening of certain consonants that did not occur in its sister languages of Welsh and Breton. The *Old Cornish Vocabulary*, dated to about 1200, actually shows the language of the time to have been in a transitional state in which some entries are in assibilated form and some are not. A document from nearly 300 years earlier should not have shown any assibilation at all, and yet the St Buryan 'charter' shows place-names such as *Bosegham*, *Bosselynen* and *Ponsprontiryon*. If genuine, these should have been presented (in corrected form) as *Bodseghan*, *Bodselevan* and *Pontprontiryon*. Furthermore, the document, purportedly signed at Kingston-upon-Thames by Athelstan himself with several witnesses, is dated to the year 943. This would have been a miraculous achievement indeed, considering that Athelstan had died three years earlier, on October 27th 940, at the age of 44.

Domesday itself, in 1086, makes no mention of any royal connection with St Buryan, which was then held solely by the 'Canons of St Berriona'. The purported Charter mysteriously appeared only when Bishop Briwer of Exeter unsuccessfully attempted to falsely elevate the church's status to a Royal Free Chapel in 1238, and the transitionally assibilated forms of the place-names it contains are wholly consistent with that date. Briwer's forgery proved useful in 1300 when, on the death of Earl Edmund, the Earldom of Cornwall - under which the Deanery of St Buryan fell - temporarily lapsed to Edward I. The Crown, using the forgery as 'evidence', proclaimed St Buryan as the Royal Free Chapel it had never been, and placed it under the jurisdiction of William de Hameldon, Dean of York. Bishop Bytton of Exeter immediately began legal proceedings to place a stop on this fraudulent claim and appointment. With the Crown digging in its heels, this led to half a century of legal wranglings, with successive Bishops of Exeter contesting its claims, and even a bout of fisticuffs between Dean John de Maunte and his prebendary Richard. Eventually, the Crown forced its will on Bishop Bronescombe in 1350, and the opposition collapsed. St Buryan was formally declared a Royal Donative, with all Episcopal rights extinguished, and all on the back of Bishop Briwer's forged 'Charter of Athelstan'.

The first genuine charter of the period involving Cornish land was made at an undetermined date during Athelstan's reign, but by a Cornish landowner with the Celtic name of Maenchi, and described as *comes*, 'count', granting the estate of Lanlawren in the parish of Lanteglos-by-Fowey, to the church of St Ildiern at Lansallos. For reasons unknown, Maenchi was at Athelney in Somerset when he signed this charter, perhaps through an arrangement with the clergy as a church was to be the beneficiary of his gift. No other charters gifting Cornish land were made until the reign of Edgar (959-975).

Athelstan was nothing if not arrogant as, at the time when he nominated Bishop Conan for the Bishopric of Cornwall, including the church and estate of St Germans, he termed himself *rex totius Albionis*, 'king of all Albion', reviving an ancient name for Britain, first apparent in the Iron Age. He was not, and never would be, king of all Britain, although he could claim to be king of all of what had then become England. This did not include Cornwall.

From King Huwal, and his 927 treaty with Athelstan, onwards, the position of the Cornish ruling dynasty had become progressively weakened and undermined to the point where English kings could acquire lands west of the Tamar with apparent impunity, usually by way of the Church, and had even assumed the right to gift them to others unchallenged. In this way, estates large and small could end up in English hands and it is very likely that Cornish bondservants being freed in the records of the Bodmin Manumissions had been held in thrall on those very lands.

Athelstan died childless in 940, and his throne passed to his half-brother Edmund. The Church in Cornwall, finally subservient to Rome, now considered itself loyal only to the English king recognised by Canterbury, rather than to any Cornish king, and so the earliest of the manumissions recorded at Bodmin between then and 946 were carried out in Edmund's name only.

The English Kings Edgar (959-975) and Edward II (975-978) also felt entitled to give and receive lands in Cornwall that had almost certainly once belonged to the Church and, in this way, more and more Cornish land was ending up in English hands. During the subsequent reign of Aethelred II ('Ethelred the Unready'), the church of St Stephen at Launceston was operating a small mint producing coins featuring that king, although only one coin from this mint has ever been found. A more productive mint was already established at Lydford in Devon, but the St Stephen mint was yet another sign of the stealthy erosion of authority from the native Cornish ruling dynasty. In 994, Aethelred authorised the Diocese of Crediton to be split, giving Cornwall its own diocese with its seat at St Germans, and under the patronage of Saints Germanus and Petroc. Canterbury immediately appointed an English bishop, Ealdred, to it. This effectively ended the dominance of the priory at Bodmin as it was stipulated that 'the place and rule of St Petroc always be in his (Ealdred's) power and that of his successors.'

As it was to turn out, the Diocese of Cornwall was to be short-lived, and Ealdred would have only two successors, both of them Englishmen: Bishops Aethelred and Burhwold. When Burhwold died in 1043, Lyfing, Bishop of Crediton, was ordered to re-absorb Cornwall into his diocese. Cornwall would not be granted its own diocese again until 1876, and in 1050, Edward the Confessor moved the See at Crediton to Exeter, and ratifed the merging of the dioceses of Devon and Cornwall. 'Devonwall' had begun.

In 981, and before the creation of the Cornish diocese, King Aethelred had angered the Cornish by appropriating lands at Downinney, Warbstow; Linkinhorne; Rame; Sheviock; and Stoke Climsland, all in areas where Saxon settlement on Cornish soil had begun, and giving them to the newly formed Abbey of St Mary's at Tavistock. This had been founded by Ordgar, Ealdorman of Devon, in 961 and completed by his son Ordwulf, who also inherited that title, twenty years later.

Perhaps this stealthy programme of attrition drove the Cornish into reviving an old alliance. During the 830s, when Ecgberht had been King of the West Saxons, the Cornish had almost certainly been providing Danish longship fleets with safe havens from which they could mount raids on the coasts of Wessex, and had even mounted a joint force with the Danes to unsuccessfully attack Ecgberht in 838. In 981, the Vikings were back. This time, according to the *Anglo-Saxon Chronicle*: 'St Petroc's Stow was ravaged and in the same year much damage was done everywhere along the coast, both among the Devon men and the British.' It is of interest that Padstow Priory, dominated by the English priesthood, was attacked and destroyed, but the Cornish bishopric of St Petroc at Bodmin was not.

In 997, the *Chronicle* also records that: 'This year the raiding fleet went about Devonshire (*Defenanscire*) into Severn (*Saefern*) mouth and plundered among the Cornish (*Cornwealum*), Welsh (*Northwealum*) and in Devon (*Defenum*). Then they went up to Watchet (*Wecedport*) and there wrought much evil with burning and manslaughter. Afterwards they coasted back around Penwith promontory (*Penwithsteort*) to the south side and, turning into the mouth of the Tamar (*Tamermutha*), went up until they came to Lydford (*Hlydanforda*), burning and slaying everything that they met. Moreover they burned to the ground Ordulf's Minster at Tavistock (*Taefingstoc*) and brought incalculable plunder back to their ships.'

Which Cornish targets were plundered by the Vikings? Highly vulnerable and defenceless native coastal settlements such as Mawgan Porth, occupied at this very time, were completely untouched. Had the Vikings, at Cornish request, singled out ecclesiastical targets again? The most interesting part of this account concerns the destruction wrought at Lydford, the site of the burh and mint founded by Alfred of Wessex, and at the Ealdorman of Devon, Ordwulf's, Abbey of St Mary's at Tavistock. How did the sea-going Danes know that these places far inland even existed, let alone how to locate and reach them, unless they had onshore advice and guidance from their old allies, the Cornish? It would have involved them turning their fleet up the Tavy river, and still have required a respectable overland trek across totally unfamiliar territory to reach Lydford. The only reasonable conclusion is that it could not have been achieved without guidance from those who knew the lie of the land, and who wanted payback for the Cornish estates that had been handed to Tavistock.

Just 16 years after the raid on Lydford and Tavistock, and 320 years after the first Viking raid on Britain at Lindisfarne, the Danes finally achieved success in 1013 when Sweyn Forkbeard overthrew the weak Athelred II ('the Unready'). Sweyn had little time to capitalise as he died in the following year, and Aethelred was briefly restored to the throne of England. In 1015, Sweyn's eldest son Cnut ('Canute the Great') invaded. Aethelred died in 1016. Cnut then forced his son Edmund Ironside to surrender half of his realm, then took the rest when Edmund died later in November of the same year. Cnut was now, in effect, an emperor, ruling England, Denmark, Norway and parts of Sweden. He was to reign until 1035, when an attempt was made by another of Aethelred's sons, Alfred, to retake the English throne, but was foiled by Earl Godwin of Wessex, a supporter of Cnut's son Harald Harefoot, who took the throne for the next five years.

It was clear that Cnut regarded the Celtic peoples of Britain in a very different light to its English inhabitants. He introduced a tripartite division of the country, in which separate laws applied: Danelaw, Mercialaw and Wessexlaw. These did not include Wales or Cumbria where Celtic remained as the main language, and it is notable that Cnut also did not extend Wessexlaw into Celtic-speaking Cornwall, which confirmed that Cornwall had never been absorbed into Wessex.

Evidently, the debt of gratitude for the old alliance had not been forgotten by the Danish king.

This legislative division, with Cornish exemption, continued in use throughout the 11th century, surviving the Norman conquest and was included in the *Leges Henrici*, or the Laws of Henry I (reigned 1100-1135). Writing of this tripartite arrangement, and Cornwall's absence from it c.1105, Simeon of Durham added that: 'in Cornwall are seven small shires,' referring to the *keverangow* or 'Hundreds'. The number appears to suggest that Wivelshire had, by then, been subdivided, while Trigg, Lesnewth and Stratton had been amalgamated, and the mention of 'seven small shires' suggests that Cornwall still retained a legislature of its own into at least the 12th century.

Had Cornwall been absorbed into the Saxon kingdom of Wessex, its exemption from the English legislative areas would never have occurred; nor would Athelstan have seen fit to fix his southwestern border at the Tamar's east bank.

A postscript to the link between Cornwall and the Isles of Scilly, and the Vikings, involves a Norwegian named Olaf Trygvasson, an experienced raider whose ships called in to Scilly in the year 986. At that time the northern part of the islands were owned by a group of hermits said to have descended from priests exiled there from Spain by Magnus Maximus, c.385, for the crime of heresy. Trygvasson is said to have encountered one of these priests who foretold his accession to the throne of Norway, but warned of mutiny aboard his own ship in which he would receive severe wounds. This duly came to pass. The priests tended to his wounds and nursed him back to health but, in the meantime, converted Olaf to Christianity and baptised him.

From then on, Olaf Trygvasson ceased his raiding. He lived in Ireland for a while, where Norse settlements had been established, and then returned to Norway in 995, where rebels had turned on the usurper Haakon Sigurdasson. Trygvasson, a descendant of Harald Fairhair, the first king of Norway, persuaded the rebels to support his succession to the throne and, in that same year, he became King Olaf I of Norway.

Perhaps ironically, the ownership of Scilly would, in 1193, during the reign of Henry I, be passed to the same Tavistock Abbey that Viking forces had sacked in 997.

In the late 10th, or in the early 11th century, uplands that had been abandoned in the Late Bronze Age due to climatic deterioration, began to be resettled in parts, with an improvement in conditions. This is most noticeable on Bodmin Moor. Already in the eastern parts of Cornwall, the English language was making significant inroads and this was reflected by the names given to these new moorland holdings in which English names such as Leaze, Fernacre and Stannon predominate, while the older Cornish names tend to cluster around the periphery of the moor. There was also an upturn in industrial activity throughout Cornwall, particularly in tin extraction. Two methods were common: alluvial streaming from river valleys, and eluvial streaming in areas where tin-bearing gravels had washed down from high land to collect in gullies and folds of the landscape. It may have been at this time when the Stannaries of Cornwall, and of Dartmoor, came into operation, although an even earlier origin cannot be discounted. Sadly, the record does not tell us. Nonetheless, the Stannaries would have a significant bearing on the centuries yet to come.

The Normans are coming!

AFTER HARALD Harefoot, the reign of the Danish kings continued through Harthacnut (1040-1042). With his death, the sequence ended. The throne then passed to Edward the Confessor, who was half-brother to Harthacnut. Cornwall remained relatively unaffected, although Earl Godwin's part in supporting Harald Harefoot were rewarded by his gaining some lands in Cornwall, most likely to have been lands under the ownership of the Church, and which passed on to his son Harold Godwinson, after Godwin's death in 1053. This Harold would be the very one whose extremely brief rise to prominence would end on the battle-field of Senlac Ridge against Duke William of Normandy. An Anglo-Saxon would never sit on the throne of England again.

In the years running up to the Battle of Hastings, the 12th century *Gesta Herewardi* has the young Hereward of Bourne, later known as 'the Wake', outlawed by Edward the Confessor, spending some of his exile in Cornwall. It claims that he befriended an otherwise unknown prince named Alef, and saved an unnamed local princess from an unwanted marriage. However, various aspects of this tale, including an Irish connection, suggest that the monk who wrote this episode was influenced by the stories of Tristan and Eselt that were also popular in the 12th century, so that this tale of Hereward is rather more likely to be fiction than fact.

The Norman Conquest of 1066 was to change the whole of British society and administration, and form the basis of the very system of governance we have today. The compilation known as *The Laws of William the Conqueror* continued the tripartite legislatures of England set out under Cnut, earlier in the 11th century. West Saxon law continued to cover Devon, Dorset, Somerset and the Wessex shires to the east, but not Cornwall which was, once again, left to carry on as a separate legislature as it would remain into the time of Henry I. This distinct Cornish legislature was of great importance, as it would later form the basis of the peculiar laws that seem to have existed throughout the Earldom of Cornwall, to then be enshrined within the Duchy of Cornwall Charters of 1337-38, and perhaps also of Stannary Law, both of these remaining intact to the present day.

William of Worcester, writing in 1478, tells us that, at time of the Conquest, Cadoc (or Candorus) was ' a survivor of the Cornish royal line', but also the apparent last of a dynasty whose entire status and power had been systematically undermined, weakened and reduced to the point where the Normans were to refer to him as *Eorl*. King William left him in place. It may be that Cadoc was nearing the end of his life, for in 1068 William appointed Brient, Count of Brittany, as Earl of Cornwall to succeed him. That he should appoint a Celtic-speaking Breton with a retinue of Celtic speakers was a masterstroke of diplomacy. It is Count Brient who is believed to have begun the construction of Launceston Castle and, if Athelstan had cleared the Cornish out of Exeter, it may well have been Count Brient who allowed them to resettle the quarter of the city known as Bretayne. Brient had been involved in the 1068 Siege of Exeter in response to an unsuccessful revolt against William I by Devon, Dorset and Somerset Saxons, who had gathered in the walled city under the leadership of Gytha Thorkelsdóttir, mother of the slain Harold Godwinson.

Even though we know next to nothing about him, there is no good reason to doubt the existence of Cadoc, who was also mentioned by Camden, Carew, Borlase and Whitaker. However, stories of him having a son whose daughter and heir Agnes married Reginald, Earl of Bristol and a bastard son of Henry I, can be discounted as fanciful, as records conclusively show that Reginald married a completely different person.

Cadoc's descendants, said to have resided in Bodmin and the Hundred of Pydar, are claimed to have included Thomas Flamank, co-leader of the Cornish revolt against Henry VII in 1497.

Count Brient's brief spell as Earl of Cornwall gave way when he was thrown out of office after taking part in a baronial revolt against the King in 1073. His place was taken by the King's half-brother, Robert, Count of Mortain, who was to act as *de facto* Viceroy to govern Cornwall on behalf of the King, an act that William did not repeat elsewhere in the conquered parts of the island.

In 1085, William I, 'the Conqueror' held a conference at Gloucester with his senior counsellors and undertook to send out agents to compile a survey of his realm. Their brief was to identify landholdings, how much each contained in land and livestock, and what each was worth for taxation purposes. This would be called 'Domesday', a variant spelling of Doomsday because it would be 'the final word'.

Cornwall was to be included but, curiously, the Isles of Scilly were not. The survey duly went ahead, with its findings published just a year later, in 1086. The holdings that were listed have become known as 'manors'.

The general perception today is that a manor was something rather grand and of high status and, where some indeed became so, the reality was generally rather different. The word *manerium* was coined by the Norman administration and merely denoted a landholding. One often hears of previous Saxon 'manors' but, in truth, there was no such thing. The term was not used in pre-Norman Britain and, instead, charters and other documents of the period referred only to *land*, and the Latin term *villae* to describe these estates.

The Domesday 'manors' of Cornwall varied hugely in size and value, from vast estates to tiny farmsteads, and few were actually referred to as *maneria*. At the high end of the scale were estates such as Tywarnhayle, taken by the Count of Mortain from St Petrock's church at Bodmin, which covered some 12 square miles of the present parish of Perranzabuloe. In direct contrast were entries such as Trelan, St Keverne, with just 4 acres, one cow and 15 sheep and hardly of grand proportion or status.

That the survey took only a year to complete does suggest that the result was likely to be skimpy at best, and so it was. Taking West Penwith as a sample area, only six estates are listed in Domesday: *Bret* (Brea);

Chelenoch (Kelynack); *Alwaretone* (Alverton); *Eglosberrie* (St Buryan); *Landicle* (Lanistly, Gulval); and *Luduha* (Ludgvan). Together, these account for less than half of the total land area of the peninsula. Not a single one of the score of ribbon holdings in Zennor parish, averaging 182 acres in extent, features in the Domesday list, yet these had been in existence for a thousand years, and would continue to exist for another thousand. Nor is Zennor parish alone in failing to appear in Domesday. By extension, this would suggest that more than half of Cornwall was never surveyed at all, and Scilly not at all, and that the farms and estates contained in those unlisted areas remained under native ownership.

The lands that were listed fell under the control of just seven landlords: the King; Robert, Count of Mortain, the king's half-brother and de-facto Earl and Viceroy of Cornwall; the Bishop of Exeter; the Abbey of St Mary's, Tavistock; the Churches of various saints; the Breton noble Iudhael of Totnes; and an obscure nobleman named Gotshelm. These last two held just one small estate each. Most of these owners had appointed managers to oversee the estates, and many of those had several estates under their supervision. Researcher Kevin Cahill has rather bluntly described the Domesday Survey as not being so much a list of land and landowners, but more of: 'a robber-king's swag-list, as the same king elected himself to be the only landowner, having everyone else as tenants.'

In fact, the biggest landlord in Cornwall by far was its new overlord, the Count of Mortain, who held no less than 285 of the 350 estates that were listed. 36 of these he held directly, with ten of them managed by tenant farmers. The remainder provided him with the revenue from their rent. The Priory of St Petroc at Bodmin held 18 manors: six in their direct ownership, nine held under them by the Count of Mortain, and three by other individuals. Seven more estates were taken away from the Priory by the Count, who held them under his own name. Tavistock Abbey held six manors, with four more claimed to have been taken away from it unjustly by the Count. The churches of St Carantoc (Crantock), St Achebran (St Keverne), St Buryan, St Constantine, St Neot, St Piran and St Probus held one estate each. The church of St Stephen at Launceston had four estates. The King's own large manor of Winnianton, on the Lizard peninsula, contained twenty sub-manors that were all placed under the Count of Mortain's control. He, in turn, appointed others to oversee them.

Under Robert of Mortain, Reginald de Valletort was given control over no less than 39 manors; Richard FitzTurold had another 29. Other estate managers included Hamelin (22 manors); Turstin the Sheriff (27); Joinus (13); Berner (12); Nigel (11); Osferd (10). In addition, Alured and Brictric had control over seven manors each; Algar, Brient, Ermenald and Odo had six each; Alnoth, Blohin and Roger five each; Alward four; Andrew, Erchenbald, Levenot and Ulsi three apiece; Alwin, Alric, Doda, Godwin, Griffin, Osfil and Rabel two each, and 29 others held one estate apiece. Several of these names are Saxon, but Norman, Breton, Flemish and Cornish names also feature. Brictric, also named Brictric *Walensis*, was certainly a native Cornishman, and had held the substantial manor of Conerton from the time of King Edward before 1066.

That, under Norman rule, Cornwall was still considered as a separate entity from England is shown by the exemption from tax given to lands held by the Cornish-based churches, whereas churches situated outside Cornwall, such as Exeter Cathedral or Tavistock Abbey, were required to pay the full taxes on their Cornish territories. Similarly, lands in Devon owned by the Cornish church of St Petroc, were liable for taxation.

A further indication of this separate identity was that, in Norman times and later, the output of tin from Cornwall was ten times that of Dartmoor, but was taxed at twice the rate in accordance with the policy then exercised with regard to goods from foreign sources. Medieval Cornish tin would be much in demand for the casting of bronze church bells.

The face of Cornwall would soon change, too. It had never taken on West Saxon characteristics, but would soon adapt to Norman practice. Few Cornish settlements had ever consisted of more than a dozen dwellings and dominant Norman influence was to introduce a concept that had been alien to the native population: the town. Shortly after the Conquest, Cornwall had three towns: Helston, Bodmin and Launceston, and six markets, three in those towns plus Marazion, Liskeard and St Germans. By 1200, those had expanded to ten towns and additional markets. Those markets owned by the Church at St Germans and St Stephen at Launceston were undermined when the Count of Mortain started his own at the neighbouring castles of Trematon and Dunheved.

The first round of castle construction took place in both the 11th and 12th centuries as motte and bailey types at Dunheved (Launceston),

Dunheved Castle, Launceston: One of the very first Norman castles to be built in Cornwall, and to function as a border post from its lofty position above the River Tamar.

Trematon, Cardinham, Tregony, Kilkhampton and Eastleigh Berries. Ringwork castles were constructed at Restormel, Week St Mary, Penhallam, Bossiney, Upton and Truro. Castles of unknown form were built at Helston and Liskeard: these may only have been defended manor houses. In some cases, the building of a castle gave rise to the development of a town. In English regions, castle-building was distributed around the countryside in a manner designed to monitor and subdue the population, but in Cornwall, the very earliest of the Norman castles were built along the Tamar, effecting border control.

Although Cornwall was now solely under Norman control, there is every indication that its Celtic population was treated more favourably by its new overlords than the Saxon English. The presence of Celtic-speaking Breton lords and administrators was one such sign and, perhaps, the Viking connection between the Normans and old alliances of the Cornish people also played a part. William I was clearly no fool and, in Cornwall, he adopted and built upon the system of government that was already established. This curried favour from the Cornish people, and there are hints in the 12th century writings of John of Cornwall that the Cornish came to regard the Normans almost as new allies against an old and common enemy: the Saxon English.

The system of ecclesiastical parishes that survive to this day probably took shape in the 11th century, their boundaries largely determined by geographical features such as rivers and streams, and also established trackway routes whose own origins lay far back in prehistory. Although the high cross beside Perranzabuloe's second church was standing as early as 960, the wayside crosses for which Cornwall is renowned, probably date from no earlier than the 11th century. These marked the route of churchway paths leading to the church from outlying parts of the parish, and were often placed on land-ownership boundaries. The parish priests were supported by meagre incomes deriving from tithes and burial fees.

Following the tenure of Robert of Mortain, the Earldom of Cornwall passed to his son William in 1095, and until 1104. A hiatus followed until the shortlived appointment by King Stephen of another Breton to the Earldom of Cornwall, Alain de Bretagne, in 1140. Alain was the nephew of Count Brient who had earlier held the position. From 1141, it would be another seven years before another was appointed, Earl Reginald de Dunstanville. It would seem that the Earldom was run in a similar fashion to the succeeding Duchy of Cornwall where there may not be a Duke for a period of time, but there is always a Duchy.

* * * *

MICHAEL WOOD, in *Domesday* (1986) wrote that, under William I, the Cornish: 'were left under their own dynasty to regulate themselves with West Welsh (Cornish) tribal law and customs; rather like Indian princes under the Raj.' This sums it up rather well and, indeed, the Earls that were appointed to run Cornwall on behalf of the King in the 11th century were the equivalents of the Viceroys appointed to run India on behalf of the British monarchy eight centuries later. This constitutional and legislative independence, that had been recognised and preserved by Cnut in 1018, continued throughout the term of the Earldom of Cornwall and into the Duchy of Cornwall created in 1337, in which laws unique to Cornwall survive to the present day.

Cornwall was not alone with regard to its legal status during the medieval period, for separate legislative states existed for the Palatine County of Durham, the Palatine Earldom of Chester, the Marcher Lords of Wales, the Palatine County of Pembrokeshire, and others, retained their own courts distinct from the Courts of England for a long time, but one by one, these lost their status, particularly during the centralisation process led by Thomas Cromwell under Henry VIII. Cornwall, however, did not.

Cornwall's Stannary Law, intact to this very day, has been recognised in the courts as having truly ancient origins. 'This jurisdiction is guided by special laws by customs and by prescription from time out of mind,' said Lord Coke in 1605. Professor Robert Pennington, in 'Stannary Law' (1973), agreed and added that: 'It is, moreover, one of the oldest parts of the law, for its origins predate the Norman Conquest.' Dr John Kirkhope has stated that: 'Stannary Law includes principles which are alien to English Common Law, for example the principle of usufruct. This suggests that its origins are ancient indeed. Certainly it predates the famous Charter of William de Wrotham in 1198 which is always quoted as the first written evidence of the Stannaries.'

In 1508, Henry VII issued the Charter of Pardon, which gave an astonishing power to Cornwall's Stannary Parliament: the right of veto over Acts and Statutes issued by the government at Westminster. Of this, Professor Pennington wrote in 1973, that: 'no other institution has ever had such wide powers in the history of this country.' Nonetheless, it took Westminster only 41 years to trample all over that right by viciously enforcing Archbishop Thomas Cranmer's Act of Uniformity. In Cornwall, that also meant imposing an alien language (English) that many Cornish worshippers did not even speak. The veto was duly issued in the form of Articles of Demand that were ignored by London, and this led to the uprising that developed into an all-out and very bloody 6-week war. This was the third Cornish uprising against the English authorities within half a century (and the Cornish would rise up against those authorities three more times between 1549 and 1715).

In July 1549, under the command of Sir Humphrey Arundell of Helland, a makeshift Cornish army marched resolutely into Devon, took Plymouth without a shot being fired, and besieged the walled city of Exeter for five weeks. London's response was to send in their own army under Lord John Russell and Lord William Grey; an army swelled in number by mercenary forces hired in from Germany and Italy. Five of the most vicious battles ever fought on British soil followed, along with one of the worst atrocities in the island's history when 900 prisoners from Cornwall and the Dartmoor Stannaries had their throats cut by Lord Grey's German *lanzknechts*. Without a trained cavalry, the war would have only one eventual outcome for brave little Cornwall. The Cornish leaders were captured and executed, and death squads under the appalling Provost-Marshal Sir Anthony Kingston were sent across the Tamar to exact London's revenge. The estimated death toll of the conflict and its horrific aftermath was 11% of the male Cornish population, and a possible overall loss of a fifth of the Cornish people. It remains a frictional bone of contention that English Heritage refuses to recognise the five major battle sites of this campaign, or to enter them into the Register of British Battlefields.

Even after such a shocking reverse, the fully legislative Stannary parliament of Cornwall, and its right of veto, remained. It last met in 1753, after which successive Dukes of Cornwall allowed it to lapse. However, the right to reconvene it remains intact at law, as does that right of veto, both facts being confirmed by Attorney-General Lord Elwyn Jones in 1977 in answer to a question in the House of Commons. Of that final meeting in 1753, historian Peter Berresford Ellis wrote in *Celtic Dawn* (2002) that: 'its right of veto was surprisingly reaffirmed by the monarch. However, in 1888, the County Councils Act determined that elected councils would take over the duties of the justices of the peace and, for the first time, Cornwall was redesignated as an 'English' county. This was not confirmed until a year after the other county councils came into being because of the unique constitutional position of Cornwall, and lawyers continue to argue that the institution of Cornwall as a county was not in accordance with constitutional law.' Indeed, this very point was touched upon by the Royal Commission on the Constitution in 1973 (Kilbrandon Report), which further recommended that Cornwall be referred to by its official title of Duchy, rather than the legally dubious 'county', with its modern connotations of humdrum status and common uniformity.

With the continued appointment of a Lord Warden of the Stannaries by the Duchy of Cornwall, Stannary Law is inexorably linked with the

Duchy itself, which continues to exercise legal and constitutional rights and privileges within the Cornish borders that do not exist elsewhere. In the autumn of 2015, the sad news was announced of the tragic death of the Duchy's High Sheriff Anthony Fortescue of Boconnoc, remembered for delightfully exercising his right of office to drive a flock of sheep over London Bridge. It came as a great surprise to many to learn that Cornwall's High Sheriff is the only one in the United Kingdom that is not appointed by the Crown. Instead, it is an appointment that is uniquely made by the Duchy of Cornwall.

At this point we return to the mention in the foreword to this book of Kevin Cahill's *The Second Domesday* (2013): 'The Crown is not the only absolute owner of the land in the UK. In 1855, the High Court ruled that: 'the whole territorial interest and dominion of the Crown in and over the entirety of Cornwall is vested in the Duke of Cornwall.' So, Cornwall is a separate kingdom!' Although the term 'kingdom' might be stretching a point a little ('realm' might have been a better term), this does, indeed, confirm Cornwall's peculiar and unique constitutional position. As we have seen, it is one that can trace its origins way back into prehistory.

More research is now being carried out into Cornwall's constitutional status than at any time in the recent past. Clearly, it cannot be simply dismissed or blindly accepted as an English county, but as something rather more distinct. Foremost among current researchers is Notary Public and expert in constitutional law Dr John Kirkhope, to whom the author is grateful for his advice and assistance. In assessing what that status might be, Dr Kirkhope explains that it is unique or, as he has put it, 'in a category of its own.' In many ways, it resembles both a Palatine State, and a Crown Dependency, but conforms to neither one. It is, quite simply, a totally unique entity with its closest parallel to be found in the Seignory of Sark in the Channel Islands.

Where the Promontory People go from here remains to be seen, although there is a groundswell of opinion towards a degree of autonomy under a National Assembly on the lines of that which currently adminis- ters its larger sister Celtic nation of Wales. The Promontory People remain a proud, innovative and ambitious people, with 12,000 years of heritage and development behind them and, one day, the attention of Westminster will not only have to address the 'West Lothian Question', but the 'Cornubian Question' as well.

Postscript: *It's all in the genes*

THAT a difference exists to this day between England and the Celtic West is undeniable. However, this is not simply an English-Celtic divide, but a distinction that is far older. It actually goes right back to the original post-Glacial colonisation of Britain, where migration came into the west from one direction, and into its east from another.

This cultural difference between east and west remains in place today. From the very beginning, the west has been closely related to the Atlantic seaboard of Europe, while the eastern side of the island was most heavily influenced by European cultures across the Straits of Dover and the North Sea. The import of cultural styles and technologies into each side of the island tended to be missed out on by the opposite half. Influences on the west from Atlantic Europe, e.g. megalith building and Maritime Bell Beakers, are largely confined to the west, and the reverse was also true. Post-Roman inscribed stones are also confined to western Britain. All that was culturally common to the two sides of Britain was the shared use of Celtic as a community language from c.2,000 BCE to the Roman period.

Environment also plays a large part in shaping the characteristics of peoples. Much of eastern Britain lacks the rugged landscapes of the west, and faces what is essentially an inland sea rather than the wild vastness of the Atlantic Ocean. As geography, geology and similar factors vary from place to place, so too will the characteristics of the people who live there.

To some, venturing into the world of genetics is to play a game that may be open to misinterpretation. This can be understood when faced with irresponsible headlines such as that presented by the Telegraph on 17th June 2012: 'Welsh and Cornish are the purest Britons'. To many, this distastefully smacked of 'genetic purity' and 'master-race' mentality. Had it read, as it should: 'the oldest, or most ancient, of Britons', readers would have not been given cause for such concern.

Of course, there can be no such thing as 'genetic purity'. Every single one of us consists of a mixture of gene clusters and sub-groups. Far from being a sinister concept, genetic research is of immense value in providing vital information about our past. From British viewpoints, it can tell us about how we got to this island in the first place, from where, and when. It can clarify aspects of history that were previously far from clear, and has indeed helped to answer questions that have perplexed archaeologists and historians for a very long time.

In 2015, the results of a ten-year genetic survey of the British population by Oxford University under Sir Walter Bodmer, were published. Based upon samples taken from some 10,000 people, this greatly expanded and improved upon previous and valuable work in the subject by Dr Bryan Sykes and Professor Stephen Oppenheimer. The results were not only astonishing, but provided a much clearer picture of our past, and our diversities, than anything that had been previously available. Since the 1990s, archaeology and archaeo-linguistics have already gone a long way towards turning some old, deep-seated, but erroneous, ideas completely on their heads: the results of this genetic survey lent strong support to the findings of this recent work.

British prehistory before the Roman invasion did not consist of successive waves of invaders, and there was no 'Celtic invasion' from central Europe in the early Iron Age, as had been hypothesised for some 300 years. Instead, the colonisation of Britain after the Ice Age, and until the arrival of the Roman Empire, had actually consisted of three significant movements of people into the island, and from two entirely different directions. The first took place during the early-middle Mesolithic period between 12,000 and 10,000 years ago. The second occurred at the start of the Neolithic period 6,500 years ago (the first farmers and megalith builders), and a third at the end of the Neolithic era some 4,500 years ago (the first metal workers).

Although continual minor movements of people into and out of Britain occurred throughout the remainder of prehistory, it was a time of remarkable continuity and social stability. Only from the Roman invasion did Britain's fortunes rapidly change, receiving one wave after another of far less peaceful inward movement: Anglo-Saxons, Danes and Normans in particular.

The prehistoric inward movements came from two initial glacial refuge areas located at either end of Europe. Colonisation of western Britain and Ireland originated 12,000 years ago from a refuge area in northern Iberia and southwestern France, on either side of the Pyrenees and centred on the current Basque region. This migration is typified by a male-line genetic group known as R1b, or 'Ruisko'. Found throughout Britain, it is most dominant in the west, weakening towards the east. R1b consists of a variety of sub-groups and those most relevant to Cornwall are: R1b-5; R1b-9 'Rox'; R1b-10 'Ruy'; R1b-11; R1b-14 'Rory'; and R1b-15c. The last, originating in the Basque region, is of particular interest in that its greatest concentration in Britain is in Cornwall. The 'Rory' cluster is also of interest as its point of origin is located in Galicia, at the northwestern tip of Iberia; an area that, like Cornwall, contains tin in its geology.

The eastern half of Britain is largely influenced by the male-line group I 'Ivan', and its sub-groups I1a 'Ian', and I1c 'Ingert'. These originated from the glacial refuges in the Ukraine and northern Balkans, to the north of the Black Sea. The westward movement of these peoples was greatly longer than the northward journey of the 'Ruisko' group, doubtless with several pauses en route, before crossing the plain that is now the North Sea and entering eastern Britain around 10,000 years ago. Also found throughout Britain, the 'Ivan' group is strongest in the east, progressively weakening towards the west.

Mitochondrial DNA for females is less clear, but two main groups are identifiable. H1 'Helena' originates from that same Basque region facing the Bay of Biscay as the male line R1b 'Ruisko', moving northward into Britain and southwest Ireland via Brittany. 'Vera' has a point of origin north of the Pyrenees in an area corresponding to Aquitaine. This group appears to have moved north to the present mouth of the Seine, then across the (then) largely dry Channel basin and into the southeastern corner of Britain.

No overall 'Celtic' gene could be identified but, as Sir Walter Bodmer pointed out, the modern Celtic peoples, including the Cornish, do all share a particular variant of the Melanocortin 1 receptor gene. That Celtic peoples have differing genetic profiles should not come as any surprise, as the term 'Celtic' properly describes peoples sharing an ancient Atlantic seaboard provenance and linguistic/cultural heritage, rather then being of a common genetic type. The genetic variation between an average Cornish person and one from North Wales can be seen in the table below.

Neolithic movements into Britain, from the south and from the east, involved peoples from the same approximate locations as those of the initial Mesolithic colonists, and were derived from the same diverse genetic roots. The Oxford survey identified 17 principal genetic clusters in Britain, of which the Cornish show up as a clear group west of the Tamar-Ottery line, and clearly distinguishable from the Devonians who, in turn, are distinct from the group to the east of the line running along the Axe and Parrett Rivers. This latter group, the most widely spread cluster of all, occupies the whole area of southern and eastern England, from Dorset to the Humber.

These 17 clusters could be broken down even further and, at 23 clusters, the Oxford survey identified a clear sub-group that is confined to the Land's End peninsula. No further detail of this sub-group has been forthcoming, but it is extremely tempting to suggest a likelihood of it being a Late Neolithic or Early Bronze Age settlement of Galician origin, and a direct link with the beginning of Cornwall's 4,500-year history of metalliferous mining.

Genetics is a complex subject, but it is not intended to tie readers of this book into scientific knots. To that end, the survey results are here broken down into three main categories that emphasise provenance, in order to compare the typical genetic profiles and origins of the Cornish, the Devonians, the overall English group (excluding Cornwall and Devon), and the northern Welsh. These categories are as follows:

EAE: Early Atlantic Europe (10,000 BCE to 2,500 BCE)
ENE: Early Northern and Eastern Europe (8,000 BCE to 2,500 BCE)
LNE: Late Northern Europe (400 CE to 1066CE)

CORNISH	DEVONIAN
60% EAE	52% EAE
28% ENE	32% ENE
12% LNE	16% LNE

ENGLISH	NORTH WELSH
41% EAE	47% EAE
42% ENE	42% ENE
17% LNE	11% ENE

The Cornish 60% EAE result is the highest in the whole of Britain, and only three other groups (NW Scotland, South Pembroke and Devon) exceed a 50% reading. Anglo-Saxon content is difficult to determine from the LNE results, as they blur into other LNE clusters and can only be approximated. While the North Welsh have no Anglo-Saxon content at all, for Cornwall an estimated presence of 6.5% Anglo-Saxon genes is to be expected. This is because of the concentration of West Saxon settlement in parishes north of the River Ottery in the Duchy's northern corner; and in Tamarside parishes south of Launceston. and also clearly evidenced by the predominance of English language place-names in those areas. Further movement of people into Cornwall from the east, from then until the present, will also enter the equation. Even then, the figure for Cornwall only amounts to about half of the estimated Anglo-Saxon content of the Devonian structure.

It comes as a surprise that the Anglo-Saxon count in central and southern England is unexpectedly low, varying from around 12% to as much as 40% in East Anglia. It is currently thought that the number of Anglo-Saxon, or proto-English, colonists into eastern and southern Britain, from the mid 5th century CE, may not have far exceeded 200,000. Even so, that number still amounted to around 15% of Britain's total population at that time.

Roman and Norman genes were not noticeable, but this can be explained by the fact that very few of the Roman troops in Britain during the 400-year occupation were actually Roman, or even Italian. Most were recruits from other parts of the Roman Empire, especially Gaul and Iberia, and a few from Germania. These are hidden in the R1b and I genetic groups that were already dominant in Britain. The Normans largely consisted of Viking (Danish) descendants, Germanic Franks, and Celtic Bretons and, again, are concealed in the same larger genetic groups.

The most astonishing discovery to emerge from the Oxford University genetic survey was the fact that, until very recently, British people have tended not to move away from their ancestral regions of 1,400 years ago. The colour-coded map of British genetic clusters, that was included in the report, clearly defines the Cornish and Devonian clusters which also, in partnership, define the Celtic kingdom of Dumnonia. A distinct group in the east Lancashire-Pennines area still clusters within the borders of the ancient kingdom of Elmet. Similarly, the extent of other old kingdoms such as Gwynedd, Rheged and Bernicia are also clearly visible on the map of modern genetic clusters. This remarkable finding had not been expected by either the geneticists or the archaeologists, but it clearly shows a modern Britain that remains firmly in touch with its past.

References

ASHE, Geoffrey. *The Discovery of King Arthur* (1985)

BODMER, William, et al. *The Fine-Scale Genetic Structure of the Population of Britain* (2015)

CAHILL, Kevin. *The Second Domesday* (2013)

CARPENTER, Rhys. *Beyond the Pillars of Hercules* (1973)

COOKE, Ian McNeil. *Mother and Sun: The Cornish Fogou* (1993)

CORNWALL ARCHAEOLOGICAL SOCIETY: Cornish Archaeology (annual journal 1962-present)

CORNWALL ARCHAEOLOGICAL UNIT: The Archaeology of Scilly (1989)

– St Michael's Mount: Archaeological works 1995-8 (2000)

– Bodmin Moor's Archaeological Heritage (2001)

CUNLIFFE, Barry. *Iron Age Communities in Britain* (1975)

– *The Extraordinary Voyage of Pytheas the Greek* (2002)

– *Britain Begins* (2012)

DEACON, Bernard. *Cornwall's First Golden Age* (2016)

ELLIS, Peter Berresford. *Celtic Dawn* (2002)

GRIMMER, Martin: Saxon Bishop and Celtic King (2001)

HENDERSON, Charles. *The Cornish Church Guide* (1925)

INSLEY, Charles. *Kings and Lords in Tenth-Century Cornwall* (2013)

INSTITUTE OF CORNISH STUDIES: Cornish Studies (annual journal 1972 to present)

KIRKHOPE, John. *Cornwall: A Category of its Own* (2015)

McEVOY, Brian, et al. The *Longue Durée of Genetic Ancestry: Multiple Genetic Marker Systems and Celtic Origins on the Atlantic Façade of Europe* (2004)

NATIONAL TRUST, The. *An Archaeological Evaluation of St Michael's Mount* (1993)

OPPENHEIMER, Stephen. *The Origins of the British* (2006)

PAYTON, Philip. *Cornwall – A History* (2004)

PEARCE, Susan. *The Kingdom of Dumnonia* (1973)

PENHALLURICK, R.D. *Tin in Antiquity* (1986)

RIVET, C & SMITH, A.L.F. *The Place-Names of Roman Britain* (1979)

ROSS, Anne. *The Pagan Celts* (1986)

ROSS, Anne & ROBINS, Don. *The Life and Death of a Druid Prince* (1989)

RULE, Margaret & MONAGHAN, Jason. *A Gallo-Roman Trading Vessel from Guernsey* (1993)

SNYDER, Christopher A. *An Age of Tyrants* (1998)

SYKES, Bryan. *Blood of the Isles* (2006)

THOMAS, Charles. *The Character and Origins of Roman Dumnonia* (1966)

– *Exploration of a Drowned Landscape* (1985)

– *Celtic Britain* (1986)

– *Tintagel: Arthur and Archaeology* (1993)

– *And Shall These Mute Stones Speak?* (1994)

– *Penzance Market Cross: A Cornish Wonder Re-wondered* (1999)

THORN, Caroline & Frank, eds. *Domesday Book: Cornwall* (1979)

WEATHERHILL, Craig. *Belerion: Ancient Sites of Land's End* (1981)

– *Cornovia: Ancient Sites of Cornwall & Scilly* (1985 and 2009)

– *Cornish Place-Names and Language* (2007)

WOOD, Michael. *Domesday* (1986)

Index